Equal Protection of the Law?

STUDIES IN CRIME & PUNISHMENT

David A. Schultz, Christina DeJong, and Gregg Barak
General Editors

Vol. 1

PETER LANG
New York • Washington, D.C./Baltimore • Bern
Frankfurt am Main • Berlin • Brussels • Vienna • Oxford

Mary Welek Atwell

Equal Protection of the Law?

Gender and Justice in the United States

PETER LANG
New York • Washington, D.C./Baltimore • Bern
Frankfurt am Main • Berlin • Brussels • Vienna • Oxford

Library of Congress Cataloging-in-Publication Data

Atwell, Mary Welek.
Equal protection of the law?:
gender and justice in the United States / Mary Welek Atwell.
p. cm. — (Studies in crime and punishment; vol. 1)
Includes bibliographical references.
1. Women—Legal status, laws, etc.—United States—History.
2. Women—Crimes against—United States—History. 3. Sex discrimination
against women—Law and legislation—United States—History.
4. Sex role—United States—History. I. Title. II. Series.
KF478 .A94 342.73'0878—dc 21 2002005692
ISBN 978-0-8204-5502-0
ISSN 1529-2444

Bibliographic information published by **Die Deutsche Nationalbibliothek**.
Die Deutsche Nationalbibliothek lists this publication in the "Deutsche
Nationalbibliografie"; detailed bibliographic data are available
on the Internet at http://dnb.d-nb.de/.

Cover design by Dutton & Sherman Design

The paper in this book meets the guidelines for permanence and durability
of the Committee on Production Guidelines for Book Longevity
of the Council of Library Resources.

29 Broadway, 18th floor, New York, NY 10006
www.peterlang.com

Printed in the United States of America

TABLE OF CONTENTS

Appendices

ACKNOWLEDGMENTS

Thanks to Radford University for the faculty development leave that provided a semester free from teaching responsibilities to work on this manuscript. I appreciate the research help of graduate assistants Traci Smart Arwood, Traci Pridgen, Jen McKeldin, and Amanda Hinshaw. I have been fortunate indeed to work with them.

I thank my husband, Dick Pennock, who has listened patiently as I regaled him with my concerns about violence against women.

For about twenty years, my daughter, Mary Stewart Atwell, and I have had an ongoing conversation. Much of it has been, I think, about women. As she grew up, went to boarding school, college, and graduate school we have talked—and sometimes argued—about women's issues. We've told stories, examined friendships, shared outrage at injustices, and laughed a lot. Through this process, I have not only come to know her but to know myself better and to understand more about this puzzle of gender. I am grateful for her, for her help with and interest in this manuscript.

INTRODUCTION

The title of this book purposely includes a question mark. The answer to the question—Do women enjoy the equal protection of the laws in the contemporary United States?—is ambiguous. At the beginning of the semester, when I ask students in my course on Race and Gender in Criminal Justice what changes are necessary for women to enjoy full legal equality, the answers tend to fall into several general categories.

- Women currently are fully equal. The students give examples of women's entry into criminal justice professions or comparable prison sentences.
- Women are not legally equal but are, in fact, advantaged by such "chivalrous" practices as lighter sentences.
- Women would experience real equality if we would just enforce existing laws. This is the most popular option.
- There are some troublesome areas in the law where women's interests are not really represented (perhaps as victims of rape or domestic violence or in promotions in criminal justice agencies) that seem to reflect some deep-seated assumptions about gender.
- The Supreme Court has not interpreted the Constitution to provide for full gender equality. This option typically requires a bit of prodding and some familiarity with legal history or women's history.

This book is written to explore and discuss these options, although it will focus mainly on the last two answers to the question about gender, equality, and justice. The sense that inequities are deeply embedded in the structure of American society is the first acknowledgment that we operate in a patriarchal system. The following pages will define patriarchy, examine how patriarchal institutions have evolved and survived in the United States, and give particular attention to the intersection of patriarchy, the law, and the criminal justice system. It will also examine how the Court has approached gender issues during the last century. Some would argue that without either an Equal Rights Amendment to the Constitution or a clear statement from the Court that the Fourteenth Amendment requires gender equality, women will continue to stand on uneven constitutional ground.

Understanding the depth of tradition and attitudes that maintain a patriarchal system requires bringing a historical perspective to the inquiry. It often becomes clear in class discussions that students tend to divide the world into two historical periods—"back then" and now. The former seems to include everything from Adam and Eve up to the time the speaker became conscious of the world—perhaps fifteen years ago. There is a certain delightful quality to such a self-referencing view of the universe, but it can lead to some pretty muddled notions of reality. Even so, such a perspective is more understandable in young people than in serious academic work. Yet it is not unusual to read criminal justice studies that create the impression that women's legal position had been static until the last several decades. Then inequities were finally "discovered" and women's issues gained attention. The failure to bring a historical framework to the inquiry means that one does not understand that issues, attitudes, and institutions are in a constant state of evolution. It neglects the dynamic interactions among values, laws, and social institutions. It fails to take into account the courageous efforts of women and men in the past to bring about social change. And it also ignores the persistence of patriarchy which, like racism, often manages to crop up in new forms. Therefore it fails to grasp the idea that changes in deeply embedded social structures that foster inequality occur only as a result of collective efforts. Without a historical approach, we are unlikely to learn from our forebears how to institutionalize positive changes. It will be a major purpose of this work to analyze issues related to gender and justice as part of a historical process, one that can and will change, and one that we who are students of criminal justice can affect.

CHAPTER ONE

Definitions, Examples, and Analytical Tools

Sex/Gender

At the most basic level, it is possible to distinguish sex as a set of biological and physiological qualities that fall into two general categories, male and female. Gender, on the other hand, is a social construct. Societies, for economic, religious, and other reasons, ascribe sets of characteristics to males and females. From birth onward, every person is immersed in socially developed definitions of what it means to be a boy or a girl, a woman or a man. These definitions are socially learned and they are not static. On the contrary, because societies evolve and change, so do certain gender expectations. Nonetheless, as Clinton and Gillespie note, "Gender roles, social conventions, and sexual orientation are embedded in nearly all aspects of public behavior, providing very distinct sets of expectations that shape and stylize human conduct."[1] How a society labels acts as legal or illegal, good or bad, deviant or normal often depends on who commits the act. Not infrequently, gender is the determining factor.

Patriarchy

As every society develops a set of definitions and characteristics associated with appropriate appearance, behavior, and life options for males and females, these socially constructed gender roles are connected to differing notions of power, notions that virtually always associate more power with masculinity. This unequal distribution of power between men and women is the fundamental element of patriarchy. Scholars argue about the precise meaning of the term. Does it refer to a political system where the state is modeled on a type of family organization in which fathers exercise absolute or near absolute authority? Does the term have a universal meaning or is it subject to cultural variability?[2] This work will adopt Lynne Goodstein's definition of patriarchy as unequal distribution of power and privilege.[3] Patriarchy includes both formal and informal authority in political, economic, social, and family life. In addition, feminist scholars have emphasized that a standard feature of patriarchal societies is the separation of life into the public and the private realms. On the one hand, the public sphere—mainly government and commerce but also the management of schools and churches—has been and still is disproportionately run by men. The private sphere—home and family—ostensibly the area where women are most present. But it is vital to recognize that even in the private areas, the public world exerts control. For example, it is through a public process—law making and court interpretation—that the criminal justice system came to define the home as off limits to the laws against assault that governed behavior among strangers in the outside world.

Some would argue that the law is a vital element in establishing and maintaining a patriarchal system. Carol Smart asserts that law not only acts on gendered subjects but that law is part of the continual reproduction of gender differentiation, part of the process of fixing people in distinct gender roles. Law affects us not only in time of crisis—when we find ourselves in court—but it "frames our lives in terms of possibilities available to us or...it operates as a discourse which constructs legal subjects." She terms law a "significantly powerful discourse because of its situation in the hierarchy of knowledges and its power to subjugate other discourses."[4] For example, the version of rape described in law may not conform with a real woman's experience of rape. The legal version is, however, the one that "counts" if a rapist is to be punished. But Smart argues as well that law is a "fruitful site" on which to dispute the meanings of gender.[5] The opposing arguments in the courts, in Congress and state legislatures, in regulations governing police behavior, all are places where gender issues can be argued and reargued.

Elizabeth Schneider sees an ongoing dialectic between law and social movements. In other words, she emphasizes the notion that law evolves in response to public pressures and actions. Schneider believes law is made in many ways and in many places (certainly not only in the legislatures or the Supreme Court). It is not separate from but reflects and is reflected in the popular consciousness. Her view is that the formation of law is a chaotic and uneven process. For example, the process of defining women's relationship to the state, of pulling domestic violence, sexual harassment, or acquaintance rape from behind the curtain of privacy and into the realm of criminal behavior is a lengthy and ongoing process that has responded to changes in popular consciousness.[6] Thus law reflects social change—including changes in gender roles—as well as it fosters social change. As has happened with social changes related to race, it is often those who are victimized by injustice who are the most effective advocates of change. And as is true of struggles for racial justice, legal changes promoting gender justice have encountered fierce resistance, retreats as well as advances. Built into the historical framework supporting this book is the understanding that law can promote both equality and inequality and that, unfortunately, the story of women in America is not a tale of unbroken progress toward a more just society. Rather it is a story of advances and setbacks, of bravery as well as indifference, of lessons learned, forgotten, and relearned.

Feminism

A bumper sticker states that "feminism is the radical notion that women are people." If people are defined as intelligent, autonomous, capable, and entitled to full participation in human society, then feminists do accept that radical notion. Feminism is both a way of looking at reality and a commitment to social change. The term suggests a worldview that uses gender as a category of analysis. What this means is a willingness to put women's lives and experience at the center, to define them not in relation to men but on their own terms. Simply put, feminists would not ask, "Why didn't women do things like men?" but "Why did women do what they did?"

Feminists do not necessarily agree among themselves when it comes to either analysis or strategy. Some prefer to focus on the ways in which women and men are basically alike. From this point of view, the best approach is to emphasize equal rights and to pursue opportunities for women to compete with men on an equal footing. Much of the civil rights struggle of the 1960s and 1970s followed this model. Another approach looks at the reality of differences between women and men. From this perspective, justice does not demand identical treatment regardless of sex but takes the different situations of males and females into consideration without privileging the male position.

One insight common to most feminists of the last generation is a sense that although women per se have common interests and experiences, race, ethnicity, and class also distinguish women from each other. One must be careful of generalizations that apply to all women, just as one is careful of generalizations that apply to all men. Karen Offen describes the situation well when she says that emphasis on women's commonalities is a call for solidarity rather than a precise description of reality.[7]

Analytical Tools

Randall Kennedy in *Race, Crime, and the Law* provides some concepts that are also useful in pursuing an analysis of gender and justice issues.[8]

Kennedy argues that African Americans have been the subject of both unequal protection and unequal enforcement of the law. In other words, as victims and as suspects and offenders, black Americans have been the recipients of differential treatment based on their race. If the authorities treat crimes against blacks less seriously than they do crimes against whites, then those victims are experiencing unequal protection. It is not the task of the criminal justice system to decide which victims are worthy of protection and which are not, yet according to Kennedy's persuasive analysis one might find multiple examples when police, judges and juries, and the structure of law itself placed African Americans in a more vulnerable position. Two examples illustrate his point. During slavery, there was no law protecting slave women from rape. As property of their owners and consequently required to act with absolute obedience, they had no legal recourse when white men used them for sexual or power gratification. A raped slave woman did not exist in the eyes of the law. She was not entitled to protection. Similarly, black men who were lynched by mobs in the nineteenth and twentieth centuries seldom enjoyed the protection of the authorities. In fact, all too frequently the police and other members of the criminal justice community were active and enthusiastic participants in the lynching.[9]

It is easy to see how the concept of unequal protection is applicable to women of all races. Historically crimes against women have frequently been treated lightly by the criminal justice system. Victims of wife battering, marital rape, sexual abuse, acquaintance rape, and sexual harassment have often found themselves without legal recourse. In addition, the race and class of the victim seem to be part of the calculus of her value. Later in this book, we will examine the victimization of women in greater detail. Kennedy's concept of unequal protection will be a useful tool in that analysis.

Most people are familiar with the concept of unequal enforcement, the position that the various parts of the criminal justice system take race into account when people are charged with lawbreaking. Kennedy and many other scholars can document in detail the ways in which police, courts, the juvenile justice system, and corrections institutions have discriminated against racial minorities.[10] Lynching can also provide a historical example of unequal enforcement. Those who were the victims of lynch mobs were often unjustly accused, denied due process, and punished in horrible ways while their assailants were seldom charged, and if charged, generally acquitted. The case of Emmett Till illustrates this concept. In 1955, Till, an African American boy fifteen years of age from Chicago, was brutally murdered by several white men in Tallahatchie County, Mississippi. Till had been visiting relatives and, unaware or oblivious to the racial codes of the rural South, he flirted with a white woman. He also claimed that he dated white girls back in Chicago. Emmett Till's apparent violation of the segregated practices of Mississippi so infuriated the woman's husband and brother-in-law that they kidnapped him from his uncle's house, beat him to death, tied a heavy piece of machinery to his body, and threw him into the river. His body was so badly mutilated his mother could not recognize his face. At most Till had violated local custom, yet he was executed for that "crime." Those who killed him and publicly bragged about their crime? They were acquitted by an all-white jury. It would be hard to argue that the law was equally enforced for Emmett Till and his white murderers.[11]

In what sense does unequal enforcement occur on the basis of gender? Scholars often cite prostitution as a case in point. Prostitution is one of the few crimes for which women are arrested at a higher rate than men. Yet every prostitute has clients (and likely a pimp as well). Those characters are at least co-participants in the offense, yet they are much less likely to be held accountable. Beyond the individual transaction involved in prostitution, one might also argue that women involved in commercial sex are also victims of other economic and social inequities that draw them into the life in the first place. Later chapters will examine women as offenders and pay special attention to the link between victimization and offending. We will find the theme of unequal enforcement helpful in that inquiry.

In addition to the concepts of unequal protection and unequal enforcement developed from Randall Kennedy's work, another useful analytical tool in studying gender and justice is a continuum provided by Samuel Walker et al.[12] In *The Color of Justice*, Walker and his coauthors address the question—how do we account for the disproportionate number of minorities brought into the criminal justice system? To examine why, for example, 58% of those incarcerated are African American at a time when African Americans make up approximately 13% of the population, Walker et al. suggest that the answer lies somewhere on a continuum of discrimination which ranges from Pure Justice at one end to Systematic Discrimination at the other. According to their scheme, the range of possibilities is as follows:

Pure Justice—a system that works fairly. The guilty are punished and the innocent go free. If more minorities are punished, it is because minorities commit more crime.

Individual Discrimination—some people who work in the criminal justice are prejudiced. There are always the bad cops, like Mark Furman, the racist judges, the overzealous prosecutors. If, however, we can get rid of these "bad apples," the system will work fairly.

Contextual Discrimination—there is bias in certain places and in certain processes in the criminal justice system. Perhaps whole agencies in certain geographic locales operate unfairly—usually for political reasons. Perhaps some processes (legal representation, for example) disadvantage minorities.

Institutional Discrimination—policies that on their face seem to be neutral actually target members of minority groups. The policy decision to fight the "war on drugs" on the streets of the inner city rather than on college campuses means that more poor minorities will be caught and charged.

Systematic Discrimination—the whole system of justice is permeated with prejudice. The laws and their enforcement do not reflect the experience of minorities and thus cannot be fairly administered.

Walker's continuum is useful for examining the issue of racial prejudice. We will also find it a practical way to analyze issues of gender. The final chapter of this book will return to these concepts. Given the material in the intervening chapters, the reader can decide for herself or himself how to evaluate the criminal justice system.

Two Court Cases as Examples

Two cases recently decided by the United States Supreme Court serve as examples of ways in which patriarchal themes are embedded in the law. *United States v. Morrison* (2000) and *Ferguson v. Charleston* (2001) provide illustrations of unequal protection and unequal enforcement. Even a case such as *Ferguson v. Charleston*, where the Court's holding supported the petitioners' arguments, reveals assumptions about women's rights.

United States v. Morrison

In 1994, when Christy Brzonkala was a freshman at Virginia Tech, she was allegedly raped by two football players, Antonio Morrison and James Crawford. Although Brzonkala did not report the rape immediately, by the time she talked with counselors at the university Women's Center, she had shown many of the classic symptoms of rape trauma syndrome. She had retreated from her friends, lost interest in her academic work, cut off her hair, and attempted suicide. Brzonkala ultimately decided to bring charges against the men through the campus judicial system. After several hearings, Crawford was totally acquitted, and Morrison was found guilty of using "abusive language." His punishment was deferred until after he graduated.

Given this unsatisfactory outcome, Brzonkala next decided to use the newly passed federal Violence Against Women Act (VAWA) to sue her assailant in federal court. VAWA provided that freedom from violence based on gender is a civil right, and as with other civil rights violations, victims could look to the federal government for a remedy. Although no court ever considered the merits of Brzonkala's accusations against Morrison, two lower courts and the U.S. Supreme Court found the relevant provision of the Violence Against Women Act unconstitutional.

The Court held that Congress had exceeded its constitutional authority in two ways. First of all, Congress had passed VAWA under the Constitutional provision allowing it to regulate interstate commerce. The arguments in favor of its passage were based on three years of evidence gathering by Congress, showing a mountain of evidence that women's participation in the economy was affected by gender-based violence. Numerous statistics showed that fear of rape or domestic violence may limit women's job opportunities, their freedom to travel, or their educational pursuits. The data also showed that violence against women costs public and private health care organizations millions of dollars a year. This evidence was enough to convince Congress that gender-based violence had a significant impact on interstate commerce. Five Supreme Court justices—Rehnquist, O'Connor, Kennedy, Scalia, and Thomas—were not convinced.

Congress had also created VAWA based on its authority to enforce the Fourteenth Amendment's guarantee of equal protection of the laws. Here again, the legislators heard substantial evidence that states were not providing appropriate or sufficient responses to victims of rape and domestic violence. There were numerous examples of failures of police to respond, jurisdictions to prosecute, or courts to convict men who abused women. Therefore, again Congress was persuaded that if women have a civil right to be free from gender-based violence, and if the states are not safeguarding that right, it is only justice to allow a victim to go to federal court and claim damages from her assailant. Again the Supreme Court disagreed, finding the remedy not congruent and proportionate to the offense. Thus the provision of VAWA allowing victims to sue their attackers in federal court was declared unconstitutional, and Christy Brzonkala never had the opportunity to have the facts of her case tried in court. Symbolically, her name was even removed from the case before the Court rendered its opinion. When the arguments were made before the Supreme Court, there were two separate cases—*Brzonkala v. Morrison* and *United States v. Morrison*. The Court chose to combine them into one case and to drop Brzonkala's name from the title. As part of a separate action, she had also sued Virginia Tech under Title IX of the civil rights act which prohibits sex discrimination in universities. Virginia Tech settled out of court. They paid Brzonkala $75,000 but admitted no fault.

What is the larger importance of Christy Brzonkala's case? At one level, it is a snapshot that reveals differing analyses of gender relations in the contemporary United States. In the opinion of the majority of the Supreme Court, violence against women seems to consist of isolated, individual acts motivated by an infinite number of circumstances. In the view of many of VAWA's supporters, however, violence against women is part of a structure of inequality, patriarchy, in which women are undervalued and in which gender-based violence is tolerated by the legal system. Supporters argue that women have a right to be free from violence based on gender and that this right is necessary for women to be full citizens. Therefore, violence against women is a civil rights violation requiring federal remedies just as violence based on race can be a civil rights violation. As long as the justices see violence against women as an individual offense, like shoplifting or auto theft, they will not agree that a different type of response is needed.

In the absence of legislation such as the Violence Against Women Act, are women likely to experience unequal protection?

Ferguson v. Charleston

During the mid-1980s, reports circulated widely that a new epidemic of crack babies was the latest manifestation of the nation's drug problem. Fueled by reports on the evening news and earnest discussions among pundits, many Americans became concerned that drug-addicted mothers were giving birth to babies who were likely to show severe mental, physical, and emotional disabilities. The mothers usually shown in these news stories were young, poor, and black. Thus the concern with crack babies meshed with another popular issue—out-of-wedlock pregnancy among African American teenagers and criticism of the welfare system.[13] The state of South Carolina responded to these problems in two ways. In 1995, the state Supreme Court held that ingestion of cocaine during the third trimester of pregnancy constituted criminal child neglect. Thus a pregnant woman could be criminally prosecuted for cocaine use or addiction. Meanwhile, the Medical University of South Carolina (MUSC) set up a procedure whereby certain pregnant patients would be tested for drug use. If the results came up positive, the test would be turned over to the police, who could then arrest the patient. Altogether thirty patients tested positive, were arrested and charged under the South Carolina law. Of these patients at a public hospital, serving primarily poor inner city clients, 90% of those who tested positive for cocaine were African American.

Crystal Ferguson and several other patients who had been arrested sued the hospital and challenged its policy. The specific constitutional issue was a Fourth Amendment question about the legality of the "search." In other words, evidence was obtained from the pregnant women without a warrant, without their consent, and without probable cause. How did the hospital decide which women to test for cocaine? A patient would be tested if she met one or more of the following criteria: no prenatal care, late or incomplete prenatal care, interuterine fetal death, preterm labor, interuterine growth retardation, previously known drug or alcohol abuse, or unexplained congenital anomalies. The significant point is that most of those criteria are associated with lack of adequate health care, which is associated with poverty. At least during the early stages of the program, if a test was positive, police were notified and the patient was arrested. She could be offered the opportunity to enroll in treatment. However, the policy made no mention of changes in prenatal care or of any special treatment for newborns. Thus although the program was ostensibly developed to promote infant health, in reality it was a program that punished mothers.

When the mothers brought their case to court, the lower courts upheld the South Carolina policy. The Fourth Circuit Court of Appeals found the testing only a "minimal intrusion on the privacy of the patients." The members of the Supreme Court who dissented from the opinion—Justices Scalia, Thomas, and Chief Justice Rehnquist—belittled the patients' right to privacy in their dissent. And although six members of the Supreme Court agreed that the MUSC policy was an unconstitutional violation of the women's Fourth Amendment rights, the program itself may also serve as a contemporary example of unequal enforcement. These women—poor, pregnant, and African American—were subjected to a violation of their constitutional protection against illegal search and seizure through a poorly thought-out program that was likely to encourage other pregnant women to avoid prenatal care altogether. But on the positive side, an otherwise powerless group of women was able to challenge an unfair program all the way to the Supreme Court and to win.

CHAPTER TWO

Citizenship, Constitutional Rights, and Equality: Elusive Goals

It is an historical fact that most law in America has been made and interpreted without participation by women. Although Abigail Adams cautioned her husband, John Adams, at the time of the Declaration of Independence to "remember the ladies," most making of law and applying of law has been done by men who made assumptions about women rather than by women who could draw on their own experience. That these assumptions may have become more enlightened during the last two hundred years is no doubt true, but that women did not speak *for themselves* in the legislatures and the courts is also true. To acknowledge this fact is not to blame or "bash" individual men for women's legal inequality but to understand the history and consequences of a system that may have been intended to be "for" women but was definitely neither "by" women nor "of" women.

In *Planned Parenthood of Southeastern Pennsylvania v. Casey*, a 1992 Supreme Court decision, the justices stated, "Women do not lose their constitutionally protected liberty when they marry."[1] Both parts of this sentence are significant—women have constitutionally protected liberties, and those liberties belong to them as individual citizens, not as female relatives of male citizens. If this seems obvious to the twenty-first century reader, an examination of the evolution of women's legal position in the United States makes it clear that such a guarantee would have been unthinkable through much of our history. The stories of women and the law that form the background of the contemporary world are part of a long process of struggle that took place at multiple levels in a society where gender has defined a different sets of obligations and rights for women and men.[2]

There are many approaches to understanding how women's relationship with the law has evolved. This chapter will examine in some detail how the Constitution has been interpreted with respect to gender issues, how these interpretations have both reflected and influenced women's exercise of rights and opportunities. The chapter will also consider how gendered legal principles are reflected in the application of law to everyday life.

For almost two hundred years, laws typically embodied assumptions that distinguished the public aspects of life from the private, the male sphere from the female sphere. With those distinctions came definitions of differing rights and responsibilities, protections and obligations. Among other things, such laws assumed that the male experience was the norm, that the ways in which women's lives differed from men's could not only explain but could justify differing legal statuses. Until the mid-twentieth century when advocates for women modeled their struggle on the civil rights movement and the Fourteenth Amendment became a more effective instrument to challenge gender discrimination, women stood in a different relationship to the state than men. This is not to say that women's legal status was unchanging from the founding of the United States until the modern era. Rather the point is that *full* citizenship has been a long-sought and very elusive goal. The courts have zigzagged along a course where an expanded interpretation of women's status has often been obstructed or reversed. Those who interpret the law have found it difficult to free themselves from the snares of patriarchal thinking.

Early American Institutions

The English settlers who came to the American colonies in the seventeenth and eighteenth centuries brought with them strong patriarchal convictions. Most colonists accepted the worldview that the family and the government were analogous institutions, dependent on one another. As the state was ruled by a fatherly lord, the family was ruled by a lordly father.[3] Governments were modeled on the family where God had given the father power over a wife and children. Likewise, God gave rulers authority over their subjects. Inequality was a natural state, divinely ordained and meant to exist both within and outside the household. In the family, status was based on a person's sex and relationship to the father. In the outside world, women and children assumed the rank of the head of the household.[4] There was a place for everyone and everyone had his or her place.

The ideas of the American Revolution challenged part of this worldview. When the framers of the Declaration of Independence wrote that "all men are created equal," they rejected the notion of a God-given aristocracy. They did not, however, go very far in questioning the notion of a hierarchy within the family. As Linda Kerber says, white men freed themselves of the public patriarchy but maintained and elaborated the system of private patriarchy. As the differences among men lessened, the differences among men and women grew.[5] The Founding Fathers knew the work of John Locke, which divided the world into two realms—the realm of politics and society, which was the more important, all-male domain, and the sphere of family where both men and women functioned but where women played a subordinate role.[6] The founders of the United States clung to the ideas about marriage and family laid down in the British common law which provided for a legal marital relationship called *coverture*. A married woman was known as a *feme covert*, which literally means "hidden woman." This status meant many things for women—but essentially it defined a type of domestic relations in which a woman had no direct relationship to the state. Her position vis-a-vis the political order was only through her husband. In other words, only men had a civic identity and the rights and responsibilities that went with it. Women stood in the same relation to the state as infants or aliens. Whereas men had civic obligations such as paying taxes, serving in the military if called, and assuming jury duty, women had obligations only to their husbands and families. The state asked nothing of them, other than that they refrain from treason. On the other hand, the state offered them few rights and few protections. They were meant to seek their rights and protections within the family. Accordingly, if the head of their family failed to protect them or abused his power, they had little recourse outside the home in the public sphere.[7]

Under coverture, the private world of the home was separate from the public world of business and government. Yet the laws developed in the public sphere were a vital part of the structure that kept the home walled off. The law of domestic relations supported the authority of the husband over his wife and children as well as the authority of masters over servants. In a sense, it solidified unequal gender relations as well as a hierarchy of class. In a practical sense, the status of *feme covert* meant that married women could not hold property or control their own earnings, make contracts or wills, chose where to live, or formally approve of arrangements to send their children out as apprentices. They certainly could not vote. A prominent authority on nineteenth-century American law explained how "asymmetrical property relations" of coverture were necessary to a husband's well-being. If women could own property, make contracts, or control their own wages, they could be sued and brought into court. "A husband would be deprived of the company of his wife, which the law would not suffer."[8] The law could not dispossess a husband of a wife's "company." In other words, he had an absolute right to her presence, her body. The law could not interfere with that right. It is easy to see in the system of coverture how the notion of unfettered control over a woman's body gave a husband the right to restrict her movements, to use force to "discipline" her behavior, and to have sexual access to her on demand.

Many historians have argued the relative advantages and disadvantages to women growing from the nineteenth-century division of life into the public (men's) sphere and the private (women's) sphere. It is undeniable that this separation was accompanied by great lip service to the importance of motherhood and praise for the contributions women made to men's domestic well-being. It is also undeniable that the insulation of the women's world from the legal order in reality devalues women and their functions. More important this insulation leaves them without formal remedies when they need to turn to the law for help.[9] Jean Baker Elshtain notes that women's status is lower in societies with "firm differentiation between the public and private spheres and where women are isolated from one another and placed under one man's authority in the home,[10] and Linda Kerber argues that as long as married women were perceived "to owe virtually all obligations to their husbands, they could make no claim of rights against the political community."[11] But this situation did not remain unchallenged. The very notion that women as a group were quite different from men led some women to identify common interests. In other words, in a society that made a point of differentiating people on the basis of sex, it was not surprising that women came to believe that working together they could change their legal and social position. It was this belief that led to the formation of the women's rights movement in the middle of the nineteenth century.

Women Challenge the Law of Domestic Relations

On July 20,1848, about 300 women and men met at a church in Seneca Falls, New York to address issues of women's position in the United States.[12] The unprecedented meeting was the idea of Elizabeth Cady Stanton, who would become one of the major leaders of the nineteenth-century women's movement, and Lucretia Mott, a Quaker leader in efforts both to abolish slavery and to extend women's rights. Stanton, as a judge's daughter and a lawyer's wife, had long been both fascinated and outraged by the unequal position of American women under the laws of domestic relations. It was at her urging that the participants at the Seneca Falls convention debated and adopted a declaration and a number of resolutions listing a series of gender inequities and recommending action to rectify them. (An edited version of the document is included in Appendix One.) Here it will be useful to examine a number of the issues raised at Seneca Falls, both to demonstrate a contemporary critique of nineteenth-century patriarchal society and to determine which of the points remain relevant to gender relations in the twenty-first century.

Stanton and Mott purposely modeled the Declaration of Sentiments on the Declaration of Independence. They realized that their audience, both those at the convention and those who would later read published versions of the document, were familiar with Jefferson's words and that many found the statements of equality inspirational. They also realized that the ideals of the Declaration of Independence needed clarification. The Founding Fathers had lived in a gendered world and assumed that in writing a list of their grievances they had covered everything. The participants at Seneca Falls had some changes to make.

The Seneca Falls Declaration begins with words identical to the Declaration of Independence but includes important amendments in the second paragraph:

> We hold these truths to be self evident: that all men *and women* (my italics) are created equal; that they are endowed by their Creator with certain inalienable rights; that among these are life, liberty, and the pursuit of happiness, that to secure these rights governments are instituted, deriving their just powers from the consent of the governed.

Stanton differed from Jefferson, not only in adding the words "and women" but in omitting the statement that governments are instituted *among men*. These are not small changes but efforts to establish women's rights as full participants in the body politic. Americans believed that a just government was based on a social contract whereby people gave certain powers to the state in exchange for the state's protection. The women at Seneca Falls rightly identified the problem that women had been left out of that equation. By not being among those who *instituted* the government—even though God had made them equal—they were not included in the group whose rights were protected by the government. Following that logic, it is clear why the first grievance mentioned in the Seneca Falls Declaration is that women have been deprived of the right to vote. They have not been real participants in the social contract, so every other deficiency of their status flows from the patriarchal structure that keeps them one step removed from real citizenship. They argue that men—as a group—would exercise tyranny over women—as a group. In other words, the social structure stands on a system of gender inequality.

The document went on to provide a list of women's injuries. Some of these are specifically directed against the law of coverture, others against women's lack of social opportunities, and still others against the assumptions that allow men to exercise power and dominance over women.

The critique of coverture noted that women could not own or control property, even their own wages. Marriage involved a promise that wives obey their husbands. This requirement degraded women in two ways—they were not legally responsible for their own actions (like children), and their husbands were allowed to "chastise" them. In the interest of insuring his wife's good behavior (by his definition), a husband could be within his legal rights in using physical force. Governments were complicit in this arrangement for although they prevented women from owning property, they willingly accepted their taxes—presumably to pay for perpetuating a system that kept women in second-class status.

Some of the grievances listed in the Declaration of Sentiments criticized the lack of opportunities for women, many of which stemmed from assumptions about female inferiority and dependence. Colleges and professions were closed to women. Most churches refused to consider ordaining women to the ministry. Without access to these avenues to power, how could women challenge an unequal society? Where would they find the forum to argue for and influence change?

Finally, other points contested basic assumptions about gender roles and male dominance. The double standard of morality—devised by men—condemned women for sexual immorality while tolerating the same behavior in men. The division of the world into appropriate male and female spheres was the work of mortal men. If such a division were to exist, it should be defined by men, women, and God. And—in a modern-sounding psychological statement—the declaration takes men to task for destroying women's self-confidence and self-respect, making them willing to lead "a dependent and abject life."

Significantly, all of these grievances are preceded by the point that women have been excluded from participation in public life, that their voice has been absent in making laws and in the social conditions that have resulted. Although they did not use the terms, it is clear that the delegates at Seneca Falls regarded women's unequal and subordinate position in American society as a systematic problem. They were not advocating just an enumeration of amendments to the laws that would provide a few specific reforms, they were calling for an end to patriarchy and a reordering of the structure of dominant and subordinate gender roles.

The Seneca Falls Declaration is, in many ways, a revolutionary document that even today provides a feminist agenda. It set in motion a "rights discourse" by which women challenged the status quo. They no longer wanted to ask their husbands to grant them rights but rather to make claims that they were entitled to *civil rights*—that they had claims of rights against the state. According to Reva Siegel, for the nineteenth-century feminists, domestic violence or "chastisement" provided an insight into the whole realm of women's rights. Domestic violence "exposed the fiction of women's protection by man," and therefore women could argue that they needed "social, civil, legal, political, and ecclesiastical power to protect *themselves*." She believes there was always a link between women's subordination in the family and the agenda of the women's movement.[13]

The nineteenth-century women's movement, growing from its roots at Seneca Falls, did achieve some important objectives. There are at least two principles to consider here. First, the reforms resulted from the collective and persistent action of organized women and men attempting to change things. As long as each woman saw her situation as an individual problem with an individual remedy, no changes in the social climate would occur. Second, although laws were modified—for example, most states adopted Married Women's Property Acts, allowing women to own property and control their earnings—many old assumptions about male superiority and female inferiority persisted. Sometimes these assumptions disguised themselves in new language.

Siegel argues, for example, that the laws regarding domestic violence demonstrate how old convictions can reemerge with updated rationales. In the second half of the nineteenth century, partly in response to the women's movement and partly as a general trend away from physical punishment and a redefinition of status relationships, many states passed laws disclaiming the right of husbands to use physical force against their wives. Nonetheless, despite changes in the law, as Chapter Four will discuss further, wife battering persisted, and the legal system did little to hold batterers accountable. The rationale based on coverture was replaced with a rationale based on the privacy of the home and family relations.[14] This rationale effectively allowed the legal system to deny women access to many aspects of citizenship—not because women did not exist in the eyes of the law but because they were different from men. The fundamental fact of those differences identified women with domestic life, and this domestic life was private—beyond the arm of the government to control.

Constitutional Challenges

Changes in women's legal position came about partly through organized efforts to influence legislatures to amend specific statutes. But change could also be pursued through the courts, especially through appeals to the United States Supreme Court, which is charged with interpreting the meaning of the Constitution. It is not surprising that during the latter half of the nineteenth and all of the twentieth century, struggles over women's constitutional status would reach the highest court. It is neither possible nor necessary to examine every case that dealt with definitions of gender. Instead the remainder of this chapter will examine a number of cases—some famous and others not well known—to see what the Supreme Court contributed to the history of women's pursuit of full citizenship. Sometimes the Court's rulings reflected popular gender stereotypes, sometimes they seemed to challenge those stereotypes, and sometimes the Court's statements are ambivalent. [Portions of the selected cases are included in the Appendices.]

Many of the cases dealing with women's issues arose under the Fourteenth Amendment, added to the constitution in 1868 after the Civil War. The first section of the Fourteenth Amendment states: "No State shall make or enforce any law which shall abridge the privileges or immunities of citizens of the United States; nor shall any State deprive any person of life, liberty, or property without due process of law; nor deny to any person equal protection of the laws." Although the amendment was originally intended to ensure that the states did not deprive the former slaves of their rights as citizens, it quickly became clear to many activist women that the amendment might also serve as a means to address issues of gender equity. Could the Fourteenth Amendment serve as a mechanism to dismantle the common law traditions that made women, particularly married women, stand in a subordinate position before the law?

Running through many of the Court's early decisions on the subject of gender is the notion that men and women are more unlike than they are comparable and a devotion to the ideology of separate spheres. For the most part, these convictions, coupled with beliefs about the need to protect marital privacy, meant progress toward equal citizenship would be slow and difficult.

The first such example comes from the story of Myra Bradwell. Her case is *Bradwell v. Illinois*.[15] Mrs. Bradwell who had read the law in her husband's office and edited a law journal was denied a license to practice law by the Supreme Court of Illinois because she was a married woman. She appealed to the Supreme Court, on the grounds that as a citizen of the United States, the Fourteenth Amendment's guarantee that no state could abridge privileges and immunities protected her right to choose a profession. The majority of the court rejected her argument on the grounds that admission to the practice of law is not related to United States citizenship but is strictly a matter for each state to determine. Illinois was within its rights to decide who could get a law license and to decide that women would not be eligible.

The most widely quoted part of the *Bradwell* decision is not the majority opinion, written by Justice Miller, but a concurrence written by Justice

Bradley. (See Appendix Two) The concurring opinion is an unusually explicit statement of women's legal subordination, cloaked in the language of the common law and the separate spheres. Bradley argues that the law, "as well as nature herself, has always recognized a wide difference in the respective spheres and destinies of man and woman. Man is, *or should be* (italics added), woman's protector and defender." Following this reasoning, women's position is fixed by the law and by nature as dependent on the likelihood that a man will take care of them. Bradley claims that God's law (the divine ordinance) has established a specific type of family organization, one in which "the domestic sphere...properly belongs to the domain and functions of womanhood." He refers to the common law tradition when "a woman had no legal existence separate from her husband, who was regarded as her head and representative in the social state." Under the common law, a woman could not sign contracts without her husband's consent. With that disability, how could she possibly practice law? Justice Bradley and those who shared his point of view believed women's subordinate position was permanently fixed and beyond the ability of the law or a constitutional amendment to change.

In 1908, the court addressed another issue that related to women in the workforce in *Muller v. Oregon*.[16] (See Appendix Three) Oregon had a law prohibiting the employment of women in industry for more than ten hours a day. The law was challenged by Muller, a laundry owner, who was charged with requiring a female employee to work more than ten hours. Three years earlier the court had declared a New York state law regulating men's working hours unconstitutional. Would they come to the same conclusion about the Oregon statute, or were the differences between the sexes sufficient to reach a different conclusion?

The justices acknowledged that women's status had changed from the days of coverture, "It is the law of Oregon that women, whether married or single, have equal contractual and personal rights with men." Nonetheless, they noted "a widespread belief that woman's physical structure, and the functions she performs in consequence thereof, justify special legislation restricting or qualifying the conditions under which she may be permitted to toil." Women need special care because of their "maternal functions." The state has an interest in assuring that mothers are healthy and in preserving "the strength and vigor of the race." Thus, it is not unconstitutional for a state to pass protective legislation that applies differently to women and men. In other words, the law can classify persons on the basis of sex and use that classification as a basis for differential treatment.

Many contemporaries and historians have argued that in the short run, women derived practical benefits from *Muller v. Oregon*, as employers were regulated in their demands for long working hours. Others see the decision as another example of stereotypical thinking in the law that had the effect of perpetuating women in traditional and subordinate roles. They point to such statements as "Even though all restrictions on political, personal, and contractual rights were taken away and [women] stood, so far as statutes are concerned, upon an absolutely equal plane with [men], it would still be true that she is so constituted that she will rest upon him and look to him for protection; that her physical structure and a proper discharge of her maternal functions...justify legislation to protect her from the greed as well as the passions of man." The court seems to be saying that even if women are partially liberated from the bonds of coverture—to the extent that they have some economic rights—because of their maternal roles they are necessarily dependent upon men. The law presumably supports these different gender roles by protecting women from the greed and passions of men who would take advantage of their weakness. But, as a decision in 1910 would demonstrate, the Court was not willing to extend its protective arm into the family.

Jessie Thompson and her husband, Charles, were residents of Washington, D.C. In the early twentieth century, all laws for the district were made by the United States Congress. One such law provided that married women had the power to make contracts, to sue and be sued. A provision of the law referred to the women's power to sue "for torts committed against them, as fully and freely as if they were unmarried." (A tort is a legal term for a harm done to someone for which they may collect damages.) Mrs. Thompson sued her husband for $70,000. He had, she charged, assaulted her on at least three occasions over a period of three days. Charles Thompson knew his wife was pregnant at the time he battered her. Could she sue him for committing a tort against her?

Even though the law seemed clearly to give her that right, the majority of the Supreme Court justices in *Thompson v. Thompson* (See Appendix Four),[17] found the concept too radical. They refused to believe that Congress would permit such a lawsuit. "The statute was not intended to give a right of action as against the husband, but to allow the wife, in her own name, to maintain actions of tort which, at common law must be brought in the joint names of herself and her husband." In other words, the Court's opinion held, that even though the law didn't say so, it meant to give women the right to sue everyone but their husbands. They settled on this interpretation for several reasons—divorce already provided one remedy for abuse. The criminal courts provided another. They were aghast at the possible harm that could be done if they were to "open the doors of the courts to accusations of all sorts of one spouse against the other and bring into public notice complaints for *assault* (italics added), slander, and libel." The idea that these marital disputes would come into public notice seemed to concern the justices more than the fact that the harms occurred. The majority maintained that if Congress intended to "revolutionize the law" to give wives the right to sue their husbands, they would have said so with "irresistible clearness." To permit otherwise might involve "emphasizing and publishing differences which might not be serious." If a battered woman could collect damages when her husband assaulted her, she might expose these "differences" and reveal behavior that was better hidden.

Three justices dissented from the majority in *Thompson*. They believed that Congress chose to use inclusive language giving women the right to sue for damages regardless of who was responsible for the damages. If they wanted to make an exception for husbands Congress would have said so. The dissenters acknowledge that this law would be a radical change in the common law relations of men and women, that it "destroys the unity of the marriage association as it had previously existed." But they argue that is the only logical interpretation of the words in the statute. Otherwise, a woman would be permitted to sue her husband for the recovery of property, but would be denied "the right or privilege to sue him...for damages arising from his brutal assaults upon her person."

Had the Court ruled differently in *Thompson v. Thompson*, it might well have set a precedent for other challenges to the remaining vestiges of coverture and to the arguments that marital privacy prohibited state action to protect women. Instead, a series of cases in the first four decades of the twentieth century provide a record of constitutional setbacks rather than advances for women.

Quong Wing v. Kirkendall[18] arose under the equal protection clause of the Fourteenth Amendment. It concerned a Montana law requiring that all persons engaged in hand laundry businesses pay a $10 license fee. Businesses consisting of one or two women were exempt from the tax. Chinese laundry owners challenged the law as discriminatory believing it was aimed at them because they owned most of the hand laundries. They further argued that a distinction based on the sex of the workers had no legitimate relation to the tax. The Court majority disagreed, stating that if a state wanted to make a distinction on the basis of sex, it was entitled to do so. The ruling seems to remove women from the protection of the Fourteenth Amendment, which prohibited states from depriving citizens of equal protection. Much as the Court allowed that racial segregation was not unconstitutional in *Plessy v. Ferguson*,[19] *Quong Wing* appears to hold that distinctions based on sex are purely a matter for the states to decide. "...The 14th Amendment does not interfere by creating a fictitious equality where there is a real difference. The particular points at which that difference shall be emphasized by legislation are largely in the power of the state."[20] Thus the states were free to make whatever legal distinctions they chose between men and women. At this point they were not even expected to justify those distinctions as "reasonable."

Three years later the Court issued a ringing defense of the principles of coverture in *Mackenzie v. Hare.*[21] Ethel Mackenzie was married to Gordon Mackenzie, a British citizen. She had asserted her right to vote as a citizen born in the United States and residing in California. Although California had already granted women the right to vote, Ethel Mackenzie was not allowed to cast a ballot because the election officials claimed she was not a U.S. citizen. Congress had passed a law in 1907 stating that a woman who married a "foreigner" took the nationality of her husband. Mrs. Mackenzie challenged that termination of her citizenship, but the Supreme Court upheld the law. They found it was based on long-standing legal doctrines. "The identity of husband and wife is an ancient principle of our jurisprudence. There has been, it is true, much relaxation of it, but in its retention as in its origin, it is determined by their intimate relation and unity of interests, and this relation and unity may make it of public concern in many instances to merge their identity, and give dominance to the husband." Thus Ethel Mackenzie was not only denied the right to vote, her case gave the Court an opportunity to reaffirm the judicial doctrine that the identities of husband and wife were "merged" and that the husband was to be dominant.

Having made that ruling in 1915, it is rather startling that in 1923 the Court would find a minimum wage for women unconstitutional, largely on the grounds that women operated as independent agents and did not need special protection from the law. In *Adkins v. Children's Hospital of the District of Columbia*[22] (See Appendix Five) the majority found that "the ancient inequality of the sexes...has continued with diminishing intensity [since their ruling in *Muller v. Oregon*]. In view of the great—not to say revolutionary—changes which have taken place since that utterance, in the contractual, political, and civil status of women, culminating in the Nineteenth Amendment, it is not unreasonable to say that these differences have now come almost, if not quite, to the vanishing point." Reading these words, one would believe that women stood on a totally equal footing with men before the law. Several times the opinion refers to this supposed equality. "We cannot accept the doctrine that women of mature age... require or may be subjected to restrictions upon their liberty of contract which could not lawfully be imposed in the case of men under similar circumstances. To do so would be to ignore all the implications to be drawn from the present day trend of legislation, as well as that of common thought and usage, by which woman is accorded *emancipation from the old doctrine that she must be given special protection or be subjected to special restraint in her contractual and civil relationships.*" (italics added) The Court seems to be saying clearly that women have been freed from the "old doctrine," presumably coverture, that provided special protection and restrained their civil rights.

Another interesting set of themes twist through *Adkins*. The law reviewed by the Court required that employers pay women adequate wages to "maintain them in health and to protect their morals." It suggests that women stand in particular need of moral supervision, assuming a likely connection between low pay and "immorality." References to immorality and women almost always referred to violations of conventional chastity, especially prostitution. Thus one could argue that legislators found a justification for protective laws for women, not only in their maternal functions (as in the Oregon law upheld in *Muller*) but in their vulnerability to vice, as argued in the minimum wage law. Both rationales stem from gendered assumptions; both seem to contradict the Court majority's claims of "revolutionary" changes in women's positions.

The dissenters in *Adkins* disagreed with the court's conclusions but expressed some interesting gender views themselves. Chief Justice Taft believed the majority's holding that the Nineteenth Amendment had changed all things for women to be overblown. "The amendment did give women political power and makes more certain that legislative provisions for their protection will be in accord with their interests as they see them. But I do not think we are warranted in varying constitutional construction based on physical differences between men and women, because of the amendment." Taft appears to realize the significance and the progressive potential of giving women a real voice in laws that apply to them. On the other hand, he also notes that a constitutional amendment can only do so much. It cannot obliterate the physical differences between the sexes. He is stating in a nutshell a modern feminist argument and a dilemma. The sexes cannot and should not be made the same by a legal proclamation. In fact, constitutional interpretation and law must reflect women's perspective as well as men's. The law needs to account for both difference and real equality.

Breedlove v. Suttles[23] affords a look at unequal treatment that appears to privilege women, but which, in fact turns out to be another assertion of a patriarchal outlook. The case concerns a Georgia law that required males to pay a $1 poll tax each year whether they voted or not. Women and blind people were exempt from the tax if they chose not to register to vote. The poll tax could be a real hardship, especially for poor tenant farmers and sharecroppers who seldom had cash. They would find it especially difficult to accumulate enough money to pay delinquent poll taxes for the years they missed.

Breedlove, who was a twenty-eight-year-old white man, challenged the law as a violation of the Fourteenth Amendment equal protection clause. He essentially claimed sex discrimination, refused to pay his assessed poll tax, but demanded to register. The Supreme Court dismissed his equal protection claim, noting that women were "naturally entitled" to special consideration. It was reasonable to exempt women from poll taxes "in view of the burdens necessarily borne by them for the preservation of the race." Thus the state of Georgia appeared to be giving women an advantage, a relief of a tax burden. The opinion goes on, however, to explain that this benevolence is not really intended to benefit women but to promote the strength and values of the patriarchal family. "The laws of Georgia declare the husband to be the head of the family and the wife to be subject to him. To subject her to the levy would be to add to his burden. Moreover, Georgia poll taxes are laid to raise money for educational purposes, and it is the father's duty to provide for education of the children." The implication seems to be that husbands, legitimately, control whether their wives' poll taxes get paid and, therefore whether their wives vote. It is hard to reconcile this opinion with the assertions in *Adkins* that women stand on an equal legal footing with men.

Many significant social changes occurred between 1937 and 1961, yet the court seemed to hold on to some very traditional ideas about women's roles. Thousands of women had served in the armed forces, and six million women had gone out to work, many in heavy industry, during World War II. Young women were attending college in record numbers. They were involved in all phases of social reform. Rosa Parks had sparked the civil rights movement. Eleanor Roosevelt had persuaded the United Nations to approve an International Declaration of Human Rights. The world had not stood still and women's roles continued to evolve. Yet *Hoyt v. Florida*[24] (See Appendix Six) reads like the Court was in a time warp.

As late as 1961, the Supreme Court echoed the themes noted in *Breedlove*, the notion that women were "excused" from their civic duties because the demands of their private domestic role superceded their public obligations. It is critical to remember that these privileges were not legislated *by* women but allegedly *for* women by men in public life.

The case concerned Gwendolyn Hoyt, convicted by an all-male jury of killing her husband. In *Hoyt v. Florida*, the court examined two issues. Was it a Fourteenth Amendment violation for women to be relieved of jury service unless they registered voluntarily? Was Ms. Hoyt deprived of her right to an impartial jury? Thus the law was evaluated both from the perspective of women's right to serve on juries and the perspective of a female defendant's right to have women included on her jury.

It had been a struggle to get women on Florida juries at all. The first bill proposing voluntary jury service for women was proposed in 1943 (23 years after women had won the right to vote). The bill was defeated at that time by a legislature that claimed every possible chivalrous reason to spare women from their civic responsibilities. For example, even though Florida maintained a strong system of racial segregation, opponents of female jury service raised the specter of "respectable" white women being closed up on juries with black men. They also argued that these respectable women would be exposed to filthy evidence—shocking things that they should never hear. They would be distracted from concentrating on the evidence because they would be worrying about their children left at home. And the state would be required to add women's restrooms in the courthouse and to hire female bailiffs to escort the jurors.[25] (Assuming that Ms. Hoyt was not the first woman defendant in Florida, the restroom issue raises some puzzling questions.) In any event, in 1949 Florida passed a law providing that women could register their names with the circuit court clerk if they wished to volunteer for jury service. At the time Ms. Hoyt was tried in 1957, 220 women had registered for jury service in her jurisdiction. There were ten women's names in the pool from which her jury was selected. When asked why only ten women's names were on the list, the circuit court clerk replied that they had always listed ten women.[26]

Were Gwendolyn Hoyt's constitutional rights violated by this jury selection process? Were the women of Florida deprived of their constitutional right to serve?

The Supreme Court said no to both questions.

Ms. Hoyt claimed that the nature of her crime, the murder of her husband who had abused her and been unfaithful over a period of years, demanded a jury including women who could empathize with her situation. The killing was, she asserted, an act of temporary insanity brought about by a long history of cruelty. The Court held, on the contrary, that a defendant was not entitled to a jury "tailored to the circumstances of a particular case." They referred to the killing as part of a "marital upheaval involving, among other things, the suspected infidelity of appellant's husband, and culminating in the husband's final rejection of his wife's effort at reconciliation." Hoyt was viewed by the Court as a woman scorned, but perhaps women would have seen it differently. Hoyt's claim, however, was not so much that women did not end up on her jury. Rather she argued that the

Florida process made it almost impossible for any jury to include women. The Court did not seem to grapple with that point.

As to the second issue, whether the Florida law violated equal protection because its differential treatment of men and women for jury service was "unreasonable,"[27] the Supreme Court thought not. "Despite the enlightened emancipation of women from the restrictions and protections of bygone years, and their entry into many parts of community life formerly considered to be reserved to men, *woman is still regarded as the center of home and family life.* (italics added) We cannot say that it is constitutionally impermissible for a State, acting in pursuit of the general welfare, to conclude that a woman should be relieved from the civic duty of jury service unless she herself determines that such service is consistent with *her own special responsibilities.*" (italics added). In other words, in 1961, the Supreme Court still found that the assumption that women were, by definition, circumscribed by the domestic sphere was reasonable. Furthermore the Court denied that such generalized definitions of women were comparable to discrimination based on race. In their view, the "benevolent" exclusion of women from public duty was distinguished from the discriminatory exclusion of African Americans.

By the time the next significant equal protection case, *Reed v. Reed,*[28] came before the Court in 1971, many of the gender stereotypes that underlay *Hoyt v. Florida* would be challenged in every area of American life. Historians and legal scholars tend to regard *Reed* as something of a turning point. In that case, a unanimous Supreme Court found differential treatment based on sex to be a violation of Fourteenth Amendment equal protection guarantees.

The facts of the case are not nearly so dramatic as Gwendolyn Hoyt's murder trial. Rather *Reed* concerns a provision of Idaho law having to do with administering the estate of someone who dies without a will. Richard Reed died in 1967, leaving about $1,000 worth of personal property. Both of his adoptive parents, who were divorced from each other, applied to be administrator of his estate. The Idaho law established an order of preference for estate administrators, based on their relationship to the deceased. Spouses would have first preference, followed by children, parents, siblings, etc. If two persons with the same relationship applied, the male would always be preferred over the female. As both Sally and Cecil Reed had the same relationship to Richard, the choice would be based on the applicant's sex. The Idaho court named Cecil Reed administrator and Sally appealed.

The Supreme Court found the mandatory preference for men over women in the Idaho estate law to be unconstitutional. The justices found that if a state classifies people on the basis of sex, the classification must be "reasonable." Reasonable means, in the Court's language, that the classification must have a *fair and substantial relation* to the purpose of the legislation. Here the purpose of the legislation was to select a qualified administrator of an estate. Why should that choice be based on sex? The state of Idaho argued that choosing men over women relieved the state of the burden of holding individual hearings to decide who was more qualified. That was not a good enough reason for the Supreme Court to permit a classification based on sex alone.

The principle that came down as a result of *Reed v. Reed* was that when a law treats men and women differently, the state must be able to demonstrate that the classification is reasonable—that it serves a fair and substantial purpose. When the court demands this level of explanation of a distinction, it is said to be subjecting that law to *judicial scrutiny*. Not until this case, did the Court state that sex discrimination would be subjected to judicial scrutiny. Earlier the Court had ruled that race discrimination would be subjected to its most rigorous test. The justices examine laws that include racial classification with *strict scrutiny*. That means that the state must demonstrate that the discrimination serves a *compelling* interest and that the means used in the law are *narrowly tailored* to achieve that purpose. Proponents of gender equality have hoped ever since *Reed v. Reed* that the court would apply the same strict test to sex discrimination. They came closest to doing this in a 1973 case, *Frontiero v. Richardson*,[29] (See Appendix Seven) but ultimately retreated from that conclusion.

Many things about the Frontiero case demonstrate how old stereotypes of patriarchy and separate spheres had become obsolete. Sharron Frontiero's career was untraditional. She was a lieutenant in the United States Air Force. She applied for dependant benefits, an increased housing allowance and medical coverage for her husband. When Frontiero encountered a military regulation that applied different criteria to servicemen and servicewomen applying for benefits, she challenged the policy in court.

A married serviceman had only to ask for benefits for his wife. She was assumed to be his dependant. A military woman, on the other hand, was required to demonstrate that she provided more than one-half of her husband's support if he were to qualify for benefits. Was this unconstitutional sex discrimination under the Fifth Amendment?[30] There were two parts to Frontiero's challenge. A woman in the military service was required to prove the extent to which she supported her spouse. A military man was not. This was procedural discrimination. Second, a serviceman received benefits for his spouse regardless of her personal wealth or income. A servicewoman did not. So the law also had a different impact on women and men.

Eight justices agreed that the policy was discriminatory and unconstitutional. The only member of the court who disagreed was Justice Rehnquist, now Chief Justice. However, among the eight in the majority, only four supported the idea that laws that discriminated on the basis of sex should be subject to strict scrutiny. A majority of five justices would have been required to make *strict scrutiny* the rule for all future sex discrimination cases. The opinion contains some of the court's strongest statements to date about gender. "There can be no doubt that our Nation has had a long and unfortunate history of sex discrimination. Traditionally, such discrimination was rationalized by an attitude of 'romantic paternalism' which, in practical effect, put women, not on a pedestal, but in a cage." What Justice Brennan here calls "romantic paternalism" is another term for a patriarchal ideology that idealized the separate spheres. He found that women still faced "pervasive, although at times more subtle, discrimination," but such discrimination violated "the basic concept of our system that legal burdens should bear some relationship to individual responsibility." Furthermore, "the sex characteristic frequently bears no relation to ability to perform or contribute to society," and laws that classify people by sex "often have the effect of invidiously relegating the entire class of females to inferior legal status without regard to the capabilities of its individual members."

The three justices who concurred in the result of the case but did not accept the strict scrutiny standard explained that they preferred to leave the decision to the political process. At the time of the *Frontiero* ruling, Congress had passed the Equal Rights Amendment (ERA) to the Constitution, and the states were deciding whether to ratify it.[31] The three concurring justices did not want "to preempt by judicial action a major political decision which is currently in process of resolution." In other words, they chose to wait and see whether the ERA was ratified before laying down a rule about sex discrimination. As the required number of states (37), never approved the ERA, the constitutional status of gender discrimination remains problematical. Decades after *Frontiero*, the court has certainly not presided over a dismantling of sex discrimination. Several cases have resolved questions regarding such specific issues as jury service. Other cases have offered some clarification of the standard to be used in evaluating classifications based on gender. To date, however, a majority of the court has not agreed that sex discrimination merits strict scrutiny.

They next revisited the scrutiny issue in *Craig v. Boren*.[32] This time the court applied a standard of "intermediate" or "heightened" scrutiny to sex discrimination under the Fourteenth Amendment. In the mid-1970s, Oklahoma's alcohol laws provided that males under the age of twenty-one were prohibited from purchasing nonintoxicating 3.2% beer. Young women, however, were permitted to purchase 3.2% beer at the age of eighteen.[33] Clearly the law made a distinction on the basis of sex. The Supreme Court found this discrimination "invidious." States may not use "gender as an inaccurate proxy for other, more germane, bases of classification." They must be careful of "outdated misconceptions" and "loose-fitting characterizations," in other words, gendered assumptions as a basis for treating men and women differently. Classifications by gender must "serve *important* governmental objectives and must be *substantially* related to achievement of those objectives." (italics added) This phrase defines a higher standard than *Reed*, which required only that classifications be *reasonable*.

According to the arguments from Oklahoma, the 3.2% beer law was designed to promote traffic safety. They argued that young men between eighteen and twenty-one posed a greater threat behind the wheel as they were inclined to drink and drive and had a higher rate of traffic accidents. The court rejected this rationale, finding little statistical support for it. The law failed to meet the heightened scrutiny test necessary to treat eighteen-year-old men differently from eighteen-year-old women.

Two jury cases, one in 1975 and the other in 1994, showed that the Court had moved 180 degrees from its position in *Hoyt v. Florida*. Whereas that case had allowed a state to assume that women's domestic responsibilities were sufficient reason to excuse them from jury service, *Taylor v. Louisiana*[34] found such treatment unconstitutional. Billy Taylor had been convicted of aggravated kidnapping. From the start of the proceedings, Taylor's attorney argued that his right to a fair trial was violated because women were "systematically excluded" from the jury under the Louisiana law that required women to volunteer if they wished to serve. His argument was that this process denied him a jury that truly represented the community.[35] The Supreme Court agreed.

The law had the effect of excluding virtually the entire population of women from jury pools. Thus, a trial jury would not represent a cross-section of the community—a test which the court found "an essential component of the Sixth Amendment right to a jury trial." There is a statistical argument that there should be some women in a representative jury pool as they made up 53% of the population in the jurisdiction where Taylor was tried. The Court believed, too, that women brought different perspectives to the deliberations, also a necessity if the jury were to represent the *whole* community. "If the shoe was on the other foot, who would claim that a jury was truly representative of the community if all men were intentionally and systematically excluded from the panel?" That question highlights the old assumption so prevalent in the legal system—men could speak for women, but women could not speak for men. At least in 1975, the Supreme Court disagreed. "The truth is that the two sexes are not fungible; a community made up exclusively of one is different from a community composed of both."

As for those "distinctive" domestic duties, the idea that these should exclude *all* women, seemed "untenable" to the justices. "If it was ever the case that women were unqualified to sit on juries or were so situated that none of them should be required to perform jury service, that time has long since passed." If individual women needed exemptions because of their occupation, the state could excuse them as it did men.

Taylor v. Louisiana effectively overturned *Hoyt v. Florida*. Although the specific constitutional issues in the case are related to jury selection, one can see it as part of the progression of rulings that questioned the validity of gender stereotypes. One may make the same claim for *J. E. B. v Alabama.*[36]

Strangely enough, *J. E. B.* also involved a male petitioner raising a sex discrimination issue. Alabama filed a paternity and child support action against J. E. B, on behalf of T. B., the child's mother. When the case came to trial, the state used nine of its ten peremptory strikes to remove men from the jury.[37] The case was heard before an all-female jury. The state admitted to removing all the male jurors because men were more likely to be sympathetic to another man in a paternity suit. But the state also argued that this procedure met the "reasonableness" test and was, therefore, constitutional.

The Supreme Court rejected this reasoning and, in effect, made the points Gwendolyn Hoyt had argued in 1961. "Jurors as well as litigants have an equal protection right to jury selection procedures that are free from state-sponsored group stereotypes rooted in, and reflective of, historical prejudice." Although the Court had previously ruled that using peremptory challenges to remove jurors on the basis of race was unconstitutional, here they extended the same protection to gender bias. "Gender, like race, is an unconstitutional proxy for juror competence and impartiality." The state had engaged in intentional discrimination on the basis of sex—clearly an equal protection violation—and the discrimination "serves to ratify and perpetuate invidious, archaic, and overbroad stereotypes about the relative abilities of men and women." This discrimination violated the rights of those on trial, those in the jury pool, and the whole community. "The litigants are harmed by the risk that the prejudice which motivated the discriminatory selection of the jury will infect the entire proceedings....The community is harmed by the State's participation in the perpetuation of invidious group stereotypes and the inevitable loss of confidence in our judicial system that state-sanctioned discrimination in the courtroom engenders."

Not only did the Court reject Alabama's argument that its gender-based assumptions were founded in fact and reasonable, they found it fell far below the requirement for heightened judicial scrutiny, an exceedingly persuasive justification.

A considerable part of the majority opinion is devoted to examining the history of sex discrimination, particularly in the courts, and comparing it to race discrimination. The justices refer to the prospect that prejudice and stereotypes in jury selection will lead to public cynicism, "particularly...in cases where gender-related issues are prominent, such as cases involving rape, sexual harassment, or paternity. Discriminatory use of peremptory challenges may create the impression that the judicial system has acquiesced in suppressing full participation by one gender or that the 'deck has been stacked' in favor of one side."

By the time this opinion was handed down, many women had expressed cynicism about the fairness of the judicial system. Supported by experience as well as considerable academic research, the suppression of women's participation and the "stacking of the deck," especially in cases where women were the victims, were well known and well documented. Upholding equal protection standards for jury selection would provide an improvement, but many deep-seated biases remained.

The Court referred to *J. E. B. v. Alabama* as a "pathmarking" decision when it ruled in the 1996 case, *United States v. Virginia*.[38] Virginia Military Institute (VMI) was sued by the United States Justice Department for violating the equal protection clause of the Fourteenth Amendment by its male-only admissions policy. VMI, one of only a few state-supported single-sex colleges in the country, argued that its unique mission—training citizen soldiers—its physically demanding standards, and its adversarial method of education justified its continuing exclusion of women. (See Appendix Eight)

It was obvious that the state of Virginia was affording different treatment to men and women at VMI. The Court noted that such gender-based government action required that the state provide "exceedingly persuasive justification." The classification based on sex must serve "important government objectives and the discriminatory means [must be] substantially related to the achievement of those objectives." The justification for the differential treatment could not be "invented" in response to a lawsuit, not could it "rely on overbroad generalizations about the different talents, capacities, or preferences of males and females." The Court acknowledged some inherent differences between men and women but declared that the differences could not be used "as they once were, to create or perpetuate the legal, social, and economic inferiority of women." They found VMI's argument—that coeducation would have a negative effect on both its mission and its method of education—far short of "exceedingly persuasive justification." In fact, VMI's evidence for excluding women was based on exactly the sort of "overbroad generalization"—that women did not do well under the adversative model of education—forbidden by the Court's Fourteenth Amendment jurisprudence. Harkening back to *Bradwell v. Illinois*, Justice Ginsberg's opinion pointed that just the same type of generalizations about women's different and inferior abilities had kept women from legal education and admission to the bar.

In an equally strong statement about women's citizenship, the Court referred to VMI's mission, to educate citizen soldiers "imbued with a love of learning, confident in the functions and attitudes of leadership, possessing a high sense of public service, advocates of the American democracy and free enterprise system, and ready...to defend their country in time of peril." Surely, the justices said, "that goal is great enough to accommodate women, who today count as citizens in our American democracy equal in stature to men."

If we compare the majority opinion in *United States v. Virginia* to the position of American women under coverture or if we place it beside the demands of the Seneca Falls Declaration, we can see how constitutional law developed in the definition of women's access to equal protection. Two hundred years before the VMI case, a woman had no direct relationship with the state but only an indirect association through the male head of the family. The women at Seneca Falls spelled out some of the implications of this inferior status—exclusion from the political arena, lack of opportunities in education and the professions, assumptions about women's limited abilities, a subordinate standing as citizens. According to *United States v. Virginia*, this inferior status was forbidden by the Constitution. If that case were our final piece of evidence in examining women and the law, we would end with a ringing endorsement of equality.

The next chapter, which considers women's participation in the criminal justice system, will cause the reader to question that equal status.

CHAPTER THREE

Participating in the Criminal Justice System

The last chapter considered the evolution of women's legal status in the United States from their position as non-citizens with only an indirect relationship to the state to the recognition that women were, in many instances, covered by constitutional guarantees of equality. Among other things, we discussed the issue of jury service as part of the struggle for full citizenship. This chapter will look at jury service, along with other types of active participation in the criminal justice system—in law enforcement, corrections, and the courts—as these matters serve to further illustrate struggles over the meaning of gender and equality. It will examine why women have wanted to be part of the system, retrace the history of their participation, and address the meaning of their involvement for women and for criminal justice.

The law and the organizations that exist to enforce the law and punish its violators—in other words, the institutions that make up the criminal justice system—protect the status quo. As discussed earlier, during much of American history, the status quo meant that the system functioned while excluding women from participating in making, interpreting, or enforcing the law. When the women at Seneca Falls declared, "He has compelled her to submit to laws, in the formation of which she had no voice," they were talking about more than the vote. They also recognized their separation from the whole apparatus of the legal system.

The legal establishment both reflected and perpetuated gender hierarchies. It is not surprising, therefore, that some of the greatest opposition to women's involvement in the public sphere centered on whether and how women might function within these institutions. The three component areas of criminal justice—the courts, police, and corrections—were organizations "structured to reflect the culturally dominant images and power relations of gender, race, and class."[1] Arguments against allowing women into this privileged sphere frequently took the form of profoundly gendered stereotypes. Some held that women were not rational enough to understand the abstract principles of the law and therefore could not be attorneys or jurors. Others believed that women would be exposed to shocking stories of crime and evil and could not stand the distress. Many charged that all females lacked the physical strength to subdue criminals or inmates. Underlying such assertions that women needed to be protected from the seamy side of the justice system, however, was an intense reluctance to share the actual power of applying the law, the power to control the public sphere.

Studies of the criminal justice system sometimes tell the story of women's participation in law enforcement and corrections in a fairly simplistic way. According to this version, women, motivated by a somewhat sentimental effort to do good for the unfortunate, worked as volunteers in prisons and courts in the late nineteenth and early twentieth century. When they were hired as salaried workers, they were "relegated" to work with women and children, assigned the less important work that the male professionals did not want to do. The conventional view is that this generation made little impact on the criminal justice system, and it was not until the modern era that began with the 1960s and 1970s that women were able to enter courts, law enforcement, and corrections as real professionals.

The reality is more complicated, more interesting, and more a part of the larger story of women's ongoing challenge to reorder a patriarchal society. Within that framework, this chapter will first examine how women become involved in policing and corrections. It will then turn to the courts and finally address the influence women may bring to criminal justice.

Law Enforcement and Corrections

In 1910, Alice Stebbins Wells became the first sworn female police officer in the United States when she joined the Los Angeles Police Department. "Women and children have a right to representation in the police departments," she said.[2] That simple statement challenged the existing arrangement that excluded women from the process of enforcing the laws. The women who pioneered in police work in the early part of the twentieth century, and to a large extent their counterparts who worked in corrections, were part of a generation who brought to American public life a definite perspective—what Sheila Rothman has called "educated motherhood."[3] They rejected the traditional view of the separate spheres and believed that the outside world would be humanized if women brought the virtues of the home into untraditional places. As Linda Kerber and Jane

DeHart note, the generation of women who came of age in the first decades of the twentieth century moved from the domestic sphere to the public sphere and "in the process changed both."[4] In effect, they undermined some of the patriarchal structure. These women embodied a sense of optimism about the possibilities of social change, organizational skills, experience gained in women's colleges and other female institutions, and tremendous energy. Why did policing appeal to a segment of such women?

In the first decades of the twentieth century, most urban police forces were made up of working class men who typically got their jobs as rewards for political activity. In general, they were expected to have few qualifications, received little training, and tended to see their main role as suppressing disorder, often through the use of a little "curbside justice" administered at the end of a nightstick. The female reformers who sought employment as "policewomen" brought a different and dynamic vision to the profession. They saw themselves as uniquely qualified to be responsive to women and children—both victims and offenders. They hoped to infuse police work with their "womanly values," with their compassion and problem-solving skills. Most of the women who joined police forces in this period were well educated, often with graduate degrees. They were thus familiar with criminological theories that emphasized the environmental causes of crime. They hoped to address conditions that would allow for more crime prevention and less punitive approaches. In general they hoped to raise the level of intelligence of policing.[5] They especially hoped to protect and serve women, who were misunderstood, ignored, and insulted by male police officers.

One could argue that this generation was part of an organized movement to bring women into all professions. But they did not come into those professions asking to be just like their male counterparts. As New York policewoman Mary Hamilton wrote, women were "not just little men,"[6] nor did they wish to be. On the contrary, they were convinced that they could transform the organizations because the old patriarchal patterns were both ineffective and unjust.

Standards for becoming a "patrolwoman" were high. They included a written civil service exam that asked questions about the role of drugs in juvenile crime, venereal disease, statutory rape, and what would today be called sexual harassment. Educated applicants with backgrounds in the social sciences were attracted to policing. Like Mary Hamilton, many believed that "most criminals are made, not born, and it is bad environment that makes them. Study the case histories of any group of prison inmates and it will be found that invariably behind the prison record is a long series of reformatory records, and preceding that a period of unsupervised street life and bad home conditions."[7] Her analysis is remarkably similar to the contemporary criminological theories that connect deviance in girls and women with abusive homes, running away, and encounters with the juvenile justice system. (See Chapter Five). Such an understanding of criminal behavior was something the first generation of female police officers believed they were uniquely able to bring to the job.

Because of their sex, they argued, they also had the ability to prevent crimes where girls and women were the victims. They developed strategies to protect those groups. Policewomen did not wear uniforms, but "good plain clothes," usually a dark dress. They believed that uniforms would frighten women and children as they represented "the coercive power of the state over life, liberty, and property."[8] Dressed as civilians, they patrolled dance halls, cabarets, movies, beaches, boats, and other commercial amusements. Although some writers have emphasized the repressive aspects of the female officers' presence, others, including the policewomen, saw themselves as protecting girls and women from unwanted sexual advances. They described their work as being a friend in need to girls and the "neighborhood's friend," who helped protect young children from "flagrant sex crimes."[9] Given the poor record of the criminal justice system in responding to crimes against women and children, it is quite plausible that the first generation of women officers identified a real problem and staked out a set of responsibilities for themselves that no one else was addressing.

Alice Stebbins Wells argued that point as she spent much of her time speaking to civic clubs and women's groups explaining the advantages of having female officers. She described women deserted or beaten by their husbands and girls who were abused, all of whom were afraid to go to a policeman for help. For the policewomen, their work with women and children was not a limitation or an inferior duty but an acknowledgment that male officers could not do the whole job. Because this generation believed strongly in the value of their work for the future well-being of the country, they would have been shocked to hear that they were "relegated" to work with women and children. They not only believed that theirs was the most important work in the world, they convinced many influential women in the community to support them. Appier argues that when middle class women's organizations invited policewomen to speak, they were so impressed they pressured chiefs to employ more women. By 1935, 290 jurisdictions had hired a total of 850 policewomen, often at the insistence of citizens' groups.[10]

One innovation supported by policewomen was the separate women's bureau. Believing that female victims of crime were intimidated by regular station houses, some cities authorized policewomen to create alternative facilities open 24 hours a day to provide services for women and children. One such model headquarters was set up in New York in 1921. Policewomen were allotted an old station house in the very high crime area of Hell's Kitchen which they transformed by washing and cleaning, painting and renovating the building so it no longer resembled a regular police station. Inside it had a reading room and dormitory, something like a shelter. It invited visitors with geraniums in the window. On those premises, the first priority was the decent treatment of women and children. The goal was to create an environment in which they could come forward without fear or intimidation but where they would find respect and concern. There is no doubt whatsoever that the policewomen who created these alternative institutions did not believe they were being kept out of the "real work" of policing. Rather they believed they were creating a model that could transform the profession. The women of this generation had no desire to be integrated into the existing structure of police departments. They fought to remain separate because they believed they could do their job better that way and because they thought separate women's organizations could both equalize and reconstruct social institutions.[11] Eventually, they hoped the world would look at their model of policing and find it superior to the status quo.

The first group of women police officers struggled at two levels and temporarily lost both battles. They represented an effort by women to move into a particularly masculine part of the public sphere, and they represented an effort to transform the work of that segment. They hoped to prove that crime prevention was more important than crime control and that women were better at prevention. If that were true, policing would indeed become a totally different profession.

If we see the early policewomen not as docile or bumbling do-gooders but as competent professionals with an alternative agenda, the mutual hostility between them and the traditional agencies takes on a different meaning. Their efforts both to advance women's opportunities in policing and to change the nature of the work failed temporarily, but this was largely because of outside social forces that stifled their aspirations. During the 1920s and 1930s, the crime control model of law enforcement came to dominate. Some attribute this shift to the public's fear of "crime waves" played up in the media and promoted by such public figures as J. Edgar Hoover. Prohibition and the Great Depression also shifted police priorities. During the 1930s, as budgets for local governments declined, female police officers were often considered dispensable and the first to be fired. For all of these reasons, the pioneering group of policewomen was largely forgotten or misrepresented as either misguided "child savers" or hatchet-faced Amazons. Both images served to discredit their work, and therefore, later generations would need to rediscover the value of some of their principles, especially their focus on the importance of attention to women and children. In the meantime, the crime control model dominated policing for several decades.

The crime control approach was generally effective in making police agencies less corrupt. As organizations were centralized and a military type of command structure was adopted, departments were less subject to partisan political control. Another aspect of the crime control style, however, was a greater reliance on force to overcome resistance and to subdue suspects. Some have argued that this model of policing reinforced male working-class culture and values, and by implication was especially unfriendly to women as coworkers.[12] The major police organizations, the work culture within agencies, and individual officers tended to believe that masculine characteristics such as physical strength, and masculine strategies, such as aggressiveness, were required to do *real* police work. By definition, women would be excluded. If they wanted to work for law enforcement, women would have to take on "appropriate" gendered jobs—usually office tasks. The difference in the separation of women and men in policing in the middle of the twentieth century from that in the earlier period, is that by the mid-1900s women were assigned female tasks by others. They did not define those jobs for themselves.[13]

The civil rights movement of the 1960s and 1970s ultimately led to another examination of gender roles in the criminal justice professions. In 1964, Congress passed the Civil Rights Act. Title VII of the law prohibits employment discrimination on the basis of sex as well as race. Ironically, the provision against sex discrimination was added by opponents of the bill. They believed the idea of forbidding employment discrimination against women was so outrageous that every rational member of Congress would vote against the legislation, and thus the ban on racial bias would go down to defeat as well. Thanks to vigorous efforts by proponents of civil rights and women's rights, the bill was passed with both categories included. Although the Civil Rights Act of 1964 is the foundation of most employment discrimination challenges, it originally applied only to private employers. Amendments passed in 1972 extended the protections based on race and sex to state and local governments, including criminal justice agencies.

Other efforts by the federal government included both pressures and incentives to expand criminal justice employment. In 1967, the President's Commission on Law Enforcement recommended that the quality of criminal justice administration be improved through higher educational standards, better training, and the hiring of more African Americans and women. The Law Enforcement Assistance Administration provided funds to local agencies to carry out those reforms, and in 1974 agencies were threatened with the loss of their federal money if they failed to provide equal employment opportunities.

Several Supreme Court cases helped to further clarify sex discrimination issues. In 1977 the court issued an opinion concerning Dianne Rawlinson's effort to be hired by the Alabama Board of Corrections as a prison guard.[14] (See Appendix Nine) Although the case concerned a corrections agency, its implications for law enforcement were quite clear. Somewhat like *Muller v. Oregon* discussed in the preceding chapter, *Dothard v. Rawlinson* both improved opportunities for women and, at the same time, reinforced stereotypes. Dianne Rawlinson was a college graduate with a degree in correctional psychology. When she applied for a position as a counselor with the Alabama prison system, she was rejected because she fell below the weight requirement of 120 pounds. The state also mandated that corrections staff be at least 5 feet 2 inches tall. The Court found that although the requirements were not intentionally discriminatory on the basis of sex, they nonetheless had a disparate impact on female applicants. Fewer than 1% of males would be disqualified by the height and weight standards, but 41.13% of females would be excluded. In addition the court found that these size requirements were not necessary for effective job performance. In other words, they were not bona fide occupational qualifications (BFOQs). If physical strength were truly related to the job, the agency could devise appropriate tests to test the individual strength of applicants. This part of the *Rawlinson* decision had the effect of forcing public agencies, including police and corrections, to eliminate height and weight requirements and replace them with criteria that would measure individual applicants' fitness for job related activities, but would not unnecessarily eliminate women candidates—or small men—from consideration.

The second part of the decision reflected some persistent, and troubling, gender stereotypes. A separate Alabama regulation established that women could not serve in "contact positions" in maximum security institutions. These were jobs that required close physical proximity to inmates. The Court upheld this policy on the grounds that women would be less able to maintain order in such facilities. The justices described the environment in Alabama prisons as "a peculiarly inhospitable one for human beings of whatever sex," characterized by "rampant violence" and a "jungle atmosphere." Women were particularly at risk as "sex offenders who have criminally assaulted women in the past would be moved to do so again if access to women were established within the prison. There would be a real risk that other inmates, deprived of a normal heterosexual environment, would assault women guards because they were women." The Court therefore found that being male was a BFOQ for working in a contact position in the Alabama prison system.

The dissenters on the Court seemed astonished at this last ruling. If the atmosphere in Alabama prisons was so inhumane and barbaric, the solution should be to require that the conditions be remedied, not to prohibit women from employment there. The idea that women would provoke sexual assaults, as the majority seemed to suggest, "perpetuates one of the most insidious of the old myths about women, that women, wittingly or not, are seductive sexual objects."

The outcome of the decision was generally positive, as agencies were forced to examine their hiring standards to ensure that they did not have a disparate impact on women candidates. The prohibition of female corrections workers from working in contact positions was narrowly written to apply only to the Alabama prisons. Presumably states whose institutions were less barbaric and more humane could not outlaw the employment of women.

Other changes in criminal justice professions in the latter part of the twentieth century also contributed to better opportunities for women in policing and corrections. In the wake of the civil rights movement and concern for racial harmony, the use of force came under public scrutiny, and most agencies adopted policies requiring more accountability and less discretion from officers. As long as those professions had emphasized the physical control of unruly, usually lower class men, they emphasized the importance of brawn over brains. In the newer version of policing that included better human relations with the community, attention to following rules of procedure, and deemphasized physical coercion, it was difficult to argue that women could not do the job. But replacing the old culture of criminal justice that focused on a masculine model has not been easy. In other words, even if reforms and professionalization expanded opportunities for women, the environment within law enforcement and corrections agencies did not necessarily become more hospitable to a female presence.

At one level, opposition to the full inclusion of women in law enforcement was based on stereotypes—they were physically weaker, too emotional, less able to exercise authority. Some male officers claimed they would be at risk if they had to depend on female colleagues for backup or that it would feel "unmanly" to call on a woman for assistance. At another level, the presence of women in police agencies could threaten the informal masculine culture. Men would need to watch their language as well as their responses to crimes with female victims.[15] Organizations sometimes created subtle but serious barriers that set up women to fail by providing them with inadequate training or uniforms that didn't fit or by failing to provide adequate bathrooms or changing facilities. Some supervisors were subjective in their evaluations of female officers, holding them to different standards than their male counterparts. In other cases, sexual harassment from superiors or fellow officers was tolerated as a part of the organizational culture. Thus, even though many of the legal barriers to full participation by women in law enforcement were removed, the traditions and environment that kept the profession as a sort of male club were more difficult to dismantle. A number of studies have concluded that the greatest barrier to increasing the involvement of women in policing is the behavior of their male colleagues. According to a 1999 study by the National Center for Women and Policing (NCWP), "hostile environments and systemic discrimination keep women from joining police agencies in more significant numbers and from being promoted up the ranks to policy-making positions."[16] The research cites four persistent factors that operate to deny women equal opportunity in law enforcement. Biased entry tests that overemphasize upper body strength eliminate qualified women, even though many studies indicate that physical power is less related to job success than conciliation and mediation skills. Such criteria violate the spirit, if not the letter, of the law interpreted by the Supreme Court in *Dothard v. Rawlinson*. Second, women are subjected to sexual harassment and intimidation. Too often supervisors look the other way. Third, recruitment policies, such as credit for prior military service, favor men. Finally, many agencies continue to encourage "an outdated model of policing by rewarding tough, aggressive, even violent, behavior."[17]

The numbers of women in law enforcement are not impressive. At the end of the twentieth century, women made up only 10.5% of sworn officers according to the Bureau of Justice Statistics.[18] The National Center for Women and Policing placed the number at 14.3%.[19] They found that at the current rate of growth, it would take women several generations to achieve equal representations in law enforcement. The gains at the higher levels are comparably small. Among top command positions, women are only 5.6% of chiefs, deputy chiefs, commanders, and captains.[20]

The NCWP argues that the under-representation of women is bad for law enforcement. Research has shown that female officers are less likely to use excessive force, yet agencies spend tens of millions of dollars settling lawsuits that involve the excessive use of force. The overly aggressive approach is also costly in terms of community relations. In addition, the small percentage of women also influences law enforcement's inadequate response to crimes against women. Domestic violence—even though greatly underreported—is estimated to account for up to 40% of calls to police and may take up to one third of police time.[21] Female officers are more effective in responding to such crimes. Thus it is likely that a greater presence of women officers would lead to greater effectiveness in responding to violence against women[22] as the first generation of policewomen were fond of arguing. Women often have good communication and interpersonal skills, which are useful in implementing the community policing model favored by many experts. Of course, many men also have such skills, but they could only benefit from the presence of competent partners. Finally, there is a good argument that if the number of women in criminal justice organizations reaches a critical mass, sexual harassment and discrimination will decrease, thus saving the cost of lawsuits and bad public relations.[23]

Integrating women fully into law enforcement is a difficult and often painful process. The traditional identification of policing with stereotypical masculine characteristics has limited both the opportunities for women and for the evolution of the profession. And yet, as long as a gendered vision of law enforcement persists, it is likely that one half the population will not experience equal protection of the laws. Susan Brownmiller asserts that the battle to achieve parity with men in law enforcement is the "ultimate testing ground on which full equality for women will be won or lost." Her argument is that when and if that parity is achieved, women will have successfully challenged the traditional belief that the use of force to maintain social order is a male prerogative.[24]

Much of the history of corrections parallels the history of policing, although as Chapter Six discusses, the establishment of female prisons in the nineteenth century meant that women gained a greater foothold in those institutions. However, the huge growth of prison populations in the latter part of the twentieth century and the adoption of a more punitive correctional approach have diminished the importance of a separate female prison culture. The same civil rights laws that prohibited sex discrimination and created opportunities for women opened the doors of employment in women's prisons to men. Today some find that although both federal and state prisons subscribe to "gender neutral" employment practices, the field of corrections remains the most sex-segregated and male-dominated part of the criminal justice system.[25] Yet as with policing, research demonstrates the success of female corrections officers. A 1996 study found that women guards in maximum security prisons were less likely to be assaulted by inmates. Male officers were attacked 3.6 times more often than female officers, apparently because although the women were just as firm as the men, they were less likely to provoke the prisoners.[26] At the same time, women officers were advised to behave more like men. Human relations training was geared more toward modifying the behavior of the female officers than of the male officers who resisted their presence. A persistent theme in articles about women in corrections stresses the need for individual officers to adapt their behavior, to strike a balance among gender stereotypes—not too tough and not too kind.[27] Such approaches see the problems women face in the criminal justice system as individual problems with individual solutions. Yet if the gender bias is built into the structure of the profession, solutions are more likely to come from collective actions and policy changes than from each woman trying, by herself, to conform to the opinions of her coworkers.

The Practice of Law

When Myra Bradwell took her case to the Supreme Court in 1872 she was told that the courtroom was far away from women's natural habitat, the home. And so it was, in the sense that the court represented a system of rules and procedures created entirely without women's participation. Perhaps for that, as well as her own professional reasons, Myra Bradwell and her fellow pioneers in the legal field sought to make their presence felt. Although Bradwell studied privately by "reading for" the bar exam, by the late nineteenth century, graduation from law school was becoming the standard route to a legal career.

The law schools did not rush to open their doors to female students. Washington University in St. Louis was the first to admit a woman when Lemma Burkaloo enrolled in 1869. Belva Lockwood was probably the first woman to receive a degree in law. She earned it from the National University Law School in Washington, D.C. But although Lockwood completed the requirements in 1871, the school delayed three years before granting her diploma. They did so only after she wrote to President Ulysses S. Grant, who was also president of the law school. With Grant's support, her degree was conferred in 1874. Meanwhile, Charlotte Ray, who was African American, became the first woman, black or white, to earn her degree from Howard University Law School in 1872.[28]

The more elite schools were much slower to admit women. Columbia did not accept women until 1927. Harvard waited until 1950. Even then, those schools maintained quotas, which meant that each class might include only three or four women. Washington and Lee in Virginia, the last law school to remain all male, admitted its first female students in 1972.

Up until the late twentieth century, law was clearly a profession of insiders. Admitting women into this "club" would, as both supporters and opponents knew, change things. It is undeniable that the experience of being a woman in a patriarchal society shaped the perspective of female lawyers and jurors. Their very presence in a court of law challenged the notions of separate spheres and undermined the assumptions that women were too different from men to enjoy equal protection of the laws. In other words, the entry of women into the legal profession was like the camel's nose under the tent of patriarchy. It threatened to topple the structure that held the gender hierarchy in place. Thus there was strong resistance to admitting women to the bar and overcoming that resistance was a necessary, but not sufficient, condition for rectifying women's legal status. The nineteenth-century supporters of women's right to a legal career recognized that they could upset the masculine atmosphere in the courtroom and disrupt the consensus between the law and other norms that disadvantaged women.[29] To them, as to the female pioneers in policing and corrections, gender was very relevant to their ability to reform an unjust society.

Unlike women who entered law enforcement and corrections, women lawyers did not initially set up separate institutions or create a female culture within the profession.

In fact, law was different from most other professions, which began with separate women's establishments and later integrated with men. In medicine, for example, several generations of female doctors in the nineteenth century were trained in women's medical colleges. Only in the 1890s were they admitted to the men's schools. In law, the first generations had to struggle for admission to the men's schools. No separate women's law schools existed until the turn of the twentieth century. For a brief period, there were several alternative single-sex institutions—the Washington College of Law at American University in Washington, D.C., and the Portia School of Law in Boston. Both had minimal admission requirements and low tuition. These schools lasted only a short time, mostly because women had better alternatives in state universities which offered stronger curricula and somewhat more prestige.[30] Thus unlike women in almost every other profession, female attorneys did not go through the stage of separate institution building with all the positive theorizing and gender identification that went along with that experience. In fact, before the 1970s when the numbers of women studying law increased significantly, women students were often excluded from the male camaraderie and the male study groups. Because of their very small numbers, they typically remained rather isolated.[31]

One reason women entering law careers followed a different pattern from other fields may be that there is less flexibility in the law. Members of the profession set the criteria, accredit schools, and design appropriate curricula. Admission to the bar involves rigorous examination. In other words getting the proper credentials means following the existing path and fitting into the established model.

The going was tough for the first generations of women lawyers even after they earned their degrees. Many preferred not to appear in court but to devote themselves to office work—research, wills, or real estate. For those who did venture there, the courtroom environment created a number of issues for female attorneys. Should a woman wear a hat in court? Should she be bareheaded like her male colleagues or cover her head like a lady? What sort of attire was appropriate for a woman? Most chose dark dresses or suits, with a slight feminine touch, such as a lace collar or jewelry. It was important to look professional and respectable at the same time. In the 1920s, a number of women lawyers decided that being called "Miss" or "Mrs." called attention to their gender. They looked for a sex-neutral term, such as "Attorney." Although these may seem to be minor matters, they represented a larger concern that gender issues not get in the way of professional performance.[32]

During the last quarter of the twentieth century, thanks to civil rights laws and the women's movement, female law students became more numerous and more visible. Cynthia Epstein refers to the 1970s and 1980s as a time of "subtle revolution" when women were accepted into the "male domains of the elite professions."[33] At another point she describes the process somewhat differently, and perhaps more accurately, stating that "men relaxed but did not release their hold on the profession."[34] In any event, it is clear that women have made dramatic numerical gains in the legal field. By the turn of the century, 51% of law students and 23% of all lawyers were women. This amazing increase raises the obvious question—have women really influenced the law in a way commensurate with their numbers as their opponents feared and as their advocates hoped?

Some changes are beyond dispute. Women are no longer oddities in the courtroom or the law office. Their presence is accepted and expected. They have proved their competence. Few would argue that women, as a group, lack the intellectual capacity to be successful members of the bar. Feminist lawyers have definitely had an impact on certain areas of the law, such as rape, domestic violence, and sexual harassment. More importantly, they have brought a perspective that challenges the assumptions of superiority and subordination upon which much law is built.

Epstein argues that female lawyers are as diverse in their goals and perspectives as their male counterparts.[35] In other words, she finds gender to be only a minor factor in a person's approach to law. Women can be found as prosecutors, defense attorneys, representing corporations and individuals on all sides of any question. There is no one "woman lawyer" model. Although some choose their cases based on feminist principles, others act like male lawyers and go where the work is. These attorneys are concerned that all sides have representation and will argue for anyone as long as they conform to professional norms. Whomever such lawyers represent, Epstein notes, they range in style from "white gloves to pit bulls."[36]

On the other hand, as a group, women do follow different career trajectories than men. A larger percentage of women enter government or public interest law or become corporate counsels. Thirty-seven percent of in-house counsels in all industries, including such traditionally masculine fields as airlines and computer companies, are women. Fewer women than men enter private practice. There is some evidence that these choices are based both on the greater stability and more predictable hours in government or corporate law, and conversely, a rejection of the overwhelming demands of private practice where the atmosphere may still be inhospitable. A report called "The Unfinished Agenda: Women and the Legal Profession" issued by the American Bar Association in 2001 finds that despite a general perception that women have achieved equality in the legal profession, many problems remain.[37] Gender stereotypes continue to prevail in the sense that feminine characteristics are likely to be undervalued while women are penalized for acting too "masculine." Women in law firms also claim they are held to higher standards than their male colleagues, that the partners evaluate them by subjective criteria, and that there is little incentive for the system to change. For example, many female associates are assigned to brief writing and other non-courtroom tasks because they are thought to have better writing skills than the male associates. But when partnership decisions are made, these women are penalized for not having enough trial experience. The ABA report also notes that young female lawyers lack the mentors who could help them negotiate the early stages of their careers. This occurs partly because there are few women at the senior ranks, and some of them do not want to draw attention to their gender by choosing to work with a younger woman. Others apparently believe that if they struggled, others should face the same obstacles. Often men are not comfortable mentoring younger women, either because they feel they have little in common or because they fear their interest would be misunderstood. Thus even in the twenty-first century, young women feel isolated in law firms. In addition, sexual harassment seems to be a largely female experience. Surprisingly, the problem persists despite laws against it, some very large damage awards to victims, and the expectation that law firms, of all places, should be obeying the law. Finally, the ABA report cites the continuing concern that women are the ones who must balance family responsibilities with work. Despite policies providing for maternity leaves, women find that if they take the leave or the flextime option, they are often penalized for not doing their share at the firm when the time comes for promotion, There seems to be tremendous difficulty in meeting the rigorous demands of a job in a law firm and motherhood at the same time. This is especially true as fathers' careers are even more at risk if they assume family responsibilities.[38]

Another way of looking at the family/work dilemma is that some women are willing to forego the male norms of success in favor of doing what they consider useful work and living a fuller life, including having children, and building relationships. Of course this approach is sometimes demeaned and trivialized. Discussion of the "mommy track" often treats it as an inferior career choice rather than as an alternative. Yet some research shows that, in general, women attorneys are more satisfied with their careers than men. It is unclear why this is so. Perhaps women are socialized to accept a different level of success. Perhaps their expectations are lower or different. They may feel that they have proved enough without reaching the top of the profession or be proud to be succeeding in several spheres.[39]

One would be forced to conclude that the overall picture for women attorneys is mixed. In 2000, they comprised 15.6% of the partners in the nation's largest firms, a number that is increasing slowly. During the 1990s, more women joined faculties (a growth from 24% to 31.5% of law professors) and became deans of law schools (a small increase from 7% to 8.2%). These professors should provide more role models for women students. More female than male attorneys work for governments, some in very high profile positions, such as Attorney General Janet Reno, the first woman to hold that position. Women have served as president of the ABA and as chair of that organization's House of Delegates.[40] Minority women are even more likely than white women to enter government or public interest practice. Many attorneys from minority groups believe they face unique challenges. They are often discouraged as girls from considering professional careers. They feel isolated both in law school and at work. Perhaps most troubling are reports of persistent attacks on their credibility as attorneys, including being mistaken in court for secretaries, court reporters, or even relatives of a defendant.[41]

Given all the ambiguities surrounding women in the law, one may ask how the profession has changed. Do women bring a different voice to the field? Carrie Menkel-Meadow cites the creation of feminist law firms based on a non-hierarchical model which involves participatory decision making. Such firms make a point of encouraging lawyer-client relationships based on values of care and mutual responsibility. They try to personalize the clients' problems, not force them into an abstract mode. It remains to be seen whether such alternatives to the usual emphasis on the adversarial model of law will have an impact.[42] A 1989 study concluded that twice as many female as male attorneys had a "general moral orientation to care." They were more likely to respond to problems in terms of people's welfare and relationships and less likely to focus on rights. Women in that study were more likely than men to experience conflicts between their personal values and the role of a lawyer.[43] Katherine Bartlett advises expanding legal reasoning to include women's perspective, in other words, to ask the "woman question." She means that female attorneys must lead the way in examining legal doctrine to uncover systematic gender bias. They must ask, when examining a law, whose experience is represented and whose experience is ignored? [44]

A final consideration regarding the law concerns the impact of women judges. Of the 210 women who have ever sat on the federal bench, President Clinton appointed 100, almost half of them.[45] Thus, because these appointments are so recent, it is probably too early to assess their influence. Research in other court systems has, however, indicated that female judges are less likely to undermine women attorneys who argue before them. They are also less likely to tolerate harassment. There is evidence that having a woman on the bench improves the attitudes and behavior of male lawyers. There is little substantive information, however, to indicate whether a judge's gender has an impact on the outcome of cases.[46] One of the few studies to address that question examined sentencing patterns in sexual assault cases among trial court judges in Detroit. Although there was no significant difference between male and female judges in conviction or incarceration rates, female judges did impose longer prison sentences.[47]

The two most visible women on the bench are, of course, Justices Sandra Day O'Connor and Ruth Bader Ginsberg, the first and second women to sit on the United States Supreme Court. Most observers agree that although she has written several influential opinions that deal with gender issues, such as *Planned Parenthood v. Casey*. Justice O'Connor is governed more by her belief in federalism and her commitment to judicial restraint than to any feminist perspective. Justice Ginsberg, on the other hand, spent most of her legal career representing and arguing women's issues. That experience appears to influence her jurisrpudence. Her opinion in *United States v. Virginia*, for example, includes a discussion of the stereotypes that kept women out of the legal profession. She compared those to the stereotypes that served to keep women out of VMI. Justice Ginsberg's life experience and her commitment to women's issues are similar to that of Justice Thurgood Marshall, who had made civil rights his life's work before being appointed to the high court. It seems logical, then, in asking whether women judges make a difference to women's issues, one must conclude that it depends upon the judge. From the small sample we have, it seems the convictions that persist through a person's lifetime are more significant than gender alone.

Jury Service

The last chapter discussed jury service as part of women's struggle for full constitutional recognition as citizens. This chapter will look again at jury service as it affords women a chance to participate in the criminal justice system. For most people who do not choose careers in law, corrections, or law enforcement, the call to be a member of a jury is their major opportunity to work within the institutions that administer justice in the United States. Thus the process by which women's legitimacy as jurors was established is an integral part of the discussion of work in the criminal justice system.

Given what we know about opposition to women attorneys, it is not surprising to learn that the presence of women on juries was equally threatening to defenders of the legal status quo. The aversion to women jurors was, in essence, a desire to preserve the existing legal culture. If women "invaded" the courtroom, it was feared that their presence would disrupt "conviviality." In other words, they could challenge the assumptions that identified the law with masculinity. A mixed jury had transformative potential, and that transformation would probably rearrange the traditional distribution of power.[48] If men were to maintain control of the public sphere, they had to claim responsibility for making the rules of society through rational debate and the assertion of universalistic principles, and to argue that women were, by definition, incapable of that lofty responsibility.[49] Supporters of women's suffrage also recognized the potential importance of jury service. For most of them, the right to vote and the right to participate in a jury were the "twin indicia of full citizenship."[50]

The adversaries of such full citizenship for women dragged out a whole range of arguments against female jurors. They raised the image of the inseparability of husbands and wives left over from coverture and the notion of the separate spheres as it was articulated by the *Bradwell* court. That position promoted the idea that women were unsuited to face "all the nastiness of the world," including such "unclean issues" as sodomy, incest, rape, seduction, fornication, divorce, impotence, and adultery. The great irony is that most of those "unclean issues" were things that occurred not out in the nasty world but in the supposedly safe private sphere. Such arguments were designed to establish that women were naturally unfit for the courtroom. In fact, they were essentially arguments based on women's subordination. The delicacy that supposedly would be offended by learning of shocking behavior was held to be inferior to men's presumed rationality.[51] Rodriguez maintains that the arguments about the appropriateness of women in court really hid the conviction that "in a court of law, where the public and domestic spheres collided, it remained the province of men to resolve the dysfunction of the private sphere according to the special professional standards set by the court."[52] This is an important insight. Opponents of women's participation recognized that many of the concerns in court actually involved "private sphere" issues. They wanted to be sure those issues were resolved from a masculine perspective rather than according to women's standards. Ultimately, those who held power in a patriarchal system hoped to hold on to that power, especially as its manifestation might be interpreted in the courts.

This significant reason for opposing female jurors was often hidden under frivolous and even insulting stereotypes. Women would be offended by foul-smelling courtrooms tainted by cigar smoke. They would neglect their husbands, homes, children, and household tasks. They would become distracted from the case by flirting with handsome men or looking at other women's hats. A woman would never convict a good-looking defendant. A woman would always believe any arguments made by attractive attorneys. They would fall ill from the strain of jury service or find it impossible to sustain the mental labor required to listen to evidence.[53] Finally opponents turned to chivalry. They would spare women the civic obligation of jury service, for no law could "clothe timid, shrinking women...with the self-reliant judgement of a man."[54]

The previous chapter explained that the courts were slow to realize the constitutional implications of excluding women from juries. In 1879 in *Strauder v. West Virginia*,[55] the Supreme Court ruled unconstitutional a law that excluded all African Americans from juries. They gave two reasons why an equal protection violation existed. The exclusion treated all black citizens with prejudice as if they were inferior and, second, the law deprived the defendant of a jury that represented the whole community. The *Strauder* court stated that although race was an unacceptable category for proscribing jury eligibility, gender was an acceptable classification. Thus, black women could not be kept off a jury on the basis of race, but could be eliminated on the basis of sex, as could white women.

From the time of *Strauder* until the mid-twentieth century, states enacted a variety of laws dealing with gender and juries. Progress toward full inclusion was not smooth. Some jurisdictions "excused" women altogether. Others required that women register if they wished to serve. Until the late 1950s, each federal court followed the practice of the state where it was located. That changed with the Civil Rights Act of 1957 which provided that women would be eligible for federal jury service regardless of state law. Four years later in *Hoyt v. Florida*[56] (See Appendix Six) the otherwise liberal Warren Court upheld the Florida law that required women to register if they wished to be included on the list of potential jurors. Hoyt's argument was similar to the African American defendant in *Strauder*, eliminating a whole group from a jury not only affected the individual accused and his or her right to a fair trial with a representative jury. It also deprived a category of citizens of their Fourteenth Amendment equal protection from exclusion.

When the Court overruled *Hoyt* in 1975 in *Taylor v. Louisiana*[57] they focused on the defendant's right to a fair trial that included a fair cross-section of the community in the jury pool. They implied that gender does make a difference in how one would view a case when they stated, "The two sexes are not fungible." Thus the Court seemed to accept the argument that women, and men, bring distinct different experiences and perhaps even different moral reasoning to their deliberations. They are not interchangeable.

The later cases concerning the peremptory challenge, *Batson v. Kentucky* that dealt with race and *J. E. B. v. Alabama* that dealt with sex, concentrated on the harm jury exclusion caused to the prospective juror.[58] These cases look at jury service from the perspective that a citizen has the right to be considered impartial, that others cannot assume that he or she will be prejudiced based on race or sex. Is there any evidence for such an assumption? There are some updated generalizations about women jurors which have been used as an excuse for excluding them. For example, stereotypes include the idea that women tend to favor defendants unless it is a case of child murder. Or women favor the plaintiff in civil cases but award smaller damages than male jurors. Some think women are less likely to favor a female defendant. Others say they are less likely to favor a female plaintiff. There is the view that women are more apt to convict rapists, unless they think the victim was at fault. And the old familiar charge continues—that women's judgement is affected by handsome men. There is virtually no evidence to support those cliches about women's behavior. Such empirical data as exist suggest the possibility that women are harder on rapists and slightly less likely to support the death penalty. But those data are not really conclusive. Thus, aside from the incontrovertible point, that men and women bring different experiences to a jury—just as they do to other parts of life—we cannot draw conclusions about how gender will affect any individual's response to any legal question. Justice Thurgood Marshall provided a reasonable explanation for why juries must be drawn from all groups of citizens. "It is not necessary to assume that the excluded group will vote as a class in order to concede that its exclusion deprives the jury of a perspective on human events that may have unsuspected importance in any case that may be presented."[59]

Justice Marshall's observation might apply equally well to all the areas of criminal justice discussed in this chapter. It is not necessary to assume that women will act as a "class" to conclude that excluding them from policing, corrections, or the courts deprives the community of "a perspective on human events that may have unexpected importance."

Those who opposed the inclusion of women in the criminal justice system feared that they would upset things, that women would challenge men for authority, and that ultimately the patriarchal structure would be threatened. Whether women's participation will ultimately have that effect remains to be seen, but it is clear that gender hierarchies will not be altered without women. One final lesson may be drawn from the historical experience of women in all facets of justice work. A number of professions have gone through similar stages. An early period of separate women's institutions allowed for advancement. Later, opportunities to join formerly all-male institutions created the appearance of female acceptance into the "mainstream." Meanwhile the female institutions weakened or disappeared. Then when reactions against women developed, they were segregated and marginalized without the base of support their earlier separate structures had provided. In other words, as historian Estelle Freedman concludes, efforts to assimilate into male institutions without a feminist basis (without a sense that women's distinctiveness is a source of strength) led women to lose both their momentum for change and their networks of support and respect.[60]

CHAPTER FOUR

Women and Girls as Victims

Violence against women is not a new phenomenon. Efforts to combat violence against women are not new either. As discussed in a previous chapter, the Seneca Falls convention spotlighted the existence of battered wives when they objected to husbands' right to "chastise" their wives. They made at least an oblique reference to rape when they spoke of condoning the "moral delinquencies" of men. They also asserted that as long as women were excluded from the legal arena, their perspectives on these and other issues would not be recognized. This chapter will examine the cultural factors that create a climate in which violence against women persists as a commonplace occurrence and the legal framework that has treated that violence as less significant than other types of violence. It will also consider changes designed to address crimes that victimize women and girls and conclude by raising some questions about additional reforms in law and criminal justice practice.

Living in a Climate of Violence

When examining the issues related to the victimization of women, it is important to remind ourselves that women experience danger and violence in a particular cultural and legal climate. In other words, the environment in which violence against women occurs reflects assumptions about men and women, and the remedies to that violence are constructed into a criminal justice system that also reflects those assumptions. That is why the issue of violence against women is inseparable from a consideration of gender inequality and patriarchy. Martha Mahoney argues that "serious harm to women results from the ways in which law and culture distort our experience."[1] At least until quite recently, the extent of violence against women was too often disguised or ignored. Rape, battering, sexual abuse, and other offenses were considered by most people to be rare or exceptional events. Both the courts and the media tell stories of violence against women filtered through cultural stereotypes—the victims are helpless or dysfunctional or responsible for their own abuse. Or the courts may equate women's experience as victims with men's experience—as if both took place within an equally matched contest.[2]

Many of women's experiences with violence did not even have names until fairly recently. Although acquaintance rape, sexual harassment, and stalking are not new—women and girls have always been exposed to such behavior—it was the modern women's movement that named those offenses and developed legal sanctions to address them. The lack of legal definition for such gender-based injuries illustrates again the point that the law tends to reflect a male point of view. As Elizabeth Stanko argues, because traditionally men were in a position to define reality, women were assumed to experience the world through male perceptions. If a woman's perception—of what constituted consensual sex, for example—was different from her partner's, she came to doubt her own understanding. Too often when it came to issues of violence and control, a woman's private assessment and the public assessment of her experience were at odds, and the female version was undervalued.[3] Much of the history of attention to and reform in the treatment of crimes of violence against women consists of a struggle to make the law and the criminal justice system validate women's experience.

What are some societal assumptions about gender and violence? Aggressiveness and even a certain amount of violence may be considered "normal" male behavior. That behavior is not assumed to be harmful or threatening to women. On the other hand, some aggression is brutal and vicious. Such actions are viewed as abnormal, aberrant, and obviously harmful to women. When does the behavior cross the line? Who decides? Who is responsible? Far too often, the law has blamed the female victim for the change from "normal" to aberrant violence.[4]

There are links between such gendered definitions of violence and social inequality. At one level, the threat of violence and the tendency to hold women accountable for it means that women are taught to live in fear of victimization. They learn to limit their lives, to restrict their behavior, lest they become a target of a sex-related crime. At another level, societies built on patriarchal frameworks have allowed violence against women to persist as an instrument of male power and control. According to Catherine MacKinnon, gender difference takes the form of gendered dominance. The differences between men and women become an explanation for a state of inequality which gives men power over women. Rape and domestic violence maintain that power and perpetuate inequality. "Intimate violence with impunity is an ultimate index of social power."[5] In other words, violence committed against women exists because there is a disparity of power between men and women in a patriarchal society. That very violence then serves to preserve the disparity of power. As Joanne Belknap demonstrates, inequality and victimization form a vicious cycle.[6] Inequality sets the stage and provides the setting for victimization, and the experience, as well as the fear of victimization, keeps women from assuming full citizenship. Inequality is perpetuated.

Many other feminist scholars would agree that the subordination of women is both a cause and an effect of the violence women suffer. Stanko asserts that the struggle against gender inequality is identical with the struggle against male violence, while Susan Brownmiller claims that "cultural sexism" is a conscious form of female degradation "designed to boost the male ego by offering proof of his native superiority (and female inferiority) everywhere he looks.[7]

The separation of life into public and private spheres as discussed in Chapter Two has been a strong element in social attitudes toward violence against women. Abuse in the home, sexual assault by an acquaintance, unwanted sexual advances from bosses or professors have traditionally been regarded as "private" matters. Not only was such behavior rationalized within the context of male/female relationships, but women who suffered such affronts often felt it was their individual, personal problem and that they were somehow to blame. As long as women believe they are dealing with an unusual, even a unique situation—rather than a widespread condition created by structural inequality in the system—they will seek to deal with the problem at the individual level, perhaps through therapy, perhaps through denial, or at most as an personal, discrete offense. As long as women feel alone in their experience of victimization, the system will not change to reflect their perspective. The changes in rape, domestic violence, and sexual harassment law have happened because groups of women came to understand that their personal "private" lives had a political dimension. According to historian Linda Gordon, deviant behavior becomes a "social problem" when policymakers perceive that it threatens the social order and conclude that social action is necessary.[8] This happens not by chance but when affected groups organize to exert pressure on the political system. Traci West writes that since the entire community is morally culpable for the deleterious consequences of male sexual and physical assault on women, women's anguish is a communal problem. Their anguish is not an isolated burden. As all participate in "socially constructing" intimate violence, all are equipped to dismantle it.[9]

Race and minority status are additional dimensions of the victim experience. Traci West describes white supremacy and patriarchy as systemic evils that devalue the human worth and dignity of African American women. She maintains that "women experience patriarchy vastly differently depending on their race, class, and other social markers of identity that are different from and interact with their gender identity."[10] In other words, women from every group occupy a subordinate role to men, but gender subordination is only part of the story. Its form may differ depending on the other aspects of one's identity. Race, gender, ethnicity, and class may all be valued or devalued. Interaction with the law, the criminal justice system, and the community will take all of those characteristics into account.

Two recent national studies examine the prevalence of violence against women. Their findings provide a statistical framework for much of the material in this chapter. The National Violence Against Women survey, sponsored by the National Institutes of Justice, included a sample of 8,000 women and 8,000 men. Among other things the survey was designed to compare the incidence of violence across gender lines. The data confirm that victimization is linked with the sex of the victim and the offender.

- Women were 10 times more likely than men to be raped.
- For women, rape was more likely to be accompanied by physical assault.
- 41% of women raped were also slapped, hit, kicked, bitten, choked, hit with an object, threatened or attacked by a gun or other weapon.
- 7.7% of women were raped by an intimate partner.
- For 61% of the women who were raped the assailant was a current or former spouse, partner, boyfriend or date. 21% were raped by an acquaintance, 6% by a relative. *Only 10% were raped by a stranger.*
- 54% of rape victims were raped before the age of 18, 86% of them by someone they knew. 99% of the women raped before the age of eighteen were raped by men. Women raped as minors were twice as likely to be raped again as adults.
- 22% of the women in the sample and 7% of the men had experienced violence in an intimate relationship. The statistical difference becomes greater as the seriousness of the violence increases. Women have a much greater likelihood of experiencing beating, choking, attempts at drowning, and violence with guns in intimate relationships.

- For 72% of the women who are assaulted, the offender is an intimate partner, for 11% an acquaintance, for 7% a relative, for 10% a stranger. The numbers are quite different for men. For 56% the assailant is a stranger, for 29% an acquaintance, for 16% a spouse or partner, for 6% a relative.
- 8% of women sampled were stalked at some time. Most knew their stalker. Only 20% of stalkers were strangers.

Several themes emerge clearly from this data. Violence against women is predominantly violence by men. Virtually all rapes were committed by men, along with 91% of the assaults and 97% of stalking incidents. For women, the risk of injury increased if the perpetrator was a current or former partner. For men, the risk of injury decreased if a female partner was involved. Thus both men and women have the most to fear from men—for women, from partners and associates, for men from strangers.[11]

In this chapter, we will examine a number of crimes against women—rape, battering, sexual harassment, and stalking—and include an examination of how at the urging of victims and their advocates, the legal and criminal justice systems have modified the response to these crimes. I will advance the argument that violence against women is a civil rights issue. As long as the state and society tolerate violence against women and treat it as a private, individual matter, women cannot be full and equal citizens. They are not receiving their "due," equal protection of the laws, from the state. This impedes women's full involvement in civic and political life and diminishes their contribution to society. Dalton and Schneider have posited this as another vicious cycle. If women's involvement in public life were not cut short by violence, perhaps we would move more quickly to reduce and eliminate violence.[12] The goal is to develop a human rights framework, with women's experiences thoroughly integrated, to alter the profoundly male perspective of the law. The right to be free of any assault on one's person—no matter what the relationship of the assailant—must stand at the forefront of any claim to equality.

Rape

In 1810 in Prince William County, Virginia, Ben, a slave was accused of the rape of a white woman, Ann Vickers. If found guilty, Ben's punishment would have been castration. It was unusual for a slave to be represented by an attorney, but Ben's owner provided him with a lawyer—perhaps wanting to prevent a valuable slave from being mutilated. The attorney turned attention from the defendant as he argued that Ann had been known to "entertain" black and white men who traveled past her home. Thus, he argued, her position was "degraded." Her claim of rape was not as serious as it would have been were she a "white woman who had not ventured outside the boundaries of acceptable sexual behavior." In sentencing Ben to a lesser punishment, the 1810 court showed its "formidable prejudices" against a poor woman who did not conform to society's conventions.[13]

The Ann Vickers story contains themes common to hundreds of rape cases in American courts during the nineteenth and twentieth centuries. One notices immediately that the victim's reputation became an issue. The accused rapist's lawyer deflected attention from his client's conduct—whatever it was—to the woman's behavior. As a poor woman, who lived an unconventional life (she had no male "protector," neither a father nor a husband), Ann had a lower status than more respectable women. Her alleged attacker was known to her, but as a slave he, too, was a person of very low status in the community. Stereotypes about black men doubtless influenced the prosecution's decision to proceed with the case. The fact that Ben was not punished to the full extent of the law may reflect his attorney's skill, his owner's influence, prejudice against Ann's lifestyle, or a combination of all those factors. The case took place against a background of a patriarchal society where white supremacy thrived. Rape, although a serious criminal offense, would be interpreted in ways that upheld the hierarchy of race and gender.

Many discussions of the history of rape law in the United States emphasize two things. First, rape was treated more as an offense against a father or husband than against the victim herself. The law made this assumption *not because women were property*, as one often reads. Nonslave women were never considered property in the United States, although their status in a patriarchal society was surely a dependent one. Rather, this attitude reflected the belief that a daughter was under the care of her father, to whom she was a valuable asset. As a young woman of good character, she might either find respectable employment or, more likely, make a good marriage. Her father had a decided practical interest in her reputation. Likewise, a husband was also expected to protect his wife. His failure to do so, most dramatically shown in someone else's sexual access to her, was a grave insult to his honor and his status as head of the family.

Second, courts even well into the twentieth century adhered to the advice of Sir Matthew Hale that "It is true, rape is a most detestable crime, and therefore ought severely and impartially to be punished with death, but it must be remembered that it is an accusation easily to be made and hard to be proved; and harder to be defended by the party accused tho ever so innocent." Accusations of rape—unless the defendant was a member of a minority group and the victim was white—were regarded with a great deal of skepticism. Victims frequently found that dealing with the criminal justice system was like a "second rape," as their privacy was invaded and they were treated without dignity or respect. The "Hale Rule" reveals one of the most persistent rape myths—that women are not to be trusted, that for reasons of their own they will lie and accuse innocent men of rape. On the other hand, a woman who made an accusation of another crime—a burglary, for example—could presumably be believed. To return to a consistent theme, such warnings were adopted into the legal system by male legislators, lawyers, and judges. As Susan Estrich demonstrates, most of the definitions and evidentiary rules in rape cases before the reforms of the last several decades are responses to men's fears of false charges—not to the crime itself or the experience of the victim.[14]

The rape laws that existed in the United States during most of its history defined the crime as "carnal knowledge, without consent, of a woman not [one's] wife." We will discuss the marital rape exemption—the notion that one could not rape his wife—in the context of domestic violence. The element of consent, with its spotlight on the victim's behavior, was the focus of most discussions of rape. How could it be proven that a woman did not consent? Traditionally, non-consent required resistance, preferably physical resistance. As the standard was set by men who knew how to fight, the expectation seemed to be that a woman whose "virtue" was threatened, would fight like a man—an especially tough requirement for a girl or woman who had always been taught to avoid violence. If she failed to demonstrate enough opposition, courts were likely to conclude that she had given in. Thus using enough physical force to break down a woman's resistance often sufficed to demonstrate that she had consented, and, therefore, no crime had occurred. Feminist scholars have repeatedly pointed out that rape differs from other crimes of violence where the law judges the perpetrator's illegal demands, not the victim's resistance. Few robbers would be acquitted if they could "prove" that the clerk "consented" to give them the money in the cash register after a severe beating.

Rules of evidence in rape cases revealed other negative assumptions about victims' truthfulness by requiring that a charge be corroborated. Needless to say, witnesses to rape were few and far between, but torn clothing or bruises might suffice to substantiate the victim's story. Courts claimed to examine the accuser's character by introducing information about her past sexual history. Such a line of questioning meant to imply that the victim was not respectable if she had relationships with other men. If she was not respectable, she might very well lie. Another inference from the examination of past sexual history was that a woman who would have sex with one man would have it with anyone. Likewise, the requirement that a rape charge be based on a "fresh complaint" was geared to the possibility of a false accusation. Demanding that a victim make an immediate complaint was based on the notion that if time passed, women were likely to make up charges, perhaps after the defendant broke up with them or after they discovered they were pregnant. All of these rules, with their focus on the victim's character and behavior, reflect the law's strong assumption that Sir Matthew Hale was right and that the defendant needed more protection in a rape case than the usual constitutional protections afforded to anyone accused of a crime.

Rape law has reflected a number of other false and unflattering notions about women—that no woman can be raped against her will, that women provoke rapists by their dress, by flirting, by living alone, by accepting a ride, and so on. Another strong and pervasive myth is that women are more likely to be raped by a crazed, psychopathic stranger who jumps out from behind a bush than by an acquaintance, date, or intimate partner. Many of the efforts to reform public understanding of rape are based on disabusing women and men of those myths and legends. Works by Susan Brownmiller and Susan Estrich in the 1970s and 1980s are credited with challenging stereotypes and expanding our understanding of rape as a crime of violence and power.[15]

Brownmiller makes the argument that rape was the original method by which men subdued women and reduced them to a position of dependence and subordination. She goes so far as to claim that rape is the "conscious process of intimidation by which *all* men keep *all* women in fear."[16] Allowing for a certain shock value in such a statement, her point merits consideration—does the fear of rape keep women limited to "safe" places and activities, and do men as a group benefit when women's opportunities are circumscribed?[17] Brownmiller is not saying that all men are rapists, as some of her critics have claimed. She is saying, however, that fear of rape (and other gender-motivated crimes) works to disadvantage women as a group. Another significant insight in Brownmiller's work is the identification of rape as a crime of violence and power, not a crime of sexual attraction. In support of this statement, she summons the history of rape as an instrument of war, an act by which a conquering nation humiliated its opponent and demonstrated control. In the twentieth century, one can find evidence of the brutal rape of thousands of women when the Japanese conquered China in the 1930s (one episode was called the "Rape of Nanking"), in the Nazi concentration camps, when India fought Bangladesh in the 1970s, during the American war in Vietnam, and most recently in the wars in the Balkans.[18] There, for the first time, Serbian soldiers were convicted of rape as a war crime before the International Court of Justice. In each of those cases, however, women's bodies served as the symbolic battleground between the winners and losers. In such cases where the victims came from all age groups and social categories, it is clear that rape was used to demonstrate power, not sexual attraction.

Brownmiller continues her argument by pointing out that if we accept that rape is not a crime of uncontrollable lust but a deliberate hostile act of degradation, the next step is to look for the cultural forces that promote and encourage such attitudes toward women, especially among adolescent males. She lists several possible candidates: the myth of the heroic rapist; the concept of male privilege; the belief that men have a "right" to women's bodies; and the notion that women's bodies can be bought—obviously though prostitution but also more informally.[19]

Estrich provided another useful category for understanding social attitudes toward rape. She argues that the criminal justice responses to any rape are related to the "appropriateness" of the relationship between the rapist and the victim. The less appropriate the connection, the more serious the offense. The more appropriate the connection, the more likely that police, courts, even friends will be inclined to excuse the behavior. For example, if the rapist is a stranger, a member of a minority group, greatly different in age from the victim—the occurrence is likely to get attention from the criminal justice system. On the other hand, if the rapist is someone with whom the victim has or might reasonably have a social relationship—a peer—rape becomes more difficult for the victim to establish. The notion of privacy reappears, and respecting the privacy of a relationship often means ignoring the complaining witness's desire for intervention.

Estrich's book, written in 1987, is a call to treat nonconsensual sex, even with an "appropriate" man, as "real rape."[20] Stanko carries this idea forward. The definition of "real rape," she says, has been a male definition, focused on women's sexuality—from a male perspective—rather than on the man's coercion.[21] Thus women have had difficulty in defining or naming what happened to them but, as Estrich notes, most women who are forced to have sex know they are victims. They may or may not know that they are victims of a *crime*.[22]

Since the work of these scholars, a great deal of attention has been devoted to defining the whole spectrum of sexual coercion that women experience. Feminist research has led to publicity about date rape and marital rape, as well as other less invasive but nonetheless offensive and disrespectful forms of sexual assault. Such scholarship has played a "subversive and transformative role in changing the representations of rape"[23] and in shifting the legal as well as the popular understanding of the crime.

Women writing about rape provided the theoretical background for the growth of an anti-rape movement. Often women meeting in consciousness raising groups, sharing their backgrounds, discovered they had a common experience with non-consensual sex. Working from the premise that "the personal is political" and arguing that violence toward women is a form of social control, an amazingly large number of women began to raise the issue of rape as a feminist and women's rights issue. In many communities, women's groups created task forces to monitor how the criminal justice system treated rape victims. They publicized the practice of victim-blaming, when police and the courts treated the woman complainant as if she were guilty and needed to prove her innocence. They started community education efforts, including "Take Back the Night" rallies and marches, and they helped to organize Rape Hot Lines and counseling services for victims.[24]

College women appear to bear particular risks as potential victims of rape. According to the 2000 report, *The Sexual Victimization of College Women*, published by the National Institutes of Justice, between 20% and 25% of women experience a rape during their college career. For every 1,000 women on campus, there are 35 incidents of rape each year. The study included a sample of 4,000 college women, nationwide. The investigators did not ask the respondents "Have you been raped?" Rather they described behaviors that are categorized as completed rapes and asked the subjects whether they had experienced those behaviors. The results reveal attitudes about rape as well as its prevalence. More than 48% of those who had experienced the behavior defined as rape said they had *not* been raped. Almost 5% did not know whether they had been raped or not. Thus researchers discovered a disjunction between college women's actual victimization and their ability or willingness to name what happened to them as "rape." Perhaps they did not understand the legal definition of rape (and imagined that it meant the stranger in the bushes scenario) or perhaps they did not want to call their date or classmate a rapist. They may have blamed themselves or feared that they would be blamed by others for what happened.

The study confirmed that the vast majority (90%) of college rapes are by persons known to the victims. Almost two out of three of these crimes took place in the victim's residence, 10% in fraternity houses, and most of the rest in other residences. After the event, only 5% of victims reported the rape to law enforcement, although two thirds of them told someone, usually a friend. The barriers to reporting the incident are probably similar to those that make it difficult to name the rape. The victim is afraid the assault was not really serious, that it was not a crime. She assumes the police will ignore her or be hostile, especially if she has no proof other than her own testimony. She may fear reprisal from the offender or his friends, or she may not want her family to know. These findings support the notion that campus rape is severely underreported, which means that victims often go unattended and offenders go unpunished. It also means that college administrators may not be treating the issue seriously enough or providing realistic advice if they underestimate or close their eyes to its frequency. Young women heading off to college are seldom warned that those who face the greatest danger of rape live on campus, are unmarried, and drink alcohol. They are most likely to be victimized when they are alone with a man they know in their own residence.[25]

The activities of women's groups and their supporters have had an impact on the way the criminal justice system responds to rape, even if the results remain incomplete. Most jurisdictions have broadened their definitions of rape to include all forms of sexual assault—oral and anal as well as vaginal and those in which an object is used. There seems a greater understanding, at least among professionals, that rape involves the forced submission of a woman to violence, not just heterosexual intercourse.[26] The passage of rape shield laws is another example of a more pro-victim attitude and, although prosecutors are more likely than in the past to be tough on assailants, courts still seem to have difficulty convicting "nice" young men of rape. The fundamental difference between a feminist view of rape and a conventional "law and order" response is that the latter consider it one of many violent crimes. To feminists, rape is, symbolically and actually, an example of women's subordination.[27]

Woman Battering/Domestic Violence

There are many names for the violence women experience from their spouses or partners. The most common term is "domestic violence," and although that phrase identifies the situation in which abuse takes place, it is misleading to interpret domestic violence as conflict between intimates. Based both on statistical data and on the experience of those who work in the field, approximately 9 out of 10 of those injured by a partner are women. Thus the term, "woman battering" is more accurate, identifying the behavior as violence against women.[28] Although this work uses both terms, it should be clear that the overriding problem is abuse directed toward women.

The history of woman battering goes back as far as one chooses to look. It is inaccurate, however, to treat the past as one consistent, unchanging picture of husbands having the legal authority to beat their wives. Too often, texts cite the "rule of thumb,"[29] which prohibited a husband from beating his wife with a stick bigger around than his thumb, as if that principle describes all there is to know about domestic violence. We have already examined, in Chapter Two, some of the issues relating to patriarchy and privacy in the United States as well as criticisms raised in the context of the women's rights movement of the nineteenth century. We misread history if we believe that domestic abuse is an issue that was just "discovered" in the last several decades or that women passively accepted their subordinate role in silence. It is true that social awareness of abuse and violence within intimate relationships has had more attention and has resulted in more legal reform in recent years. On the other hand, those changes as well as the resistance to change, make more sense when viewed as part of an evolutionary process.

Historian Linda Gordon states that family violence is inseparable from a society's norms about "family values" and from other political issues concerning race, class, and gender. In fact, she sees family violence as a "lightning rod" for various social and political perspectives. Historically interest in addressing domestic abuse rose and fell as feminist influence increased and declined. When feminism was strong, there was a public discussion of inequality between the sexes. During conservative "family values" periods, the privacy of the home was emphasized, there was less interest in protecting the individual rights of family members and more emphasis on preserving the normative, patriarchal family. Any consideration of domestic violence emphasized individual personality disorders, drunkenness, or poverty.[30]

From the foundation of the American colonies, one can find some reference and opposition to wife beating. The Puritan settlements in Massachusetts Bay and Plymouth had laws against spousal abuse in the seventeenth century, and living in close communities, neighbors watched out for family conflict. But these colonies were also hierarchical in form. If a question of domestic violence arose and came to the attention of the church or the law, it was often the wife's responsibility to prove that she was blameless. The assumption that a family head could keep his wife and children in reasonable order existed in tension with the prohibition against wife beating. As the colonial period progressed and American society became more secular and more urban, the state had less interest in enforcing morality, including domestic peace. By the late eighteenth and early nineteenth century, wife beating came to be seen as a moral rather than a criminal matter, and the privacy of the individual nuclear family replaced the community life that had existed in the smaller villages and towns.[31]

The issue of wife beating was raised in three contexts in the early 1800s—by temperance reformers, as part of a general movement against corporal punishment, and by women's rights advocates. It is not clear whether temperance advocates purposely concealed their concern for battered women behind their efforts to limit or ban alcohol. The latter was a public matter that could be debated in political forums without threatening middle class family privacy. In any event, the opponents of alcohol believed that "demon rum" was a cause of violent behavior. A drunk was likely to be a brute who lacked self-control and took out his animal passions by terrorizing innocent women and children. Such behavior was usually associated with the lower classes, immigrants in particular. In the view of the time, the upper classes were likely to be more civilized.[32]

A contemporary reform movement focused on the issue of corporal punishment and lobbied to restrict beatings in prisons, in the navy, and in schools. Proponents of reform argued that physical punishments were incompatible with democracy which was theoretically based on the individual dignity and rights of all citizens. To beat a child or an adult was to treat him as something inferior. Needless to say, this complaint was also made by northern opponents of slavery. Slaveowners responded that while they might beat their slaves, northern men beat their wives. There was some indirect discussion of domestic abuse among opponents of corporal punishment. For example, it was argued that boys who were beaten at school would be brutalized and grow up to be violent husbands. But for the most part, these reformers were reluctant to address wife beating openly. Most likely they agreed with their contemporaries that marriage was sacred, the home was a "haven of privacy," or they were reluctant to challenge the myth of domestic harmony among the middle classes. Perhaps they were unwilling to explore the connections between sex and violence. For whatever reason, they did not extend their argument that corporal punishment is an insult to a free citizen in a democracy to include women.[33]

It fell to the women's rights advocates to challenge the institution of coverture in marriage and to demand a single standard of morality that applied to both men and women. Their efforts were instrumental in dismantling coverture and in establishing certain legal rights for women, such as the right to own property. By the late nineteenth century, most states enacted laws that denied husbands the "right" to beat their wives. The image of marriage as a companionate institution rather than a hierarchical arrangement filled the literature. But with companionate marriage came a greater emphasis on the privacy of the home, and this strengthened notion of domestic privacy served to make the laws against domestic violence ineffective. If the law said that chastisement was "a vestige of another world, an ancient legal precedent of uncertain legitimacy," in practice husbands were unlikely to be held accountable.[34] Some men—usually poor immigrants or African Americans—were prosecuted for wife beating, but they were considered depraved, deviant individuals. A few states adopted the whipping post as punishment for wife beaters. The debates on the subject in Maryland, Delaware, and Oregon emphasized that battering was a crime. The state would act as a moral father punishing a brutal son-in-law, on behalf of the woman victim. It was argued that the whipping post was preferable to sending the abuser to prison because it would not destroy the family but would get the father back home quickly! Even President Theodore Roosevelt, while condemning wife beating, believed prison was not the answer, as taking away the breadwinner would only hurt the innocent wife and children.[35] In general, late nineteenth-century law criminalized domestic violence, but by treating it as the act of depraved individuals rather than as a problem of gender inequality, it failed to provide a remedy.

If the criminal law did not punish abusers, what other alternatives existed for the victims? Could a woman leave an abusive husband? Divorce statistics from the Bureau of Labor show 7,233 divorces granted between 1860 and 1878. Of these, almost half charged cruelty, extreme cruelty, or cruel and abusive treatment.[36] But even in divorce cases, the meaning of cruelty was ambiguous. Often courts cited a 1790 British ruling that defined cruelty as "actual violence with danger to life, limb, or health or a reasonable apprehension of bodily hurt."[37] It was left up to the court to decide the meaning of reasonable. Not all bodily harm within marriage met the definition of cruelty.

Lucy Stone, a leader in the woman suffrage movement, published a list of crimes against women as a weekly feature in her newspaper, *The Women's Journal*, including 500 examples of "extreme" wife beating. She argued that the law was too lenient toward the male perpetrators. Stone recommended that victims be granted custody and provided with child support, but she ultimately concluded that women would only enjoy real protection from brutality when they were legally equal to men. If women could vote, she believed, they would be able to influence the courts and the legal system.[38] Stone recognized that without women's perceptions and experience incorporated into the law, there would be no real solution to domestic abuse.

Women suffrage advocates were not the only ones to publicize wife beating. Stories on the subject appeared in many American publications, including the *New York Times* and *Popular Science Monthly*. A graphic piece called "Wife Torture in England" was reprinted at least twice in the United States after 1878. There were morality tales in McGuffey's Readers, the popular children's textbooks, telling of drunkards who beat their wives and children. Cartoons, songs, and jokes referred to domestic violence. For example, consider the following exchange between comedians, dating from at least 1845. Comedian 1: "Nothing beats a good wife." Comedian 2: "Except a bad husband."[39] Given the prevalence of these popular cultural references, one cannot argue that Americans were unaware of violence within the privacy of the home.

The development of the child protection movement in the late nineteenth century added another force to the movement against wife abuse. As caseworkers, first from private agencies, and later from public social service departments, investigated cases of child neglect, they often uncovered child abuse, sexual abuse, and wife beating in the same families. The privacy that shielded middle-class homes from public scrutiny did not necessarily apply in neighborhoods of poor, uneducated, unemployed immigrants.[40] To the social workers who usually came from the middle class, protecting children often meant exposing "evils" within indigent homes. Such exposure frequently challenged patriarchal relationships that rationalized violence within the family. But social workers were not necessarily advocates for women. They tended to promote an alternative, idealized version of male supremacy—one in which fathers supported their families, mothers stayed home and served as moral teachers, and children attended school.[41] It was a family norm based on the middle-class ideal and often out of reach of the poor.

Linda Gordon argues that it was immigrant and other victimized women themselves who developed strategies to achieve their own "right not to be beaten." They ran away, called in relatives to shame their husbands, or appealed to social services for money so they could support their children. To these women, freedom from violence would become a reality only when they had economic alternatives. They needed to become less, rather than more, dependent on their husbands. Thus although the child protection efforts of the late nineteenth and early twentieth centuries revealed domestic violence as a serious social problem and provided relief for some, the agencies' approach seldom provided lasting solutions to the victims.

Through the first half of the twentieth century, wife battering and other forms of domestic violence remained a low priority among both social service and criminal justice professionals. During the Depression and World War II, public policy focused on economic and international crises. Families were urged to pull together during difficult times. Meanwhile, experts in psychology, influenced by Sigmund Freud and his disciples, offered to explain wife beating as a result of female masochism. Women, these authorities claimed, received sexual and/or psychic gratification from violence. Or, as an alternative, they hypothesized that women provoked battering by their frigidity, their aggressiveness, or their unreasonable demands. In such a context, husbands were frustrated and weakened. It was understandable that they lost control.[42] If this was the professional diagnosis of domestic violence, it is not surprising that law enforcement and court personnel did not respond to it as criminal behavior. Police and prosecutors shared the assumptions of their contemporaries—violence against women was a family problem, and the person beaten up often provoked it.

It was the rise of the women's movement out of the civil rights and peace movements of the 1960s that opened the door to a different analysis of violence against women. These movements challenged the status quo on many levels and called into question things people thought they "knew" about the justice of the American system. When the anti-rape activists raised issues of misogyny, gender-based violence, public apathy, and criminal justice abuses, battered women identified with many of the same points. It was a fairly short step from an analysis of rape as an act of domination to an analysis of domestic violence as a form of control, to see that separating the world into the public and the private afforded little protection for women. It was this generation of women activists who publicized the notion that a woman has the right to control her own body. That control should include not only choices about reproduction but also the right to be free from assault—at home as well as on the street.

One outgrowth of the revelations about violence against women in the home was the creation of the first battered women's shelters in the early 1970s. A shelter in Harrisburg, Pennsylvania, grew from an Al-Anon group. These women, married to or living with alcoholics, believed that what they most needed was not professional help, but the support of others with similar experiences. A Boston shelter, founded around the same time, was created by a neighborhood group who recognized the need of battered women for bilingual services.[43] These early shelters had no models and operated by trial and error as they identified the needs of the residents. They afforded the women a chance to clarify their experiences, to see the need for cooperative action. Those involved in the battered women's movement often had the political goal of challenging the institutions that preserved male domination and women's subordination. Like many others involved in the women's movement of the 1970s, they looked to cultural factors, such as gender stereotypes and women's secondary status in education, the workplace, and the home as explanations for the persistence of violence. Quite significantly, they stressed that violence was not an individual problem but a social issue. It was not brought about by the pathology of the victim but by structures in society that devalued women.[44]

There were some public policy responses to battered women. The Law Enforcement Assistance Act of 1968 provided some funding for domestic violence projects. Most of the money, however, was used in diversion programs for batterers. In 1979, the Department of Health, Education, and Welfare established an Office on Domestic Violence. Most of its programs supported the notion that keeping families together was the highest priority. Little attention was given to the dynamics of violence. But even modest and sometimes misguided efforts were too much for the conservatives who took over Congress in the 1980s and eliminated all funding for domestic violence programs. As one Senator commented, the federal government should stay out of "*family matters* which are properly and more democratically represented by state and local communities."[45] The Office of Domestic Violence was closed in 1981. One might conclude that the wall between the public sphere where the government had a role to play and the private sphere where victims were without protection remained firmly in place within the expression, "family matters." The next major federal effort to address domestic violence and related crimes would be in the Violence Against Women Act of 1994.

In examining the current state of affairs with respect to domestic violence, there are several issues to consider: What do we know about its prevalence? What are some of the enduring myths and misconceptions about domestic violence? Why does domestic violence continue? How does the criminal justice system respond to domestic violence at present? And finally, what are the long-range concerns for victims of domestic violence?

The National Violence Against Women Survey, cited earlier in this chapter, revealed that 22% of the women in the sample had experienced violence in an intimate relationship compared to 7% of men. The gender difference becomes greater as the level of violence becomes more serious. Women are much more likely to be subjected to beatings and to the use of guns in intimate relationships. Seventy-two percent of women who are victims of assault are attacked by an intimate partner. Sixteen percent of male assault victims are victims of violence by intimates.[46]

Even so, some scholars argue that men are also the victims of domestic violence, and one widely quoted survey seems to support this. However, that survey asked questions about "incidents" of physical confrontation. It did not explore who started the fighting, the intensity of the act, or which acts were committed in self-defense (if someone approached me with a knife and I knocked it out of his hand, each of us would have committed an "incident of violence.")[47] The majority of research indicates that any congruence of abuse against women and abuse against men occurs only at the lower end of the scale of violent behavior. Women admit to hitting men with their hands—usually in self-defense—but men inflict many more serious injuries. According to a review of the literature by Dobash et al., 90%

of domestic violence reported to the police consists of men battering women. Likewise, women's reports of abuse are much more detailed and lengthy than those of men.[48]

Other factors make it difficult to provide a precise count of the incidence and distribution of battering across class, race, and ethnic lines. Poverty and isolation seem to add to the risk of domestic violence, but women from minority groups may be reluctant to seek help from the police, shelters, or social service agencies. Sometimes they have sought help and not gotten it. This lack of response may become a self-fulfilling prophecy: "I know the police won't take me seriously (because they think African Americans/Hispanics/Native Americans are just violent people), so I won't bother to call them." Sometimes illegal status or a lack of proficiency in English discourages an immigrant woman from reporting abuse. And sometimes within minority communities who are suspicious of outsiders, a woman who reports on her husband or partner is considered an "informer."[49] All of these cultural considerations make it difficult to know exactly where and how frequently domestic violence is occurring.

Just as society holds onto a number of myths about rape, there are comparable myths about battering. Many of these misconceptions persist in the public mind and continue to find their way into the operations of the criminal justice system.

The Batterer has Lost His Temper and is "Out of Control"

Why is he able to confine his violence to his wife? Why doesn't he lose his temper with his boss or the next-door neighbor? Why does he manage to hit her in places where it won't show? Why does he stop when threatened by someone more powerful, such as the police?

Battering is a Series of Separate Events, Each Provoked by Some Particular Circumstance

Why does battering recur in the same homes, among the same people? Why is the rate of recidivism among batterers comparatively high? Why does battering often escalate from minor to serious injuries?

Battering is a Family Matter—Just a Spat between Spouses

Why is assault within certain relationships ignored while assaults by strangers are considered a crime? Does marriage or intimacy give one person the right to abuse or control another person's mind and body?

A Man can't Rape His Wife

Is marriage a blank check for any future sex, regardless of the partner's consent? What does this say about the right of a woman to her own bodily integrity?

Why doesn't She Leave if She's being Abused?

Can we assume that abused women have the economic and emotional resources to leave? Where will she go? What will happen to the children? What if he won't let her leave?

These myths about domestic violence rest on certain assumptions. On the one hand they presuppose a patriarchal structure where a certain amount of control—even if exercised through physical force—is acceptable within an intimate relationship. They assume that what occurs within families should not be the concern of the community, and to a great extent, the myths tend to blame the victim for not stopping the behavior of the aggressor.

Most recent studies of domestic violence emphasize that the physical abuse within some relationships is actually a part of an attempt on the part of the batterer to exert and maintain power and control—power and control once permitted in a patriarchal structure but no longer acceptable. The Power and Control Wheel developed by the Domestic Abuse Intervention Project of Duluth, Minnesota, is a useful device for examining the many dimensions of an abusive relationship—of which physical battering is only one. In this analysis, domestic violence is actually an ongoing process of domination. It is misleading to look at behaviors as isolated incidents. Rather one must see domestic violence as a continuing process that includes intimidation, isolation, and denial.[50]

From this perspective, the issue of why women stay in abusive relationships leads to more revealing conclusions. A controlling spouse may deprive his wife of any economic resources. She may have no money of her own and no way to support herself or her children. If she has been isolated from friends, family, and the community, she has probably lost touch with possible supporters outside the home and may well have lost her confidence in dealing with strangers.

There is also the matter of "separation assault." A battered woman experiences the violence against her as controlling her thoughts, emotions, and actions "including her efforts to cope with the violence itself."[51] Should she attempt to leave the environment of dominance, the abuser will perceive a serious threat to his control. Mahoney has called this violence in retaliation for departure "separation assault." Naming separation assault helps to focus attention on domestic violence as an issue of power and control. If the violence stemmed from normal conflicts between equals, why would the abuser refuse to let his victim go? He would be glad to see her out of his life. But in reality, abusers see leaving as the victim's ultimate act of rebellion. It often triggers a fatal response.[52] How often have you read in the paper that a man assaulted his "estranged wife"?

In far too many cases the courts have treated these assaults and even murders not as separation assault, part and parcel of domestic violence, but as "crimes of passion." Rather than identifying the victim's history of misery and her reasons for leaving, defendants have been allowed to emphasize their emotional distress at "losing" the victim and to appeal to the sympathy of the judge and jury. Men who kill their partners in the ultimate act of power and control claim loss of self-control as a mitigating factor.[53]

In addition to the experience of control and the possibility of separation assault, women who are members of ethnic, racial, and religious minorities may also confront cultural pressures to stay in an abusive relationship. African American women sometimes feel compelled to present a "united front" in a racially biased society. If they leave and seek assistance, they may be inviting violence toward African American men. They may also believe that the criminal justice system doesn't care about them, that the police assume they are accustomed to violence, that they will be treated as if they are not really victims of domestic abuse. Churches in the African American community may encourage women to endure their suffering, to submit to their situation, and to protect black men from the system. Finally, black women also assert that they are ignored by shelter providers and thus do not find the outside support they need to leave an abusive situation.[54]

Latinas likewise face daunting prospects both within and outside their ethnic group. Many Hispanic communities maintain patriarchal stereotypes—that women must find their identity within the family, that they are dependent on men. Strong notions of privacy may prevail, supporting a code of silence about problems within the home and within the community. Like African American women, Latinas may be expected to present a united front to Anglo society. Additionally, for Hispanic women who do try to leave an abusive relationship, there are often language problems in dealing with the criminal justice system or with shelter providers. Many have experienced cultural as well as personal isolation and find it difficult to access social services. A large number of Latinas, if they work outside the home, are employed in the lowest paying service jobs or even in the underground economy. This economic deprivation adds another obstacle to leaving an abuser and setting up an independent home.[55]

Traditional Jewish women encounter other barriers to leaving an abusive marriage. Orthodox Judaism defines women as subservient to their husbands. The confluence of culture and religion means that a victim who complains of domestic violence may find hostility in her own community. Her rabbi may tell her to try harder, to maintain peace in the home. In the face of such advice, she is likely to blame herself and to feel shame for the failure of her marriage. If a woman in a traditional Jewish marriage determines to leave her husband, she is unable to have a religious divorce or a "get" unless her husband gives it to her. In other words, even with a civil divorce, without a husband's agreement, a religious Jewish woman stays married until her husband consents to the get. Without it, if she remarries she is an adulteress, if she has children with a new husband, they are bastards. With such restrictions, traditional Jewish women can find it virtually impossible to end an abusive marriage.[56]

These examples could be multiplied many times. They help to demonstrate that domestic violence cannot and should not be viewed as individual pathology or aberrant behavior, but rather as a problem embedded in a social hierarchy of male domination and female subordination. Too often the legal system fails to recognize that violence against women stems from common structural causes, that various forms of violence against women are linked, and that all are forms of discrimination against women. The failure to resolve the issue of domestic violence is a failure to redress the exercise of power and control over women.[57]

Criminal Justice Responses

Despite historical attitudes and practices that minimized or misinterpreted domestic violence, during the 1990s all aspects of the criminal justice system have undergone some reforms in their dealings with violence against women. To a great extent, these reforms have come about through publicity and pressure generated by advocates for women to create changes in the law. Law enforcement officers and courts have also been educated about domestic violence. In some instances, lawsuits have gotten the attention of criminal justice agencies and forced them to pay attention to the well-being of victims of crimes against women.

As late as the 1970s many police departments followed a non-arrest policy when dealing with domestic violence. Typically they reasoned that arrests might "aggravate a dispute" (implying two equal sides in the matter) or that intervention would be dangerous for police officers. As with many other departments, Oakland, California, police were told that if one party (presumably the woman) demanded an arrest (presumably of her male partner), they should remind her of the ramifications—loss of wages, the cost of bail, court appearances—and encourage the parties to "reason with each other."[58] Such policies clearly reflected the belief that domestic violence is a private matter in which the "law" is not implicated, that no crime was involved, and that the "parties" were probably equally blameworthy. The police simply shared the attitudes toward domestic violence that were quite common across American society.

Lawsuits in a number of jurisdictions challenged such policies. In 1976, victims of domestic violence in Oakland filed a class action suit against the police chief. They claimed that repeated domestic violence calls from women, especially black women, were ignored by the police. This neglect was, they charged, a violation of equal protection under the Fourteenth Amendment. In an out-of-court settlement, the agency agreed to change its approach. They would make arrests where there was probable cause in battering cases. In addition, police would inform battering victims of their rights (not of the disadvantages of arresting the abuser) and make referrals to shelters and social service agencies. A similar case in New York City helped to attract the attention of law enforcement agencies across the country and led many to revamp their policies.

An additional wake-up call came with the case *Thurman v. City of Torrington, CT*. There, police were held responsible for failing to protect Tracey Thurman and her son from her abusive husband. The agency was found guilty of sex discrimination in its dealings with crimes against women and ordered to pay $2.3 million to the victims.[59]

Changing public attitudes toward marriage and domestic abuse led to reforms not only in police practices but in state laws on the subject. By the turn of the century, most states had made significant changes in domestic violence law. Generally the new legislation provided for less police discretion. They were now required to arrest the primary physical aggressor, based on probable cause, even if the assault did not take place in the officer's presence. Police were also required to file written reports on every incident (suggesting greater understanding of the ongoing nature of domestic violence). Many agencies provided officers with training in documenting and collecting evidence at a domestic violence scene to assist the state in convicting the batterer even if the victim did not testify. Police dispatchers, too, were trained in responding to calls from domestic violence victims, to listen for background noises such as threats or gunshots, that serve as evidence. Some departments appointed an officer to be responsible for domestic violence cases. He or (usually) she could develop expertise in the procedural and legal issues and be responsible for following up with victims to ensure they were aware of community services. These changes in law and practice combined to make a "presumptive arrest" policy a reality in law enforcement agencies across the country. The police play a vital role as gate keepers in dealing with domestic violence. Arrest serves as "the first link in the vital chain of institutional interventions that save the lives of battered women and children, restore the community, and invite batterers to accountability."[60]

Of course, arresting a batterer is only one step in the process of protecting the victims and holding aggressors accountable. Little would change if prosecutors did not charge the abusers, if judges threw the cases out, or if probation officers did not ensure compliance with the terms of probation. Consequently, district attorneys' offices have, in many jurisdictions, adopted "no drop" policies in domestic violence cases. If there is sufficient evidence, they will proceed with charges even without the victim's cooperation, treating battering like other crimes against the state.[61] This marks a significant theoretical change in viewing domestic violence not as a private dispute but as a criminal matter. If assaulting one's spouse in the kitchen is considered as much a crime as assaulting a neighbor on the sidewalk, the criminal justice system has made major steps in its willingness to provide women with equal protection. Aggressive prosecution of abusers demonstrates that domestic violence is a public safety issue. Publicity about charges may increase public awareness and decrease public tolerance of such behavior. Prosecution also shows that batterers are not allowed to control the criminal justice system by intimidating or manipulating victims into withdrawing charges.[62]

Judges are also key players in dealing with domestic violence, and educating them about the issues is vital. If judges see battering as insignificant compared to "real" crime, or if they persist in believing that abused women who do not leave their abusers are responsible, batterers will not be held accountable but, too often, excused for their behavior. When it comes to sentencing, judges often tend to rely on treatment rather than incarceration as a sanction. Choosing a therapeutic rather than a punitive approach may indicate the belief that domestic violence is a personal problem rather than a crime. There is a definite need for both individual risk assessment of batterers before recommending sanctions and for studies examining the effectiveness of programs such as anger management.

Many jurisdictions have organized seminars for judges to learn about the dynamics of domestic violence, and separate Domestic Violence Courts have been established in some cities. Here judges have the opportunity to develop expertise in the field. These courts have also provided victims with an opportunity to pursue a number of related matters—criminal charges, custody, protective orders—in one place. The creation of a Domestic Violence Court can make a statement that the community sees the need for comprehensive remedies to the problem of battering.[63]

Many times observers attempt to evaluate more aggressive policies against domestic violence by asking "Is arrest of batterers effective?" There are several considerations in responding to that question. How do we measure effectiveness? Arrest, compared to what? What happens after arrest? Barbara Hart has listed a number of goals for measuring effectiveness: providing for the safety of battered women and children; stopping the violence; holding the perpetrator accountable; challenging the batterer's belief in his right to control his partner; restoring the battered woman to a decent life (including restitution, medical care, community resources); and enhancing agency or control in battered women's lives. These goals, she argues, should determine the criminal justice system's arrest policies.[64]

A report issued by the National Institutes of Justice in 2001 provided a new assessment of the effectiveness of arrest, although it measured mostly the deterrent effect of arrest rather than the full range of goals listed by Hart. In 1984, a landmark study done in Minneapolis seemed to demonstrate that arrest was successful in reducing further incidents of domestic violence. That research influenced many departments to move to a pro-arrest policy. However, five attempts to replicate the Minneapolis experiment—in Charlotte, North Carolina, Colorado Springs, Colorado, Omaha, Nebraska, Dade County, Florida, and Milwaukee, Wisconsin—did not seem to support the original findings. The most recent NIJ report reexamined the data from those five cities, using some standard measures of analysis. This study reached three conclusions. Arrest of batterers had a consistent, modest deterrent effect on aggression toward partners. Arrest plus incarceration, which averaged nine days, led to a 30% decrease in assaults according to interviews with victims, measuring periods of up to one year after arrest. The research found no empirical support for the concern that arrest might lead to an increase in violence. Second, a minority of batterers continued their violent behavior, regardless of the intervention. Third, a majority of batterers discontinued battering without arrest, but with other interventions, such as counseling, mediation, protective orders, or warnings from the police. The report concluded that perhaps arrest should not always be required.[65] That conclusion would place discretion in dealing with domestic violence back in the hands of individual police officers, who would have no way of knowing which batterers would respond to arrest. Hart's analysis seems to supplement the NIJ report. She argues that if arrest is a "singular intervention"—separate from other necessary services to the victim and consequences to the batterer—it will have only transitory benefits.[66] Overall, it seems clear that arrest of batterers is only one in a range of necessary responses to domestic violence. It is certainly not a silver bullet, although the message that beating a spouse is a crime with criminal sanctions should not be underestimated.

Although it is of overriding importance to treat domestic violence as a crime, victims also need a variety of civil remedies. Most states have expanded the scope of protective (or restraining) orders that require an abuser to have no contact with the victim. Courts may issue emergency or preliminary orders of protection at the victim's request. They require testimony that there are reasonable grounds to fear further danger. Under these orders, victims may be allowed possession of the home and the abuser may be required to leave. When such orders are provided and enforced, the victim may be spared the additional problem of finding housing for herself and her children. A "permanent" protective order (which actually lasts approximately two years), may be issued if a court finds evidence of abuse after a full hearing. As the name implies, protective orders are meant to keep victims safe.[67]

Are protective orders effective? One study found that nearly 75% of victims felt safer immediately after the orders were issued, and 85% felt safer after six months. The vast majority (95%) would seek protective orders again, if the need arose. The study also found that violations of the orders were most likely when children were involved, as judges often ordered unrestricted visitation. An abuser would be told by one court to stay away from his wife and told by another to visit his children who lived with her. Therefore, one recommendation is coordination between protective orders and visitation. The research also recommended that judges provide more information to victims about the enforcement of violations of protective orders, encourage victims to develop a safety plan "just in case," and inform them about community services, such as shelters.[68]

A separate study of protective orders offered several practical recommendations that would provide easier access for victims: legal assistance for petitioners, who often represent themselves before the judge when requesting the order; provision to issue emergency orders after business hours and by telephone; and elimination of fee requirements.[69] All of these suggestions would seem to contribute to the goal of increasing community safety. They would assist poor and frightened victims at the time they most need help.

Can a victim of domestic violence sue her abuser? Intentional emotional distress is grounds for civil suit, and some victims have sought damages on this basis. One problem is that to qualify for damages, a plaintiff must show that she was subjected to "outrageous" conduct. In a true Catch-22 situation, some courts find that domestic violence is so widespread that it does not qualify as "outrageous." In response, some advocates have suggested that violation of a protective order should be considered outrageous per se. In other words, if an abuser violates a protective order, he is automatically engaging in outrageous conduct, and the plaintiff would be eligible to collect damages.[70]

There are many other suggestions for legal remedies to domestic violence, including the civil rights provision of the Violence Against Women Act, which the Supreme Court found unconstitutional and which will be discussed later. Communities also address battering by providing other services and opportunities that allow victims to escape abusive situations.

According to Elizabeth Schneider, "battered women lose jobs, education, opportunities, careers, homes, and savings. They may also lose relationships with family and friends that might otherwise provide material aid. Women become homeless as a result of battering, their homelessness is made more difficult to remedy because they are battered, and they are more vulnerable to further battering because they are homeless."[71]

If domestic violence is a relationship, a process, and a vicious cycle as Schneider states, victims need help beyond the crisis when they are threatened with physical harm. The criminal justice system cannot and should not be expected to solve the problem alone. Shelters and transitional housing provide places for battered women to go when leaving an abuser. Job counseling, money management, and support groups offer assistance in developing independence. Counseling for children and parenting classes can help to break the generational cycle of violence. These services and programs are vitally important both to give victims the resources not to return to an abusive situation and to prevent domestic violence from being the revolving door. A coordinated community effort including support from employers, schools, and churches may be what turns victims into survivors.[72]

Yet the law doesn't always "get it" when it comes to victims' attempts to break free from abusers. Some vestiges of coverture can come back to haunt a woman who escapes from a violent home and tries to move, with her children, to a different city or state. In many jurisdictions, a custodial parent needs the other parent's permission to move—a policy left over from the past when husbands had the legal right to choose where their family would live. Even now, abusers can restrict women and children from relocating for a new job or to be closer to family members. Some courts chastise women who try to move and threaten to give custody to the abuser.[73]

Welfare policy also relates to domestic violence. Women on welfare experience high rates of domestic violence. Some estimate as many of 60% of welfare recipients are abused. The reasons are not clear—perhaps low-income men are more likely to resort to violence to deal with problems. Perhaps they have fewer resources to exert control. Looking at the other side of the issue, women may be on welfare because they are battered. In a relationship characterized by power and control, an abuser may refuse to allow a woman to work or she may be unable to hold down a job due to frequent injury. The federal welfare reform legislation passed in 1996 has particular implications for battered women. The law requires that a woman must try to get child support from the father as a condition for public assistance. A request for support can become an occasion for violence. The law also requires that recipients get into the work force as soon as possible by placing time limits on receiving Temporary Assistance for Needy Families (TANF) grants. For a woman who leaves an abuser and who has never been in the work force, this may be a formidable challenge. The act does include the Family Violence Option (FVO) which may allow an extension of TANF funds for abuse victims, modify the requirement for child support, and provide counseling services to domestic violence victims. However, the individual states have the power to decide who deserves FVO exemptions and for how long. As states are under pressure to reduce the number of people on welfare, this goal may conflict with the need to provide assistance to abuse victims.[74] The welfare issue demonstrates once again that domestic violence is not a private matter but one that influences and is influenced by public policy.

Even if the criminal justice system attempts to deal equitably with victims of domestic violence, race and class have an effect. African American and other minority women face particular hurdles in dealing with abuse and moving beyond an abusive relationship. A study of victims dealing with domestic violence, drawn from a sample of mostly African American women, showed a variety of coping strategies, ranging from talking to the abuser (the most common and least effective) to calling the police (the most helpful). Such a survey reveals once again that women in violent relationships are not passive but take what seem to be reasonable steps to end the abuse. Some ended the relationship, others fought back, left home, slept separately, or tried to keep the household peaceful. Seeking protective orders was found to be another effective strategy.[75]

Taking these steps to deal with abuse may be especially hard for black women who are expected to be rocks of strength and not to feel or acknowledge being hurt. They may have been conditioned to sacrifice their needs for the needs of others, to try to maintain an "honorable" (two-parent) family. The experience of racism leads many African American women to rationalize that black men have been victims of injustice themselves and therefore to justify violence. The message from some African American leaders is that a betrayal of an abuser, if he's black, is a betrayal of the race and therefore a capitulation to the white establishment.[76] Given the pervasiveness of such social pressures against resisting abuse, the variety of resistance is remarkable.

At another level, advocates for victims have raised the matter of domestic violence as a global human rights issue. Here they face again the effort to persuade the international community that domestic abuse is not a private issue or an individual problem. Rather when nations neglect to address the problem, they are failing to protect vast numbers of female citizens. Research by students of international law has demonstrated that domestic violence is not unusual, but that it exists in all societies, that the majority of violence against women happens in the home and is caused by a spouse or relative. Thus, gender-related abuse is a real human rights issue—in virtually every nation women and girls suffer assault and injury purely because they are female. Traditionally international law has focused on the exercise of rights in the public forum—freedom of speech, political expression, or rights of the accused. Such an emphasis tends to ignore the abuses that occur in the private sphere but which inhibit women from enjoying basic human freedoms. During the 1990s, the International Conference on Women as well as a number of non-governmental organizations, such as Amnesty International, have brought to light the issue of women's subordinate status and the connection with domestic violence.[77] In 1993 the United Nations Conference on Human Rights called for the "elimination of violence against women in public and private life...and the eradication of any conflicts between the rights of women and the harmful effects of certain traditional or customary practices, cultural prejudices, and religious extremism." Later that same year the United Nations General Assembly endorsed the Declaration on Elimination of Violence Against Women which included battering and marital rape within the definition of violence against women. It also warned governments against "invoking any custom, tradition, or religious consideration" to avoid their obligations to protect women from abuse based on gender.[78]

Many international covenants condemn the existence or tolerance of torture as an obvious human rights violation. Some argue that domestic violence meets the definition of torture. It involves severe physical and/or mental pain and suffering; the pain is intentionally inflicted; the pain is inflicted for specific purposes; and the official agencies of government are involved because they choose not to stop the violence. If such a definition were to be widely adopted, the international community through the United Nations and other organizations, could add its condemnation of domestic violence as a systematic violation of women's human rights.[79]

Stalking

Compared to rape and domestic abuse, stalking may seem a relatively minor crime. Yet it merits attention for several reasons. Stalking grows out of some of the same attitudes toward women that promote other forms of violence. It involves behavior that creates fear in the victim and often grows out of a sense of entitlement or possessiveness on the part of the stalker. It is one of the experiences that, by causing women to be fearful, serves to limit their opportunities and participation in a full range of normal activities. Stalking may either precede or accompany other more serious crimes, such as rape and domestic violence.

The National Violence Against Women Survey defined stalking as "a course of conduct directed at a specific person that involves repeated visual or physical proximity; nonconsensual communication; verbal, written, or implied threats; or a combination thereof that would cause fear in a reasonable person."[80] According to the NVAW definition, victims did not need to be actually threatened, but they did need to feel a high level of fear. Based on those criteria, 8% of women in the sample acknowledged that they had been stalked at some time in their lives, more than half of them by current or former intimate partners. The numbers reveal that approximately 1 million women over 18 are stalked annually in the United States.[81] Among college women the rate was higher. Thirteen percent reported being stalked each year.[82] Considering both college women and the larger sample in the NVAW, the majority of stalkers were men known to their victims.

In the wake of high-profile incidents, California was the first state to pass anti-stalking legislation in 1990. Since then, all fifty states and the District of Columbia have enacted similar laws. In 1996, as part of the Violence Against Women Act, stalking that crosses state lines became a federal crime. Thus, although the fear-inducing behavior is not a new phenomenon, the definition of it as a criminal offense is fairly recent.

Declaring something a crime is, however, only one step to controlling that activity. According to the NVAW survey, a small majority, 55% of women victims, reported the stalking to the police. When the others were asked why they did not report it, most thought it was not a police matter (perhaps they considered it "private"). Others believed the police could not help or they feared reprisals by the stalker. Stalking lasts an average of 22 months, although for some women it persisted for as long as five years. When asked why they thought the stalking ended, only 9% said it was because the offender was arrested and 15% because he was warned by the police. In all the other cases, the stalker or the victim moved away or the stalker formed a new relationship.[83]

In a number of cases, men charged with stalking have raised constitutional questions. Generally they have argued that the behavior prohibited by the laws is innocent and protected by the right of free association. In other words, the defendant has the right to be on the street, in a restaurant or shop, or to go where he chooses in a public place. Supporters of anti-stalking legislation argue that it is not the innocent movement that is criminalized but the persistent unwanted contact. The Court of Appeals in Alaska ruled that "the Constitution does not guarantee a right to threaten other people. When a person's words or actions constitute an assault—when they cause other people to reasonably fear for their own safety or the safety of those close to them—the Constitution no longer provides a refuge."[84]

Stalking is definitely a gendered crime. The fear of sexual assault or the threat from an abuser who lurks outside her home or phones her repeatedly occurs in the context of a woman's experience. Scholars have made the case that courts should apply a "reasonable woman" standard when evaluating whether a stalker's actions constituted a "credible threat" or whether they were meant to cause fear. In other words, the issue should be not whether a man would feel threatened by the stalker's behavior, but whether from the perspective of a reasonable female victim, the offender's course of conduct causes her to feel a high level of fear.[85]

Similar issues arise in discussing sexual harassment. Whose perception of unwanted sexual contact should determine whether an action is prohibited?

Sexual Harassment

Like stalking, sexual harassment is an old issue, but one that only gained a name and a legal history during the last quarter of the twentieth century. Similar to domestic violence and stalking, sexual harassment is seldom an isolated act but rather a pattern of behavior involving repeated, and often escalating, confrontations. As with other crimes that victimize women, sexual harassment reflects unequal power relationships between men and women. Carol Pateman asserts that even more than discrimination in employment, sexual harassment helps to maintain patriarchal rights in the public world. She believes it is part of a structure that subordinates women in the workplace and that the sexual language that often plays a part in sexual harassment is a language of discipline, designed to remind women of their inferior status.[86]

For sexual harassment to be recognized as illegal behavior, lawmakers and courts had to realize that it is more than just flirting or "romance in the office." In other words, as with other crimes against women, as long as harassment could be dismissed as "private," it could stand outside the scope of the law. There is, however, a major difference between mutual or desirable sexual attraction between equal partners and unwanted advances or comments designed to establish or maintain an unequal power relationship in the workplace.

Studies show that women are not just passive victims of sexual harassment. As with other offenses, they employ a variety of strategies designed to end the behavior. According to a study by Louise Fitzgerald et al., about half of victims try to avoid the harasser; 44% tell him to stop, and about 60% confide in friends or family. Only a small minority, however, lodge a formal complaint.[87] The parallels with other gender-based offenses are clear. Women feel their complaints will not be taken seriously, they fear reprisals, or they are wary of public humiliation. These feelings are not unfounded. Fitzgerald et al. found that women in the military who complained of sexual harassment discovered that reporting made their lives worse in every way.[88]

As a legal matter, sexual harassment is defined as a form of sex discrimination prohibited by the Civil Rights Act of 1964. That legislation makes it unlawful to discriminate against an employee with respect to "terms, conditions, or privileges of employment because of such individual's race, color, religion, sex, or national origin."[89] In its first sexual harassment case, *Meritor Savings Bank v. Vinson*,[90] the Supreme Court held that Congress intended to "strike at the whole spectrum of disparate treatment of men and women." As examples of this disparate treatment, they defined two types of harassment. The first is the most obvious type, quid pro quo. Here a supervisor, employer, or colleague offers or threatens some tangible consequence in exchange for sex. A woman may be promised a raise or promotion, or she may be told she will be fired or demoted. Clearly such a "bargain" is discrimination in the terms of employment based on sex. *Vinson* also spelled out the illegality of a second type of sexual harassment—the hostile environment. The Court compared such an offensive environment based on sex to harassment based on race. "Surely a requirement that a man or woman run a gauntlet of sexual abuse in return for the privilege of being allowed to work and make a living can be as demeaning and disconcerting as the harshest of racial epithets." In order to qualify as a hostile environment, the harassment must be "severe or pervasive" enough to alter the conditions of employment. Thus, while defining what sexual harassment is, the Court left it up to future litigation to determine when it crossed the "severe and pervasive" line.

The Court's next attempt to clarify this standard came in 1993 in *Harris v. Forklift Systems*.[91] Justice Sandra Day O'Connor wrote the opinion holding that a hostile environment was conduct a "reasonable person" would find hostile or abusive. The victim need not demonstrate that she was harmed—psychologically or otherwise—but only that the conduct detracted from her job performance. Justice Ruth Bader Ginsberg, in her concurrence, defined a hostile environment as "working conditions making it more difficult to do the job."

Since 1993, courts have tried to apply the reasonable person standard. But who is this reasonable person—a man or a woman? It appears that there are gender-related differences in what constitutes tolerable workplace behavior. What "reasonable" men may see as funny, "reasonable" women may see as offensive and threatening. A number of scholars have suggested—and some courts have applied—the reasonable woman standard.[92] They argue that inequality is a given, that a reasonable person standard actually privileges the male perspective, and that based on different experiences men "don't get it." Instead a perspective that asks 'would a reasonable person *the same sex as the victim* be offended?" is a more reliable measure.

In 1998, the Supreme Court addressed the matter of whether a man could be sexually harassed by other men even if none of them was homosexual in *Oncale v. Sundowner Offshore Services.*[93] Oncale, who was part of an eight-man crew on an offshore oil rig, was repeatedly subjected to humiliating, sex-related actions, including assault and a threat of rape. His tormentors claimed it was just horseplay, but the court found sexual harassment. They held that a hostile environment need not be based on sexual desire, but could be general hostility expressed in sexual and derogatory terms, that a reasonable person would find abusive. Presumably here the reasonable person is the same sex as the victim.

A number of other cases, most recently *Faragher v. City of Boca Raton,*[94] have addressed the issue of employer liability. When may an employer be held legally and financially responsible for employees in supervisory positions who abuse their position to harass other employees? The Court held that employers would be responsible unless they could demonstrate that they had taken *reasonable* care to prevent and correct harassing behavior and that the complaining employee had *reasonably* failed to take advantages of opportunities to report.

Sexual harassment can also occur in an educational setting. The familiar example is the quid pro quo—a professor offers a student a grade in exchange for sexual favors.

Hostile environment can also be an issue in schools and colleges where adding a sexual dimension to the teacher/student relationship interferes with the learning experience and constitutes an abuse of power. Students who professors treat in sexually inappropriate ways may also find their peers distrust them. Colleges and universities have a variety of policies against sexual harassment. Some discourage "romantic and sexual" relationships between any faculty member and any student. Others limit the ban to professors and students under their supervision. As the Yale University policy says, "The unequal institutional power inherent in this relationship heightens the vulnerability of the student and the potential for coercion."[95] While not specifically forbidding any type of sexual relationship, the policy recognizes the dangers of such a power differential. Probably the worst type of sexual harassment experience for a student occurs when she reports it and those in authority do not respond, creating the impression that the university approves of the behavior.

In employment cases, too, the decision to report harassment can be risky. According to an article in the *National Law Journal* in the summer of 2001, courts have dismissed a number of sexual harassment suits because women have failed to report it to management or they have waited too long to report. Based on such cases, some scholars have suggested that if employers make the complaint process difficult, harassment victims will be discouraged. If employees claim they failed to report out of fear of losing their job, courts are unlikely to find this a reasonable explanation. Thus the *NLJ* quotes a *Fordham Law Review* article that advises "Employers should not engage in or should eliminate extensive preventive efforts such as expensive sexual harassment training, or more particularly, harassment reporting hotlines."[96] The suggestion is not to deal with sexual harassers, but to disempower the victims so they will not complain.

In a related article, a federal judge in Georgia dismissed a woman's hostile environment claims because, he asserted, the whole society has become so vulgar and crude, a victim can no longer reasonably allege that exposure to such conduct is abusive.[97] In the examples cited in both articles, the "reasonable person" standard was not that of the victim but of the (male) court. Both examples illustrate the continuing difficulty women have, despite Supreme Court rulings, in establishing the seriousness of sexual harassment, especially as it reflects a power differential.

In 1991, Professor Anita Hill testified before a committee of the United States Senate that Supreme Court nominee Clarence Thomas had repeatedly engaged in sexual harassment when she worked with him a decade earlier. Hill provided graphic examples of behavior that surely met the standard for a hostile environment. Yet the majority of Senators chose not to focus on the allegations against Thomas but instead asked "Why didn't she quit?" Women around the country shook their heads in disbelief and said, "They just don't get it." Since then there has been progress in looking at harassment from the victim's perspective, but there remains a need to acknowledge that the reasonable woman's experience of harassment must be looked at through the filter of her gender.

The VAWA Perspective

In examining the many examples of how women's unequal position in American society is reflected in crimes against women, it is useful to return to the theory that underlies the civil rights remedy in the Violence Against Women Act. Supporters of the act argued that women have a right to be free from violence directed toward them on the basis of gender, and that right deserves to be afforded constitutional status. The failures of the states to adequately address violence against women—whether it takes the form of rape, battering, stalking, or sexual harassment—constitutes a violation of the Fourteenth Amendment's promise of equal protection of the laws. Throughout this chapter, we have noted how infrequently women report crimes against them to the authorities because they believe they will not be taken seriously. Surely this attitude is additional evidence that the institutions within the criminal justice system have not adequately addressed the issue of violence against women.

The Supreme Court declined to accept this view when they ruled in *United States v. Morrison*. The majority of the justices ignored the evidence gathered by Congress that crimes against women were not treated like crimes against men. In dismissing this issue without attending to the implications of violence for perpetuating gender inequality, the Court missed an opportunity to address historical and structural barriers to women's full citizenship.

Chief Justice Rehnquist was quite right when he stated in *Morrison* that if Christy Brzonkala's allegations of a "brutal assault" were true, "no civilized system of justice could fail to provide [her] a remedy for the conduct of...Morrison." But then the Court rejected Congress's remedy, which had been based on the argument that Brzonkala's civil rights were violated and did what "no civilized system of justice" ought to do. As Post and Siegel state, the Court dismissed VAWA's civil rights remedy without truly grasping it. Congress had found that the criminal justice system's traditional methods of handling violence against women presented grave problems of sex discrimination. The Court did not appreciate the systematic nature and breadth of the constitutional violation that Congress was undertaking to remedy.[98]

CHAPTER FIVE

Victims and Offenders: Gender as the Link

In this chapter, we will shift our primary focus from women who are the victims of crimes to women who commit crimes. One of the questions frequently raised by scholars who study gender issues concerns the omission of females from the study of criminology. In other words, if we look at the volumes of work that purport to examine why "people" commit crimes, we quickly notice that the vast majority of them are really asking the question why men and boys commit crimes. During the past several decades, a number of scholars have attempted to rectify the absence of women from the study of crime causation. This chapter does not pretend to be either a full review of criminological theory and its neglect of women or a new criminological explanation. Rather it is an examination of several issues that are particularly relevant to understanding some of the connections between gender and crime.

In studying women who commit crime there are really two fundamental problems: How to account for the fact that most crimes are committed by males and how to explain the small percentage of women who do break the law. No matter what set of statistics one uses—reports from law enforcement or reports from victims—the most consistent and prominent fact about crime is that the vast majority of offenders are male. Because, as Steffensmeier and Broidy note, the gap between men and women in criminal behavior is consistent across time and space, gender itself must be a part of the explanation. Why otherwise would differences in development or culture have such a minor effect on who commits crimes?[1]

It is also true that the gender gap is the widest for the most violent crimes and the narrowest for minor property crimes. Although male offenses run the gamut from lesser to greater, women's crimes cluster around "consumer crimes," such as larceny, fraud, theft and prostitution.

Few women have long-term criminal careers and few identify themselves with a criminal way of life. There is evidence that when women do commit serious crimes, they are "situationally induced," often by an abusive situation rather than as part of a lifestyle. In addition, when a woman does commit a serious crime, it is often regarded as more aberrant because of its rarity. At some level, the public, too, seems to regard violence as more "unnatural" for women than for men.[2] It seems shortsighted then, to ignore connections between gender and violence. If we knew that 90% of violent crimes were committed by left-handed people, would it not be wise to explore connections between left-handedness and crime, and between right-handedness and lawful behavior?

Our understanding of the connection between gender and crime has mirrored changes in women's social and legal position as well as academic interest in studying the importance of gender. Criminological theorists in the early part of the twentieth century looked for individual biological and psychological causes to explain deviance. For those such as W. I. Thomas, who examined female offenders, criminality was equated with sexual misbehavior. Thomas's "unadjusted girl" reflected a number of assumptions about gender. Using psychoanalysis and IQ tests, Thomas argued that a healthy, adjusted woman was characterized by sexual self-control. Girls who became delinquent were identified by precocious sexual maturity and feeblemindedness. Sexual misbehavior was not just a type of deviant behavior, it explained deviance. To theorists like Thomas, "moral imbeciles" and "mental defectives" were synonymous. Because of this convergence, these feebleminded and immoral young women must be prevented from living a life of promiscuity, unwed motherhood, and dependence on the state.[3] Such theories are interesting to modern students, not only because they could and did lead to public policies such as sterilization of "feebleminded" girls. (See the discussion in Chapter Seven). They also reflect a tendency to equate female crime with sexual misconduct and to ignore both the social causes for that misconduct and the sexual double standard.

Other major schools of criminological theory focused on social and environmental explanations for crime. Social disorganization theory emphasized links between poverty and the failure of stabilizing institutions. Strain theory stressed the notion that blocked opportunities for success lead to crime. Differential association theory looked at deviant influences that encourage criminal behavior. Labeling theory noted that society defines crime and determines who will wear the badge of "criminal," thus encouraging people to live up to their reputations. Social bonding theories examined the forces that tie a person to conventional behavior. However, virtually every criminological study was based on a male sample. Were women subject to the same influences as men? How did these factors influence women? None of the conventional theories examines why women were so often the targets of male violence. It is a fallacy to assume that what is true for men is true for women, especially in light of the statistical gaps in criminal behavior. It is also a fallacy to assume the reasons for differences without making women the subjects of criminological inquiry.[4]

Some of the earliest efforts to raise questions about gender and crime focused on sex roles. Assuming that males and females are basically similar, one may account for differences in behavior by different processes of socialization. While men are raised to be aggressive and to seek power, women are raised to be unselfish and to be nurturers. Some theorists jumped from this analysis of socialization to conclude that as women enjoyed the results of the modern liberation movement and were socialized more like men, their rate of criminal behavior would come to resemble that of men.[5] According to this perspective, greater opportunities for women would lead to higher rates of crime. In fact, there has been no empirical evidence to support this theory. Statistical evidence is quite the opposite. The proportion of male to female crime has not altered significantly despite greater legal equality for women. Also, minority women, who have generally enjoyed fewer opportunities, are disproportionately involved in crime, especially violent crime. The profile of the chronic female offender is remarkably similar to the profile of the chronic male offender, except that there are many fewer of them. But both are disproportionately members of minority groups, single, and substance abusers.[6] This may be related to differential treatment by the criminal justice system, to poverty, to the more vigorous enforcement of drug laws in inner city neighborhoods. It is unlikely to be related to the women's movement.[7]

In the last two decades, feminists have addressed questions of women and crime, and given their general focus on patriarchy and social inequality, they have found those themes applicable to criminology. In other words, they have looked to the gendered nature of society in studying crime. Women's position in relation to authority structures, both public and private, may provide a way to explain both the low rate of crime by women and the crimes that women do commit. According to Joycelyn Pollock, feminist criminology agrees on several basic points:

- Gender is not determined by nature, but is socially constructed. Although it is related to biological and reproductive differences, gender is not identical with them.
- Gender and gender relations order social life and social institutions in fundamental ways.

- Gender relations are not symmetrical. Rather, men enjoy dominance in social, political, and economic areas.
- Existing systems of knowledge reflect men's views and experience, but not women's ways of knowing, which are different.
- Women should be at the center of intellectual inquiry—not out on the periphery or added as an afterthought.[8]

Meda Chesney-Lind, one of the most prominent feminist criminologists, asked why most crime is committed by males and why sexual crimes (such as prostitution) and its "buffer crimes" (such as running away) are usually committed by females. She found that women who commit crimes are often victims of "multiple marginality." Their race, gender, and class place them on the edge of society. Her research on adult women revealed that "powerful and serious problems of childhood and adolescent victimization powerfully circumscribe girls' choices." Girls who are subjected to physical and sexual abuse—most often at home—run away. Their victimization sets the stage for homelessness, unemployment, drug use, "survival sex," and sometimes more serious criminal acts.[9] She finds that studies of women in prison seem to support this link between abuse and offending. Although 12% of males in prison had been victims of abuse, the percentage for women was 43%. Two thirds of them had been abused as children, and three fourths lived with abusive men. Chesney-Lind also noted that these victim/offenders were disproportionately women of color.[10] She cites a study of drug users that indicates that while males use drugs for thrills or pleasure, women are more likely to use them for self-medication and to get into low-level dealing out of economic necessity. For some, drug dependence can lead to the horrific life of the "crack ho," the woman who trades sex for a hit of crack.[11]

Thus Chesney-Lind's work revealing a patriarchal social structure that permitted female victimization and other social inequality provided an explanation for a sizeable proportion of female crime. She has offered an insight into the vicious cycle of victimization and crime. Girls who flee from abusive homes may be picked up for the status offense of running away. At that point, they are either returned to the home or detained within the juvenile justice system. In either case, they may feel there are no good alternatives to returning to the street. There they have no legitimate way to support themselves (especially if they are young and without a high school education). They turn to prostitution, theft, or small-time drug selling—the three crimes that most female offenders commit. Chesney-Lind notes that despite their high rate of victimization, few women resort to violence. Rather their "survival strategies" almost always involve petty offenses.

Kathleen Daly studied felony court defendants. She tested Chesney-Lind's description of "street women" and found that although some had followed this route to crime, she identified four additional pathways.

- Street women ran away from abuse or were attracted to the streets. They were involved in prostitution, theft, and selling drugs, likely had a drug habit, and were often arrested.
- Harmed and harming women were victims of physical or sexual abuse or neglect. They grew up in a chaotic environment, got into alcohol and/or drugs at a young age, and were frequently accused of being tough or acting out.
- Battered women were in relationships with abusers and in court for steps they took to fend off their abusers.
- Drug-connected women used or sold drugs usually as part of a relationship with a man.
- Others who did not fit the categories were generally involved in crimes for money.[12]

Thus Daly's work supports and expands on Chesney-Lind's links between abuse and domination in a patriarchal society and female crime. Not only street women but those in other categories had experienced abuse and relationships with violent men as well as drug and alcohol dependence and other psychological problems. Daly speaks of a "panoply of problems"—drug addiction, alcoholism, rape, physical abuse, mental impairment, and psychological problems. She maintains that the system has not only criminalized these women's survival strategies, as Chesney-Lind claims, but also their anger. Women in several of her categories were convicted for retaliating against their batterers and abusers.[13]

Joycelyn Pollock endeavors to weave these threads together into a more general criminological theory. She posits both social and biological factors to account for crime and delinquency. Individual biological and psychological factors serve as preconditions that can be aggravated by social circumstances. She summarizes the key elements that can lead to criminal behavior:

- Early childhood problems and poor parenting, including discrimination, school failure, failure to learn moral reasoning, problem solving, or empathy
- Neurotransmitter imbalances, such as low serotonin, hormone imbalances, or nervous system disorders
- Birth problems, including mother's drug or alcohol use

- Personal characteristics, such as impulsivity or a nonverbal orientation
- Chronic psychological arousal
- Association with those who approve of criminal behavior
- Weak attachment to other people

Those problems can be aggravated by such difficult social conditions as:

- Economic inequality
- Emphasis on material success
- Poverty and a disorganized community
- Racial discrimination and/or social isolation
- Stigmatization of deviants
- Media messages that encourage crime[14]

Pollock then focuses her general criminological theory on gender issues. She argues that through the evolutionary process, females have developed attachments because of the need for mothers to care for their young. Fathers are less likely to care for infants, and as a result men tend to become autonomous rather than affiliative. This evolutionary process may help women to develop a more sensitive conscience, to make more pro-social choices, and to learn more self-control. Thus, she suggests that men and women have different predispositions to crime. One then adds the social factors listed above—an environment where violence is tolerated, where social networks are weak, and where formal social supports are non-existent. Men are more likely than women to make criminal choices, and women in those negative environments are more likely than women in supportive environments to make criminal choices.[15] Pollock has offered a macroanalysis of gender and crime that complements but does not contradict the microanalysis suggested by Chesney-Lind and Daly.

Several other feminist theories address the macro issues—why are women as a group less likely to commit crime. Travis Hirschi and his followers have asked the question—Why do most people not commit crime? Based on their research on adolescent males, they have found the answer in social bonds—the factors that tie one to society and encourage behavior that conforms with norms and law. Frances Heidensohn finds this social control theory useful in explaining female behavior because gender roles create particular bonds for them. Women both exert and experience social control—forces that tie one to conformity. Women are still the primary caregivers and moral influences on children. If they do not comply with this role and fail to instill proper behavior in the next generation, mothers are blamed for public disorder. Thus, in their parenting role, women are expected not only to be bonded by lawful behavior themselves but to transmit those bonds to others. Likewise, women are, even today, expected to maintain most of the social relationships that reinforce norms, to ensure that family ties are fostered, that neighbors and communities care for those in need. These responsibilities in and of themselves serve as a constraint on women's behavior, leaving less time and opportunity to get into trouble.

But there are other social constraints that exert control over women's behavior. The tradition of separate spheres has, as discussed throughout this book, limited women's opportunities and served as a sort of "preventive detention." Heidensohn notes that the idea of domestic privacy meant that "women were banned from the men's clubs, but men were not banned from clubbing women at home."[16] Expectations of public propriety have also influenced women to behave cautiously—both because female reputations are delicate and because women have reason to fear sexual assault and violence if they stray from safe places. In other words, Heidensohn argues that female behavior is controlled by a subtly woven web, which women themselves help to weave.[17] However, as Ngaire Naffine asserts, to say that women are bound by ties to society is not to say that they are vapid, passive creatures. In fact, she notes Hirschi's argument that men who conform—who are tied to social norms—are responsible, hardworking, involved in constructive activities, and making a rational choice that such behavior is better than crime.[18] Cannot the same be said of women who conform?

The work of Carol Gilligan, who has studied gender and moral development, is also useful in examining women's lower rate of offending. Gilligan argues that there are masculine and feminine ways of approaching moral issues. Her research reveals a male tendency to make decisions based on notions of individual rights, while the female tendency is to look at the effect on relationships before making a decision. Whereas the male way assumes that people are autonomous and separate, the female way assumes attachment among persons. She summarizes that boys are raised to operate on the basis of an "ethic of rights," while girls learn an "ethic of care."[19]

Sandra Harding and Nancy Choderow, among others, have studied the process through which these attitudes are fostered. They claim that mothers are aware that sons are different from them and therefore encourage separation and individuation. Boys are taught to become independent and self-sufficient. Girls, on the other hand, experience a different relationship with their mothers—one that does not require differentiation, but continuity. They can be kindred spirits and maintain a spirit of attachment.[20] So, these scholars hypothesize, males come to see the world as made of people separate from each other, while girls see it a world of interdependence. The former makes it easier to rationalize negative behavior. These patterns help to account for a different moral sense in men and women.

Steffensmeier and Broidy offer an integrated theory of crime that includes some of the feminist insights into gender development with other social forces that influence criminal behavior. They note that the majority of male and female offenders have similar background characteristics. Both groups are disproportionately poor, poorly educated, unemployed or underemployed, and members of minority groups. Thus, one could assert that those social and structural forces affect both men and women. But, Steffensmeier and Broidy argue, other factors affect males and females differently. "Broad social forces (suggested by traditional criminology) exert general causal forces on both male and female crime." But "the organization of gender" (norms, moral development, and social control as discussed above) will determine how those social forces "play out into gender differences in types, frequency, and contexts of criminal involvement."[21]

With some of the tools of criminological theory at our disposal, we will look at three examples of victims who are also offenders—delinquent girls, battered women who kill, and prostitutes.

Victims and Offenders: Delinquent Girls

A 2001 report by researchers at the University of Pennsylvania estimated that each year 325,000 children in the United States were subjected to sexual exploitation, including prostitution, use in pornography, and molestation. Fifty-five percent of those children ran away from home, fled a foster home or institution, or were thrown out of their home by parents. The report also finds that 96% of the perpetrators of these assaults were known to the victims—47% were relatives, 49% were teachers, neighbors or other acquaintances, and only 4% were strangers. Nearly all the perpetrators were male, a quarter of them were married with children.[22]

Where do the children who run away from these abusive situations go? According to a number of studies, they end up on the street and/or in the juvenile justice system. Yet the issue of sexual exploitation of children is not a new problem. Rather it is one where notions of family privacy have led to decades of misguided policies that punish the victims, seldom hold perpetrators accountable, and play upon public fears of victimization by strangers.

Linda Gordon's study of family violence during the late nineteenth and early twentieth century finds that at least 10% of the known incidents were cases of incest, most frequently between men and female children. She finds that the patriarchal family, with its gendered relationships of power, authority, and dependency set the stage for such behavior. Social workers, however, often saw the situation through "prudish, anti-immigrant, anti-pauper" attitudes. They blamed the girl victims for being juvenile sex delinquents and their mothers for not protecting them. Rather than holding the guilty male relatives accountable, public agencies supported the notion that the real threat came from strangers who were sexual deviants.[23]

Girls who were the objects of sexual abuse within the home were victims at many levels. Besides the obvious violation of their physical integrity, they were likely to be blamed for allowing or even encouraging the illicit sex. In a patriarchal family, a daughter was expected to be obedient, but if she was obedient to demands for sex, she was immoral. If she stood up for herself, she could be labeled rebellious. The double standard was in full force in cases of sexual abuse. A girl who was sexually experienced—no matter whose fault—was "polluted" in some way. If she claimed assault from a male relative, especially a father, she was likely to be accused of lying. If she left home to avoid abuse, her morals would be questioned. Gordon notes that "the theme of girls' pollution overwhelmed that of their victimization. Locating this sexual delinquency on the streets shifted the blame onto girls' irresponsible presence in public and unrespectable spaces. This kind of problem was one for the police, who were not expected to contain predatory males but to control the girls."[24] During the early twentieth century, experts concluded that many of these "promiscuous" girls were actually feebleminded. Their alleged moral and mental retardation justified incarcerating them.[25]

Gordon's work on the early twentieth century is compatible with Chesney-Lind's studies of contemporary girls. As discussed earlier, she argues that the criminal justice system criminalizes the survival strategies of marginalized, victimized women and girls. Girls run away from home not only because they are victims of sexual abuse, but also to escape physical assault, dating violence, or pregnancy. Because others have focused on their sexual identity, they may "use their sexuality as a proxy for independence, sadly and ironically reinforc[ing] their status as sex objects seeking male approval—ultimately ratifying their status as the subordinate sex."[26] In other words, sex may allow them to declare their independence from familial control, but if sex becomes the means of survival on the streets, it is likely to be a "gateway" to other illicit activities and to involvement with the criminal justice system.[27]

The high correlation between victimization and delinquency among girls exemplifies the blurry lines between victim and offender. The historical and contemporary tendency to misidentify the problem of sexual abuse of children as the fault of the child or as a threat from strangers has sent countless girls and boys into the street—and worse.

Victims Who Become Offenders: Battered Women Who Kill

"If a woman cannot leave, death can occur, either hers or the abuser's."[28] An earlier chapter discussed the facts about domestic violence, including the threat of separation assault—the danger a victim faces when she tries to leave an abuser. This section will discuss several ways in which that scenario may play itself out, including how the criminal justice system responds.

Women commit only a small percentage of violent crimes and less than 10% of murders. Not only are women much less likely to be involved in a homicide, when they do take a life it is more likely to be an intimate and often after a history of abuse. No one would suggest that killing spouses or partners is the solution to domestic violence, but it happens. Yet the way the legal system has framed the issues and defined the crime when men and women kill a spouse or significant other has revealed gendered assumptions embedded in the law. For too long, even when laws are written in gender neutral language, their application reflects a male view of the world and a receptivity to men's stories. It has been a struggle to bring the battered woman's perspective into the criminal justice system and to reinterpret legal justifications for homicide in order to take into account the experience of abuse and its effects.

Elizabeth Stanko describes a double standard. If a man murders his wife or partner because he found her irritating, annoying, or suspected her of infidelity, courts have often found the victim's behavior to be a mitigating factor. Judges and juries have been particularly sympathetic to men who claimed they acted in a jealous rage because they knew, suspected, or imagined a wife committing adultery. On the other hand, a woman who killed a husband while defending herself or her children against the same jealous rage was much less likely to be understood. Some commentators have referred to the male "domestic discount." Murder is less serious if the victim is a female intimate. The assumption is that it was provoked.[29]

Advocates for battered women who strike back at abusers have grappled with the issue of how to explain the context in which such things take place. Some experts believe such a violent response by a woman must be abnormal—a "good" woman would accept suffering. Those who work from a "family conflict" perspective may argue that both parties are guilty of provoking violence. During the 1980s Lenora Walker developed the idea of the "battered woman's syndrome" in response to police or prosecutors or judges or juries who asked, "Why didn't she leave if the abuse was so bad?" The battered woman's syndrome was an attempt to explain that, over time, beating and fear could lead a woman to believe there was no way out for her as long as her abuser was alive.

Sometimes the battered woman's syndrome was associated with the experience of learned helplessness. This concept suggests that a person who is repeatedly abused learns not to fight back but to anticipate and even endure the brutality, as a strategy for survival. In some cases, defense attorneys presented learned helplessness as a type of "diminished capacity." From this perspective, a woman who experienced repeated battering would have lost the ability to respond in a fully rational way (leaving) and would put up with it until something drove her over the edge. Other advocates for battered women compared the experience to posttraumatic stress disorder (PTSD), a condition frequently found among combat veterans. Here, too, victims of abuse may appear to behave peculiarly. They may exhibit what seems to be too little or too much reaction. They may deny the extent of the abuse they suffered and/or react violently at seemingly inappropriate times.[30] One criticism of the "battered women's syndrome" in its various meanings as a defense strategy is that it is based on the assumption that the victim acted somehow irrationally. It suggests that she became unhinged as a result of long-term abuse and that because her perspective was distorted, her capacity to reason was diminished. Such a defense places the focus on the defendant's state of mind rather than on the batterer's actions.[31]

To put the batterer's behavior in the spotlight, other feminist legal scholars and attorneys have suggested that self-defense—interpreted to take the battered woman's experience into account—is a better defense. They would argue that expert witnesses should not talk about "battered women's syndrome" but should inform the fact finders, the judge and jury, about "battering and its effects."[32] Such an explanation may be useful to account for inconsistencies in the victim's testimony, to describe why she remained in an abusive situation, delayed in reporting a crime, or changed her story. Overall, expert testimony on battering and its effects can show that, given her individual experience, the victim acted *reasonably* when she struck back at her abuser, that her action constituted self-defense.[33]

It has been more difficult than one might imagine for battered women to claim self-defense when they assaulted or killed an abuser. Traditionally in order for a person to claim that an act otherwise considered murder was not morally or legally blameworthy because he or she was acting in self-defense, a defendant had to establish that there was an immediate or imminent threat. The image of self-defense that "the law" seems to have is two men in a bar fight. If one attacks, the other has the right to defend himself. This image suggests two similar opponents of comparable size with comparable weapons. It also conjures up an isolated event—not an ongoing relationship characterized by one person asserting power and control through a variety of means. For a battered woman, who kills her abuser to claim self-defense, she must persuade the court that her sense of threat was reasonable.[34] In other words, she must establish that a *reasonable person* would act as she did. Some legal scholars have argued that the standard should not be a reasonable person but a *reasonable woman*.[35] Would a reasonable woman, given the experience of this victim, perceive an actual threat of death or serious harm? Would she, aware of the threat of separation assault, know that she could not leave this man without endangering her life? Would she, smaller than he, knowing of his prior violence toward her, reasonably believe that he intended harm or death, even if he was not threatening her at the moment she attacked him? In the largest sense, could the victim's experience explain and justify her act—not as insanity or diminished capacity—but as the reasonable response?

According to the Department of Justice figures for spousal homicide, in the mid-1990s, while 87% of males charged were convicted, 70% of women were convicted of the comparable offense. In bench trials, 37% of women and 17% of men were acquitted. Juries acquitted 27% of female defendants but no male defendants. Of women who were found guilty, 81% were sent to prison, while the figure was 94% for men found guilty. The women who went to prison typically served shorter sentences.[36] These numbers may suggest that during the last decade, advocates for women were somewhat more successful in telling their stories to the court and in providing an explanation of, at least, why some women kill. Perhaps an even more encouraging sign is a general conclusion that there are altogether fewer murders of abusers since better resources, including shelters, are available for battered women.[37] Perhaps this section can conclude with the opposite of how it began, "If she can leave (and has somewhere to go), death is less likely to occur, hers and the abuser's."

Prostitution: The Vicious Cycle

Prostitution remains one of the offenses that involves a significant number of women. As noted earlier, several criminological theories focus on the link between abusive homes, running away, life on the streets, and commercial sex in an effort to establish that prostitution is often preceded by victimization. Works that examine the history of prostitution in the United States confirm that this link between victimization and illicit behavior is not a new phenomenon, but rather a pattern of long-standing duration. Hobson found that the profile of nineteenth century prostitutes was not significantly different from the profile of prostitutes today. They were mostly younger women for whom prostitution was a transitory phase. They usually began their life on the streets at a vulnerable time when they were seeking independence from parental dominance and seeking control over their own sexual and financial lives. If married, they were often escaping spousal abuse. Most were poor. Many were immigrants. If they left legal employment, it was often domestic service—considered a degrading job at the bottom of the occupational ladder. Thus, in the nineteenth century, as in the twentieth, women and girls who became prostitutes were already marginalized—by their history of abuse, their poverty and minority status, and their unstable and dead-end work lives.[38]

Prostitution is often called "the world's oldest profession," suggesting that in all societies there is a demand for paid sex and a group of people, usually women, available to supply it. Certainly it has been a constant feature of patriarchal societies, where women occupy a secondary status that includes separate spheres with limited economic opportunities and gendered assumptions about sexuality. But the public response to prostitution is not static. In the United States, both the definition of and the strategies to deal with prostitution have shifted many times from tacit tolerance to attempts to contain or even to abolish the offense. The one approach almost never tried was legalization and regulation.[39]

During the early and mid-nineteenth centuries, prostitution was generally treated as a public order issue. The middle class wanted clean, safe cities and regarded prostitutes as part of the dissolute, idle, dangerous classes. Women who "walked the streets" were out of their proper sphere. Their behavior posed a threat to mainstream values. Criminal law came to define prostitution as a lifestyle and a status, rather than an act. In other words, a woman could be charged, not just because she accepted money for sex, but because her inappropriate presence on the street—where a respectable woman should not be—constituted disorderly conduct.[40] The enforcement of the laws reflected class and sex biases. Charges were more likely to be brought against streetwalkers than against brothel residents, against prostitutes rather than madams. Public, not private, sexual nonconformity was punished. Landlords and financial supporters of the businesses were seldom held accountable.[41] And, as feminists have always pointed out, although commercial sex requires at least two participants—a seller and a buyer—the men who solicited the services were not prosecuted.

The women who wrote the Seneca Falls Declaration and their successors in the nineteenth-century women's movement were well aware of the double standard that excused sexual promiscuity in men while condemning it in women. They saw the double standard as one element in the patriarchal structure that allowed men to dominate social, economic, political, religious, and "private" life. Many of the female reformers drew an analogy between sexual coercion in marriage and prostitution. Both were manifestations of men's misuse of their dominant position to use women to satisfy their physical desires. Thus, it became possible for middle-class, "respectable" women to make common cause with "fallen" women, as both could be exploited in a society where gender inequality persisted. Groups such as the Female Moral Reform Society and the Women's Christian Temperance Union cast a woman's perspective on the problem of prostitution. They hoped to end it by creating a single standard of morality—one where men would be held to the same high levels of behavior expected of "good" women. They also hoped, through offering economic opportunities and alternative living arrangements to poor women, to, in effect, dry up the supply of prostitutes.[42] The next chapter will discuss some of the attempts by these reformers to alter the treatment of "fallen women" in prison. Unfortunately, the social purity crusades often had unanticipated and negative consequences for the prostitutes themselves. As, in the interest of social order and morality, police enforced laws against prostitution more aggressively, they closed down brothels and "swept up" the streetwalkers. But the root causes of prostitution—poverty, abuse, economic marginality, gender inequality—remained in place. The structure of the business changed as prostitutes often attached themselves to pimps for protection from the police. Pateman claims that the late nineteenth-century "reforms" had the net effect of making prostitution more dangerous and exploitive. It shifted from a female control by madams to male control by pimps. The girls and women in the business had another level of patriarchal control to contend with.[43]

During the Progressive Era in the early twentieth century, prostitution became a national preoccupation as journalists and politicians discovered a phenomenon they called "white slavery." The term carried some powerful imagery. It suggested that respectable "white" women might be lured, kidnapped, drugged, or seduced into a life of prostitution. It also suggested that the villains responsible were immigrants who engaged in international trafficking in women. One manifestation of the power of the white slavery metaphor was the passage of the Mann Act by the U.S. Congress in 1910. One of the first federal criminal laws of the modern era, the Mann Act made it a federal offense to transport a woman across state lines for "immoral purposes." There were few prosecutions under the law. The most notorious involved black heavyweight boxing champion Joe Johnson, who was charged in a shocking gesture of racism for paying for his white girlfriend's interstate railway ticket. In general, the Mann Act, like the entire white slavery crusade, again missed the mark in identifying and addressing the real causes of prostitution. Nor were policies during World War I more enlightened or more effective. The War Department, concerned about the spread of sexually transmitted diseases among soldiers, encouraged the arrest of thousands of "suspicious" females. Patriotism and the war effort demanded that the armed forces be protected from "vicious" young women and that "foolish and innocent" girls be saved from contact with depravity.[44]

The ebb and flow of public policy on the subject of prostitution reflect shifts in political priorities as well as in moral standards. Modern feminists have also entered the debate. Some have advocated against any laws prohibiting commercial sex, arguing that women should control their own sexuality, that prostitution is, for some, a means of economic independence, and that consenting adults should enjoy a right to whatever personal sexual expression they choose.[45] Other feminists, echoing their predecessors, assert that prostitution is a form of sexual slavery, that the patriarchal structure allows men to demand that women's bodies be sold as commodities so they can ensure access to them.[46] Some find prostitution to be a form of violence against women. Anderson and Estes believe that sexual activity without mutual desire and respect objectifies the participants and violates their human dignity. Sex becomes a form of "bodily intrusion" that obscures the distinction between a human being and a thing.[47] They further argue that prostitution accommodates men's desires for women who cease to exist when they are no longer wanted. In such a dehumanizing situation, the prostitute must detach herself from the event and often resorts to alcohol or drugs to dull her senses. Her lack of reaction may lead the client to violence or other degradation in an effort to provoke a response.[48]

We have identified several of the areas where the link between victim and offender comes into play in prostitution. Women who deal in sex for money experience both unequal enforcement and unequal protection. If a society based on gender inequity is a precondition for prostitution, then the offense is at least in part a social, rather than an individual one. Yet the individual prostitute, only rarely the client, is likely to be labeled a criminal. She is likely to be doubly blamed if she is addicted to drugs, as if that problem were not often attributable to the same conditions as prostitution. At the same time, prostitutes are often victims of unequal protection. If they are robbed, assaulted, or raped, the criminal justice system will seldom see them as innocent. Their lifestyle increases the odds that they will be victimized, and also that they will be blamed for the crimes against them. Finally, if girls were better protected from sexual and physical abuse in their homes, the streets would be less alluring. Dealing with abuse will not end prostitution, but for the girls who enter that life out of desperation, there may be better alternatives.

CHAPTER SIX

Punishing Women: The Experience of Female Offenders

Whether or not you believe that incarcerating thousands of Americans in federal, state, and local prisons is an effective way to accomplish the objectives of the criminal justice system, it is clear that the different status, experience, and needs of women raise some particular questions about that approach to punishment. Yet while both researchers and correctional professionals gather information demonstrating the failures of harsh punitive policies toward women, politicians blithely go along ignoring that data and pandering to the idea that tough measures are an effective crime prevention strategy. During the 1980s and 1990s, in response to public fears of drugs and violent crimes, state and federal legislatures passed a series of "get tough" laws intended to send brutal criminals to prison for a long time. Although the target offenders may have been violent and male, the actual effect of these laws was to sweep up thousands of non-violent girls and women into state and federal prisons. The increase in the number of women in jails and prisons is shocking and perplexing, especially when one considers that the rate of violent offenses committed by women has remained stable. This chapter will examine issues related to punishing women. It will look at the statistics describing female offenders, consider who makes up the prison population, what crimes they have committed, and discuss why so many women are incarcerated. The remainder of the chapter will look at women's prisons from an historical and a contemporary perspective. It will conclude with information about women who have been sentenced to death.

The Numbers

According to data from the Bureau of Justice Statistics report on women offenders, at the end of 1998, 950,000 women were under the care, custody, or control of a correctional agency.[1] The vast majority of these women, 85%, were under community supervision. The other 15%, about 115,000 women, were in jail, or a state or federal prison. During the 1990s, the per-capita rate of women in prison grew by 88%, while the per-capita rate for men grew by 27% during that same decade. This increase cries out for an explanation, especially when the same report informs us that the per-capita rate of women committing violent crime decreased by 25% during those years. In fact, the per-capita rate of murder by women in 1998 was the lowest recorded since 1976. Three out of four women sentenced for violent crimes had committed simple assault. So, the simple answer—we are locking up more dangerous violent criminals—is clearly false.

Where do these offenders go? During the first two hundred years of its history, the United States built 43 prisons for women. During the next thirty years—from 1970 to the end of the century—that number more than doubled. Seventeen new prisons or units for women were built in the 1970s, 34 more were completed in the 1980s, more in the 1990s—yet many facilities were overcrowded in spite of these additions.[2]

What offenses account for this growth in the female prison population? Thirty-four percent of those in state prisons and 72% in federal prisons were there for drug offenses. An additional 27% in state institutions had committed property crimes, most commonly larceny and fraud. Thus the majority of female prisoners were behind bars for low-level drug offenses or for theft.

A few other statistics help to fill out the picture of these convicts. About 70% were between the ages of twenty-five and forty-five. A significant percentage (77% of state prisoners) had never married, were separated or divorced. More than half had a high school diploma or a GED. Women in state prison had an average of 2.38 children under the age of eighteen, and about two thirds of these children had lived with their mothers prior to prison. Nearly 30% of female inmates had been on welfare before arrest, 40% had been employed full-time. Nearly two thirds of women in jail, state, and federal prison are members of minority groups, while these groups account for only 26% of the general female population. A profile of the "typical" woman in custody would show a fairly young, black, single mother. She would have a minimal education and a poor record of employment. When she went to prison, she would leave behind several minor children.

Behind the Numbers

According to Barbara Owen, the criminality of women reflects the circumstances of their lives and their struggle for survival. She cites ingrained racism and sexism, the devaluation of women and girls, and toleration of abuse in a male-dominated society as explanatory factors. A women's prison, she maintains, is a place for those with no place in conventional society, a place for those no one wants, a place for those with no place else to go.[3] Kathryn Watterson, who has studied women's prisons for more than twenty years, also argues that the women who end up in prison are those with chaotic, disorganized lives. She believes that the criminal justice system treats them with contempt and thinks of them as tramps or evil mothers. Most people forget that inmates are someone's daughter, wife, sister, or mother—probably no worse than the rest of us but stigmatized because they have been convicted of a crime.[4]

As the criminological literature discussed in the last chapter asserts, Watterson and others find a clear link between prior abuse and deviant behavior. Among many of the women she studied, abuse led to addiction, running away as juveniles, attempted suicide, poverty, and crime.[5] Other studies make the same point. A report funded by the National Institutes of Justice finds that females abused or neglected in childhood are 73% more likely than those not abused or neglected to be arrested for property crime, alcohol or drug offenses, and juvenile status offenses. Their study makes the point that both abuse and neglect are significant factors.[6] Likewise, speakers at the 1999 National Symposium on Women Offenders sponsored by the United States Department of Justice, argued that women offenders are different from men, especially regarding the role of abuse in their prior lives. The criminal justice system is not set up to take the complexity of their experience into account when sentencing them to prison but instead focuses on the single incident that violated the law. Consequently, many battered women end up in prison—not just for killing their abusers but also for other crimes coerced by a batterer, including such things as welfare fraud, selling drugs, or driving a getaway car.[7] Others at that symposium listed statistics on the prevalence of abuse among women offenders. Officials at the Bedford Hills facility in New York noted that 94% of the inmates had had at least one serious physical or sexual assault in her past. Sixty percent had been molested as children, more as adults.[8]

Other scholars agree. In her study of a North Carolina women's facility, Lori Girshick found that 68% of the women had been abused before the age of eighteen.[9] In addition to physical and sexual abuse, they had experienced other traumas during adolescence—teen pregnancy, school failures, poverty, alcoholism, and family disruptions, including the involvement of family members with the criminal justice system. She argues that girls who experience abuse and/or neglect often feel desperate for love. They go looking for it in all the wrong places and often end up with more abuse, and eventually a conviction.[10] Quite a few of the women in her study had problems with school. Some were discouraged by the low expectations for girls. Many dropped out—because of a poor academic record or the need to go to work or help out at home. Most who left school did so because of pregnancy. In general, she concluded that they had been girls in trouble without family resources to help them out.[11] Their adult lives were also disorganized and chaotic—sometimes reproducing the problems in their own families. They ended up with bad boyfriends, low-paying jobs, low self-esteem, abuse, and drug addiction. When children and bills were added to these conditions, life often got out of hand.[12]

Study after study, whether by corrections personnel or by academic researchers, discuss the role of abuse in the lives of women offenders. Few would argue that abuse or neglect or any other elements of a hard life excuse criminal behavior. Most do maintain, however, that because there is a clear link between being a victim of abuse and drug use, it should come as no surprise that the "War on Drugs" has resulted in filling prisons with women who do not fit the profile of the violent criminal.

Casualties in the War on Drugs

In 1975, the Law Enforcement Assistance Administration's Task Force on Women made a series of recommendations "to ensure that women are treated fairly in the criminal justice system." Twenty-five years later, a follow-up report found that women's needs were still "substantially overlooked" in the system and that gender bias remained. They noted especially that at the end of the century not only were there more women in corrections facilities, but that they were a different population from the women in prison in 1975. Yet the increased numbers in prison for drug offenses were not matched by "enhanced programs geared particularly for women." The lack of attention to women was particularly troubling in light of the more punitive criminal justice philosophy of the last several decades.[13]

The configuration of public policies known as the "war on drugs" is one aspect of this more punitive approach. During a number of historical periods, Americans have sought to address a variety of social problems by controlling access to substances deemed dangerous. As discussed earlier in this book, some who advocated the prohibition of alcohol in the nineteenth and early twentieth century argued that abolishing liquor would solve a host of other problems from wife battering to barroom fights to tardiness at work. Rather than looking at the root causes of violence or worker dissatisfaction, prohibitionists believed getting rid of alcohol would be a panacea. To some extent, those who supported ratcheting up anti-drug policies in the late twentieth century made similar claims. Many Americans came to believe that if we could just get the drug problem in hand—particularly through harsher punishment of offenders—property crimes and crimes of violence would diminish. It was a politically popular argument.

In 1986 and again in 1988, each time right before a November election, Congress passed Anti-Drug Abuse Acts. Those laws increased penalties for both the sale and possession of illegal drugs, eliminated federal probation and parole for drug offenders, raised fines, and provided for forfeiture of assets. State laws reflected the same tough approach, including mandatory sentences and abolishing parole. Congress provided extensive funds for local law enforcement, although only a small amount was set aside for treatment and preventive programs. By 1995, expenditures for the war on drugs amounted to $100 billion per year.[14] Anti-drug law enforcement focused extensively on street crime, resulting in the arrest of users and small-time dealers—including many of the women who fill state and federal prisons.

According to Bush-Baskette, the war on drugs intentionally targeted women who are disproportionately consumers and abusers of drugs, legal and illegal. She argues the general conditions of women's lives often lead to depression. Many women self-medicate, with alcohol or drugs. For the poor, this means going to the street to get illegal substances, where their sale and use are highly visible. As federal and state laws cast a wider net against drugs, more women were caught in the net. Policies such as sentencing guidelines, mandatory sentences, and prison for first-time offenders increased female incarceration. Additionally, the women who committed other crimes, such as theft, to get drugs or money for drugs, were also snared by the tougher policies, such as three-strike laws.[15] In its report on women in prison, Amnesty International alleges that the war on drugs is a "war on women." In addition to the factors cited by Bush-Baskette, Amnesty notes that women are seldom in a position to bargain with prosecutors to get the lower sentences that can be traded for providing material assistance. Women are usually not high enough in a drug organization to have that sort of useful information. They also argue that many drug-related crimes committed by women occur because of threats or control by abusers. The tough drug statutes do not take such situations into account.[16]

Drug laws are not the only explanation for the increase in women's incarceration, although in Girshick's study, for example, 70% of the inmates had a drug-related charge.[17] But the drug issue must be put back into the larger context of the women's lives. They have experienced economic marginalization. As women, they were likely to be segregated into low-paying jobs. Living on the edge or in the depths of poverty helps to explain crimes like larceny, theft, writing bad checks, and welfare fraud—the other big categories of women's crimes. Along with drugs, these offenses may well represent "survival strategies based on limited options," attempts to cope with the circumstances of one's life.[18]

African American and women from other minority groups have been hit especially hard by the harsh drug laws. Already disproportionately represented among the poor and among victims of domestic violence, minority women have also felt the brunt of laws that set mandatory sentences for possession of crack cocaine. The 1988 federal anti-drug act set the required penalty at five years for five grams of crack. For powdered cocaine, which is more a white drug of choice, one must have 500 grams to earn a 5-year sentence. The National Symposium on Women Offenders noted that such laws are "racist in effect if not in intention."[19]

It is clear that the increase in the numbers of women in prison can be explained, not primarily by an increase in serious female crime but as the result of policies adopted through the political process that represent a decision to fight the war on drugs on the streets of the inner city. In other words, there was nothing inevitable about the dramatic growth in the incarceration of women. Had politicians decided to fight the war on another front—college campuses, for example—it is highly likely that the prison population would look far different than it does.

Perhaps the consequences of the current policies are unintended. It may be that lawmakers did not realize that the result of their "get tough" policies would fill more than 111 prisons with mostly non-violent women. Life in those prisons has, historically, reflected social attitudes about female offenders—what was wrong with them and what sort of punishment was appropriate. The next section examines women's prisons, how they evolved as separate institutions and what life is like for inmates today.

Establishing Prisons for Women

Estelle Freedman's classic study of the development of prisons for women, *Their Sisters' Keepers*, discusses the work of reformers to establish corrections institutions that, ideally, would address the causes of law breaking and provide an atmosphere where offenders could be appropriately rehabilitated.[20] While prison development and reform occupied a great deal of public attention in the early nineteenth century, the discussion was almost exclusively about prisons for men. Even the most humane reformers ignored the horrible conditions in which incarcerated women were kept. In most cases, women who broke the law were locked up in jails and prisons alongside men. They might be targets for sexual assault or abuse. They were likely to be forced to cook for the men, to wash their clothes, and scrub their cells. Babies and children were sometimes confined along with their mothers in dark, damp, windowless spaces. Why, in a society that supposedly respected women, were these people treated so abysmally? Two reasons are generally offered. There were so few female prisoners that they were easily overlooked by administrators and politicians who focused their concern on the far more numerous male convicts. Secondly, the female inmates were usually guilty of crimes related to sexual misbehavior, such as prostitution. According to typical nineteenth-century thinking, a woman who was sexually promiscuous was irredeemable. The Victorians believed that female sexual desire was unnatural, that a decent woman had little interest or enjoyment in sex, aside from her duty to become a mother. If a woman appeared to be sexually active, she must be an unnatural woman, even a depraved woman. (Never mind that prostitutes were hardly likely to enjoy the sexual activity they engaged in.) And if she was depraved and unnatural, there was little the penitentiary could do to rehabilitate such "fallen women." They might as well be left in prison to destroy or prey upon each other.[21]

Reform-minded middle-class women discovered the plight of female inmates in much the way they discovered prostitution and other injustices. Starting with religious groups who went into the prisons to read the Bible and try to convert convicts, some reformers came to understand that the "fallen women" were not inherently different from respectable women but rather that their situation was "rooted in the social relations of the sexes." In other words, male privilege permitted men to exploit poor vulnerable girls, then to benefit from the double standard that excused masculine behavior while condemning their partners. The idea of the separate spheres, so common in the nineteenth century, allowed middle-class women to bond with their "sisters" in prison. If women were really a separate sexual class, very different from men, then all women must have common experiences and common concerns. Regardless of social class, they all shared a subordinate position. Thus respectable women could reach across the moral divide and try to help the deviant. In this case they did so by supporting the idea of separate prisons for women designed and run by female staff.[22] In such institutions, the inmates would be free from sexual exploitation, exposed to the uplifting influence of programs geared to overcome their unfortunate pasts and to teach them to be respectable, decent citizens.

The nineteenth-century prison reformers developed their theories with the young, impressionable "chastity offenders" in mind. Their institutions would be totally different from the big, forbidding, fortress structures that housed male inmates. Instead, they would build small, homey cottages away from the corrupting city in the fresh air of the country. In such an environment, called a reformatory rather than a prison, character training could succeed. There the offenders would learn to do domestic work, to live peacefully and respectfully with others, and, if they had babies, to care for them as proper mothers. The reformers believed that learning to care for children was one of the greatest aids to rehabilitation.

Despite their good intentions, there were some conflicts among the reformers' goals. On the one hand, they believed that feminine ideals such as purity and domesticity were necessary to rehabilitation. At the same time, they knew that the inmates must become self-sufficient and economically independent if they were to avoid law breaking in the future. There was also the concern that the institution itself might foster dependency.[23]

In fact, the purposes of women's prisons have always been marked by contradictions and competing pressures. They existed not as independent private entities, as the women's colleges did, but within the context of the larger political world. Like other public agencies, they had to fight for money and autonomy within the state legislature. They faced at least as much public contempt and apathy as men's prisons did. Thus the reformers' ideals about humane or feminine approaches to corrections were often submerged in the reality of insufficient funding and public prejudice. An additional issue for the women's prisons was finding qualified and committed staff after the first enthusiastic generation. Because the institutions were located away from cities, in the "wholesome countryside," staff members found themselves lonely and isolated. Low pay as public employees and questions about the respectability of their work did not improve the job's attractiveness. By the twentieth century, the idealistic notions of the earliest generation of women's prison advocates had come up against a more pessimistic reality.

During the early twentieth century, new approaches to corrections affected the development of the female institutions. Progressive reformers who influenced public policy at the local, state, and national level emphasized the environmental causes of crime. They wanted to put more resources into community agencies, such as the juvenile court, probation for minor crimes, and policewomen to work with female victims and offenders. Such a policy shift meant both that less money would be available for the residential facilities and that those who were sent to them were likely to be more hardened offenders and older women with a longer history of deviant behavior. This was not the population the nineteenth-century prisons had been designed to accommodate, and the change meant a challenge to their managers.

Other political developments affected the female prisons. In 1914, Congress passed the Harrison Act that outlawed a number of narcotics.

Then at the end of the decade, the nation adopted Prohibition, making it illegal to produce, distribute, or sell alcoholic beverages. This legislation affected so many women that for the first time the federal government needed to build a female prison to house those convicted of violating these laws. It is hard to miss the parallel with the increase in female offenders brought about by the increased severity of drug laws in the late twentieth century. At the state and local level, World War I meant stringent enforcement of anti-prostitution laws in the interests of protecting soldiers from disease and assisting the war effort. Such policies brought significant numbers of women into prisons and jails.

Thus, during the first quarter of the twentieth century, for reasons related to larger social changes, instead of offering a different corrections philosophy, women's prisons became more like men's institutions. They focused less on benevolence and understanding the inmates and more on protecting society. Rather than reforming those whom social injustices had harmed, they would control people who brought mental, medical, and social problems into the facility.[24] Nonetheless, the reformers who created the prisons for women left a legacy more positive than negative. By segregating offenders on the basis of sex and providing a female staff, they were able to reduce or eliminate sexual abuse and the exploitation of women's labor for the benefit of male inmates. For the women assigned to the institutions, there were benefits in education, vocational training, health, and even companionship. On the other hand, the reformatories were also characterized by stereotypical thinking related to race, class, and sex. The residents were often treated like children in need of guidance, instead of like adults encouraged to become independent. Sexual segregation also meant that women convicted of any offense from the most trivial to the most violent would be sent to the same institution. As the century progressed, and as the facilities became more crowded, discipline issues increased. This development was not the fault of the creators of women's prisons; rather, it posed a challenge for the later generations of administrators to try to create a prison environment suitable for a new population.

Prison Life

In December 1999, the U.S. Department of Justice sponsored a high-powered Symposium on Women Offenders. One speaker noted that it was the first major discussion of female offenders in the department's history. (The Department of Justice is one of the original cabinet departments created by President George Washington in 1789.) Aside from the obvious fact that 210 years was a long time to wait for a conference, the participants addressed the issues with clarity and enthusiasm. They included judges, attorneys, scholars, and corrections personnel, and they expressed remarkable agreement in defining problems and suggesting changes.

Almost every session began with two acknowledgments—that the number of incarcerated women was growing and that women offenders are different from men. During the last part of the twentieth century, as Americans struggled with the idea of gender equality, some insisted that it meant identical treatment. For the area of corrections, this interpretation seldom worked to women's advantage. Such a form of "equality" meant that women would be sentenced like men without regard to their different circumstances. It might also mean that women's facilities could become as cold, brutal, and dehumanizing as men's. Some scholars have called this idea "equality with a vengeance."[25]

Amnesty International sees the issue of sex discrimination in prison as a sort of double-edged sword. In some cases, inmates have won improvements by claiming violations of their right to equal treatment. In the District of Columbia, for example, women were able to get better educational and vocational programs. However, when they also claimed a right to religious services and recreational facilities comparable to men, the court found it would be too expensive to provide those to a small facility. Amnesty notes that in prison, equality with men is not enough if the men's situation is itself a violation of human rights.[26]

At the Symposium on Women Offenders, the goal was to develop policies that were "gender responsive," that take into account the ways in which female convicts differ from their masculine counterparts. For example, a high percentage of women are first-time offenders. When they do commit a violent crime, it is often against someone they know, and frequently due to domestic or family violence. A large percentage of female inmates come in with a background of mental illness, often depression and addiction; many have a history of victimization; a significant number have young children for whom they are responsible as major caregiver. Women are less violent after they enter prison and are unlikely to get into trouble over issues of power and dominance as males do.[27] How do prisons take these differences into account and what can be done to make them more gender responsive and ultimately more effective?

Watterson argues that the effectiveness of prisons as they exist is debatable. She believes the one thing they do well is punish. They strip inmates of their dignity, health, and whatever self-esteem they had. They also punish inmates' children and families. But they do not stop crime, especially the big crimes that threaten people's security.[28] Girshick also finds that adjusting to the institution takes its toll on the prisoners. The very first thing that happens is an invasive strip search, which is part of the stripping away of the person's individuality. Along with the strip search, the inmate gives up her personal possessions and dons prison clothes. The initiation rite is a sort of status degradation.[29] Some would argue that humiliation is what someone deserves when he or she commits a crime, that the old law-breaking personality needs to be broken. Others argue that for women who may already have problems with abuse or depression, such mortification can only have negative consequences.

Both Watterson and Girshick discuss how institutionalization fosters dependency. Inmates' lives, attitudes, and behavior are regulated in every way. The authorities have total power, and as Watterson notes, the more isolated the institution is from public view, the more helpless the inmates are to defend themselves. These authors claim that cultivating dependency, especially in women who have often already been victims of men determined to assert power and control, is both cruel and illogical. Fostering dependence is illogical if one of the institution's goals is to encourage responsibility when the inmates leave and also because, according to Watterson, it leads prisoners to develop other negative qualities like dishonesty, cheating, stealing, hustling, and evasiveness.[30] She quotes a guard who expresses frustration with the emphasis on controlling the inmates. "All our work in the institution is so restrictive. We have to follow all these rules and we're told we can't get too friendly with the inmates. All our time seems to be spent solving little problems—like keeping count or who wants to move where or who broke this or that rule. We don't ever get to the big problems or to things that will really help somebody."[31] The guard's comments reflect the ambivalence that characterizes the work of women's prisons, primarily because as institutions they seem to serve several, often conflicting, purposes. On the one hand, public opinion supports the idea of punishment for those who break the law. At the same time, recognizing that most convicts will eventually come back into the community, the public benefits from efforts at rehabilitation. In general, people express less hostility toward non-violent female offenders than toward "criminals" in general, but even so, they don't want to spend too much of taxpayers' money giving them a comfortable life behind bars. Those who argue in favor of punishment for its own sake, and bare-bones punishment at that, seem to have won the argument over those who argue that in the long run, rehabilitation both better protects the public and saves money.

Inmates themselves admit that there can be some affirmative aspects to the prison experience. For some, it is a chance to be safe from the abuse and control that has characterized their former lives, or a chance to get off drugs, or a chance to examine one's life and try to find ways to change. One prisoner explained to Girshick that if positive change is going to take place, it won't take a long sentence to make it happen. "You're either going to be rehabilitated in five years or you're not...[otherwise] You don't want to change. You like who you are."[32]

Marcia Bunney, serving a sentence of twenty-five years to life in California for first-degree murder of her abuser, has described how she went from being a victim to being a healed individual to becoming a peer counselor/activist/journalist in prison, with the support of fellow inmates and some sympathetic staff. Her story involves questions of control and dependence and illustrates the need for gender-responsive approaches to women's experiences.

When Bunney was tried, the court knew very little about battered women. She was unable to explain or articulate her experience of abuse, and her lawyer so misunderstood her story that he described her to the judge as a "gravely disturbed and unhappy woman." As a result, Bunney was convicted.

She determined that if she had survived years of abuse, she could survive prison without psychotropic medication or allowing herself to become a zombie of mindless routine. She looked for ways to have some control over her life. She took food from the cafeteria and combined it with what she bought in the canteen and food her family sent to make a healthier diet. She learned to crochet and knit, and was eventually able to sell some of her work in the prison craft shop as well as to make gifts for family and friends outside. Eventually she was promoted from her routine kitchen job to office work, and while there, she was encouraged to take some college courses offered on site. Bunney was able to earn an associate's degree, but more importantly, she learned that she was intelligent and capable, things she had never realized about herself. She also came to understand how women could mentor and assist one another and from that knowledge went on to start a self-help group for battered women. Bunney was also learning not to tolerate manipulation, which led her to file several grievances against prison procedures. After filing the grievances, she claims that in retaliation and contrary to policy, she was transferred to a harsher facility. Assigned to work in the law library there, Bunney studied law on her own and eventually organized a class action lawsuit, claiming the prison's medical care was below standard. At that point, she was removed from the law library, but she continued to write for newspapers and prisoners' publications.

Bunney's story is certainly one of successful rehabilitation, although she remains behind bars. Her own analysis of its lessons is informative. When asked if she feels safe in prison because she is away from abuse, she responds that the abuse hasn't stopped, but her ignorance and tolerance of abuse have ended. Her recommendation is that comprehensive assistance to victims of abuse should be a priority in all women's prisons.[33] Such programming might make the inmates less docile, but it is likely to make them better able to succeed when their sentences end.

Observers have identified a number of issues that are particularly influential in determining the quality of women's prison experience. Although some of the same concerns may apply to male inmates, gender does make a difference with respect to sexual harassment, sexuality, mental and physical health issues, and especially in relationships with children.

Elizabeth Morgan, a physician with a degree from Yale University, was sentenced to the District of Columbia jail for contempt of court when she refused to abide by a judge's order to allow her daughter visitation with the father who had sexually abused her. Morgan kept a diary while she was in jail and later published it. The facility housed male and female inmates, supposedly in separate wings. She described an atmosphere in which loud, sexually aggressive music was piped in, and in which male prisoners roamed the halls, stood at the entrance of the women's cellblock, and watched the women shower. The guards claimed that the male prisoners "needed" these activities. Morgan called it "organized degradation of women."[34] The situation she portrayed was almost as bad as those found by the prison reformers in the early nineteenth century and certainly an example of institutionalized sex discrimination and gender inequality. "The dominant members of the system," Morgan wrote, "chiefly men, accord themselves an unspoken, unwritten right to abuse their power, mainly by using physical violence to subjugate less dominant men and by using sexual violence inflicted by themselves and the men below them to dominate women."[35]

Groups such as Human Rights Watch and Amnesty International have found widespread examples of sexual abuse by staff in women's prisons. Human Rights Watch noted particular problems because inmates are unable to escape their abusers, because grievance procedures are ineffectual or nonexistent, because of a lack of employee accountability in most institutions, and because the public shows little or no concern about the problem.[36]

Amnesty International also found numerous allegations of sexual harassment, abuse, and even rape. At the federal prison in California guards took money from male prisoners to get into women's cells for "involuntary sex." When the victims complained, the white women were moved to another area. The African American women were left to fend for themselves for an additional ten days. Other investigations revealed cases where female prisoners were stripped naked and kept under surveillance for suicide observation. They had no underwear or tampons, but male guards were allowed to keep watch. In Michigan, male personnel watched women take showers and use toilets "well beyond legitimate security needs." Rape and sexual assault allegations were raised in Alabama, Arizona, California, Florida, Idaho, Illinois, Maryland, Massachusetts, Michigan, New Hampshire, New York, Ohio, Texas, Virginia, Washington, West Virginia, Wyoming, and the District of Columbia.[37]

Participants in the Symposium on Women Offenders also discussed the growing prevalence of sexual abuse by staff in female facilities. They cited intrusive frisk searches, a problem addressed by a 1993 lawsuit in federal court but obviously not resolved. At that time the judge cited prisons that permitted male guards to grope, fondle, expose themselves, or masturbate while searching female prisoners. The judge noted that common sense should reveal that intrusive, invasive searches of women by male guards both "constitute and reinforce gender subordination and offend basic human dignity."[38]

Although searches may be justified by security needs in the prison, the purposeful sexualization and degradation of such processes could surely be addressed. For the sizeable number of inmates who are already victims of sexual abuse, intrusive bodily searches could easily be traumatic.

In addition to the issues related to searches, the Symposium on Women Offenders identified "inappropriate cross gender supervision" (presumably observation in showers and bathrooms, etc.), inappropriate language, poor grievance and investigation processes, and retaliation, as other elements in the problem of sexual abuse. Perhaps the simplest response to this array of issues would be to prohibit male guards from working in women's prisons. As the reformers in the early 1800s realized, not all, but many of these problems would go away in a single-sex facility. However, the courts have interpreted Civil Rights Laws to make it illegal to discriminate on the basis of sex, in most cases, when hiring public employees. Therefore, male guards claim they have a legal right to work in women's prisons, and at present, approximately 41% of employees in those institutions are male.[39] Assuming then, that men do have a right to be employed in female prisons, what can be done to reduce the possibility of sexual harassment and abuse?

Rape is, of course, a crime in every jurisdiction, and in recent years a number of states have defined any sexual intercourse between guards and inmates as rape based on the argument that—given the disparity of power—an inmate cannot freely consent to sex with a guard. As of 1999, at least 45 states had laws prohibiting sexual misconduct in prisons although states differ in their definition of misconduct. Surprisingly in 1996, only 3 states had such legislation. It appears that sexual abuse of inmates—like acquaintance rape and sexual harassment—existed long before the legal system was prepared to define and deal with it.

But in addition to outlawing sexual assault and misconduct other reforms are needed if female inmates are to be made safe from their overseers. Often staff receive little or no training in the special needs and issues of women's prisons. Sometimes it is a cost-cutting measure to cut out the "dealing with women" portion of the training. In some states, wardens regard being assigned to the female facility as either a punishment or a stop on the way to a "real" prison. These supervisors are unlikely to be sensitive to the inmates' gender-related needs. Lawsuits have sometimes helped to alert wardens and state officials to the importance of training, but prevention of sexual assault and harassment claims would be preferable to seeking redress after the fact.

If better training were made available, it would need to include warnings against the use of demeaning and sexually charged language to and about the inmates, proper search techniques, and avoidance of improper interactions among staff members such as gossip in front of the prisoners. If men are to be employed in women's prisons, other reforms may reduce the probability of sexual abuse. A number of facilities require that a male guard going into the living areas must be accompanied by a female guard. Although in some states, unions objected to this regulation, lawsuits where guards were fired for misconduct seem to have diminished union opposition. Accountability for those who violate the policies would mean a workable grievance procedure, where inmates could file claims without fear of retaliation, a fair process of investigation, and sanctions for those who are found guilty.

Fear of retaliation is a powerful force in maintaining inmates' silence when they are victims. Guards or their friends can make life miserable for a woman who complains. They can confiscate her mail, subject her to more searches, harass her verbally, threaten her, file false reports against her, or even assault her again.[40] As discussed earlier, dependence and powerlessness are facts of life for any prisoner. Gender inequity is a fact of life for women. Those two factors combined can make prison an extension of the horrors of sexual abuse. When institutions permit such misconduct to exist and continue, they are surely violating inmates' human rights.

Mental illness and addiction commonly accompany women into prison. Because such a high percentage of inmates have been victims of abuse and because many have self-medicated with drugs and alcohol, they are particularly in need of treatment. Girshick found that depression was the most common health problem among the women she studied.[41] Some observers claim that many of the women in prison are actually there as punishment for their mental illness. Over half of them were under the influence of some substance at the time of their crime. As part of the process of deinstitutionalization in the late twentieth century, many residential facilities for the mentally ill were closed. People were released, theoretically to be cared for in community settings. Often, however, states and localities considered the closing of institutions to be a budget savings. Rather than divert that savings into community care, it often went to other projects, including prisons. The former patients were left without adequate care on the outside. After they got in trouble and ended up inside prison, in many cases they still did not get adequate care.

Treatment within most corrections settings is minimal; in fact, inmates who exhibit troubling behavior are frequently given psychotropic drugs to keep them quiet. Watterson notes a troubling contradiction in attention to psychological problems. According to her observations, prisons are kept under tight discipline for security reasons. The stringent rules make life a pain for the majority. Yet the small minority who are really dangerous because of mental illness are ignored by the staff. She found that the inmates did a better job of caring for each other than the institution did.[42] Her view seems consistent with Bunney's experience. She, too, felt her greatest help came from the other women, both through their informal encouragement and ultimately through the support groups she organized. She also mentioned her decision to resist the psychotropic drugs offered by the prison staff.[43] The issue of mental illness is ultimately inseparable from the matter of abuse and the general quality of health care in the prisons. Elizabeth Morgan documented that the sexualized and misogynist conditions in the D.C. Jail triggered posttraumatic stress behaviors in some inmates.[44] Others see the lack of treatment for mental illness as part of a larger neglect of prisoners' health.

Amnesty International notes that the U.S. Supreme Court has held that depriving people in prison of adequate medical care is a violation of the Eighth Amendment's ban on cruel and unusual punishment. However, by many measures, prisons across the country violate the constitutional standard every day. Funding for health care is not increasing in proportion to the increase in prison populations. Amnesty sees this problem manifested in the decline of drug treatment. In 1991 40% of female inmates received drug treatment; in 1997 only 18% did. Yet during that time the proportion of women sentenced for drug crimes increased. Other signs of lower expenditures for medical care included procedures that required inmates to get permission from non-medical staff before they could see a doctor or nurse. Often this meant a guard, untrained in medicine, was in the position of diagnosing whether a patient was sick. Some states began to charge inmates for medical care, while others turned prison infirmaries over to private, for-profit health care providers.[45]

Few women enter prison in the best of health. Most had a poor diet, bad nutrition, inadequate fresh air, exercise, and rest on the outside. Typically, as poor people, they did not have medical insurance, regular check-ups, or dental care. They often lacked the information or the motivation to take good care of themselves. If one adds drug and alcohol abuse, the likelihood of chronic illness such as high blood pressure, diabetes, sexually transmitted diseases, including AIDS, it makes for a prison population with serious and on-going health problems.[46] In addition, there is a set of uniquely feminine medical concerns, including the approximately 8%-10% of women who are pregnant when they are incarcerated. Girshick found that some women in her study were made to have abortions; others were denied abortions when they requested them.[47]

Morgan, a doctor herself, concluded that 87% of the medical cases she observed during her stay in jail were either refused treatment or given inadequate care. A medical director on the staff of the D.C. jail who complained of those conditions did not have his contract renewed.[48] Amnesty International documented some shocking stories, especially in the treatment of women giving birth. Many states have a policy of keeping every inmate patient who goes to a hospital in restraints—handcuffs and/or shackles—regardless of her history of violence and even though an armed guard is present. One woman in a minimum-security prison for shoplifting, with no incidents of violent behavior, was shackled during her seven-hour labor. Speaking after her release, she said, "Even animals wouldn't be shackled during labor, a household dog or a cow on a farm."[49] Another woman reported being shackled with her feet together during twelve hours of labor. Even though a guard was present, her feet were not released to be put into the stirrups. She was shackled to her bed for the three days she remained in the hospital. The report details a number of cases where restraints were left on women during labor despite doctor's orders to the contrary. It is troubling that few corrections officers were able to offer any reason for such procedures when the prisoner had no history of violence and when guards were present. Investigators were told, "It's the policy."[50]

For many women who gave birth while incarcerated, the pain of the labor room conditions was exceeded only by their pain at giving up their babies immediately. As of 1999, women under correctional supervision were the mothers of 1.3 million children. There are few programs in place to help these families maintain their bonds. More than half of the women in prison do not receive visits from their children, and most states favor the termination of parental rights for convicted offenders.[51] Incarcerated mothers fear the loss of their children. Many report anxiety when they were arrested—were their children safe? Who would take care of them? Would they be separated and put into foster care?[52]

The loss of a mother to prison is a different experience for children than the loss of a father. Many more children have lived with mothers than with fathers, so the change in a child's day-to-day life is likely to be greater. Children sometimes feel that their mother's absence is somehow their fault, that they are being punished. Girls whose mothers are locked up may be especially vulnerable. They seem angry and embarrassed that their mothers are in prison, that they get bounced around and live chaotic lives. Such girls are likely to drop out of school and may start down a path similar to their mother's. It is common for girls to blame their mothers for messing up their lives at the same time they want them out and back at home.[53] The National Criminal Justice Commission also reported that the incarceration of mothers was likely to lead to traumatic stress, developmental regression, loss of self-confidence, aggression, withdrawal, depression, interpersonal violence, substance abuse, and teenage pregnancy among their children.[54] This seems a high and long-term price to pay if those incarcerated are nonviolent offenders, convicted of relatively minor crimes.

Girshick notes that in the visiting rooms of men's prisons, one sees lots of families, wives, and children. In the visiting rooms of women's prisons, one seldom sees fathers with children in tow. One reason is that male facilities are likely to be closer to cities, so getting there to visit is easier. Women's prisons, on the other hand, are often in rural areas, sometimes in places without public transportation.[55] Over 60% of women who never had family visitors were in facilities more than 100 miles from their home.[56] In addition, fathers seem less likely to take up the obligation of visiting an incarcerated mother, perhaps an example of gendered role expectations.

Without visits or between them, phone calls provide an alternative way to keep in contact with family members. Generally access to telephones is limited, and prisoners are only allowed to make collect calls. In some states, the companies who provide service to prisons charge exorbitant rates, which must be paid by the families or friends who accept the calls. Some families have no phones; others have blocks on their lines; sometimes foster families will not accept calls. All in all, even maintaining telephone contact with children is full of obstacles.

Although much research suggests that sustaining and building relationships with their children is critical to women's rehabilitation and reduces recidivism, a variety of public policies work in a contrary direction. For example, all states permit termination of inmates' parental rights. The federal Adoption and Safe Families Act places a rigid cap on the time allowed mothers to reunite with their children before losing custody. In 1950, thirteen states allowed mothers to keep their babies for a time in prison. Fifty years later, only three states had such programs. Although in 1994 Congress authorized $20 million for programs to support keeping inmates' families together, the money was never spent.[57]

The Bedford Hills Correctional Facility in New York has resisted the trend to separate mothers and children. From its foundation in the early twentieth century, Bedford Hills has been committed to supporting families and has involved the inmates in developing the programs. A nursery on the grounds allows mothers to care for their babies for up to a year. Part of the visiting room is set up as a playroom. The institution provides bus transportation for inmates' children to and from New York City and has set up a summer program where children can stay with local families and see their mothers often. Mothers also record books on tape to send to their families. The superintendent finds that building and encouraging family ties does prevent recidivism, although she also says frankly, "Most women at Bedford Hills don't need to be in prison."[58]

Whether they should be in prison or not, the vast majority of female inmates will get out one day. Experts argue that gender-responsive programming in prisons and in the community is necessary to prevent future law breaking. Although it may be debatable whether prison is worse for women than for men, it is definitely different. The rate of recidivism is high for both men and women, but again the reasons differ. There is evidence that education and drug treatment have been successful with female inmates, yet in the punitive atmosphere of the late twentieth century, these were just the programs likely to be cut.[59] Some experts advise that effective interventions for women in prison should focus on self, relationships, sexuality, and spirituality. Such programs would support positive relationships, provide good role models and mentors, assist victims in dealing with sexual abuse and traumas as well as offering job training and education. Women have a particular need to see themselves not just as addicts, alcoholics, sluts, or bad mothers but also as people with talents and competence. Bunney's account of her success in college classes is a good example of such a positive experience. Likewise, many female inmates need help in forming healthy relationships, especially if they did not see them in their own families. Prison staff especially need training in combating the stereotypes that foster adversarial relationships with inmates based on a "combat and control" culture and allow them to see the prisoners as "those women" rather than as human beings. Staff behavior would seem very important in either reinforcing inmates' negative perceptions about themselves or in encouraging healthier attitudes.[60]

Women released from prison need readjustment aid if they are to avoid falling back into their old patterns. Many will still need therapy or treatment for addiction. They may require transitional housing, training in life skills and organization, anger management, and job assistance. To prevent the same people from rotating from agency to agency—from prison to hospital to homeless shelter, ideally these services need to be integrated in some comprehensive form that incorporates the criminal justice, health care, and educational systems.[61] Knowing that such a coordinated approach would help women avoid another trip to prison, help build families, and ultimately save public funds, it is troublesome that some recent laws seem to make rehabilitation more difficult. In addition to the laws terminating parental rights, recent welfare reform legislation provides that drug offenders are barred for life from public assistance. The same law requires that in order to receive assistance, adolescent mothers must live with their parents.[62] Both provisions clearly have a disproportionately negative effect on women, and both seem to disregard the links between poverty, abuse, and drug addiction.

It is instructive to revisit the nineteenth-century reformers who created women's prisons. Although some criticize their naiveté, many of their ideas have proved to be correct. They realized that gender inequity and sex discrimination were major factors in women's criminal behavior and that the different circumstances of women's lives demanded separate "gender-responsive" institutions. Those facilities would provide safety from abuse and help in developing healthy habits. They would pay attention to women's roles as mothers. In fact, they maintained that learning positive child care attitudes and family skills would be a factor in rehabilitation—a point repeatedly made by today's experts. Although they were limited in their perceptions of racial and ethnic prejudices, they spoke for a class of women usually ignored by respectable society.

Women on Death Row

Another group, sometimes ignored, who alternately attract fascination and repulsion is the small group of women who have been sentenced to death. A few numbers illustrate the relative rarity of death sentences handed down to women. Between 1632 when the first woman was executed in America and the end of the twentieth century, 561 women were put to death for crimes, about 2.8 % of all executions during that period of almost 400 years.[63] Today women make up 1.3% of death row inmates. Since 1976 when capital punishment was reinstated in the United States, six women have been put to death. Two of these were in Texas, one each in Arkansas, North Carolina, Oklahoma, and Florida.

An examination of the female population of death row shows similarities with both the larger population of women in prison and with the population of condemned men. Texas leads the nation in capital punishment for men and women—for both sexes, about one third of all those put to death have been in that state. The majority of executions of males and all those of females are clustered in the South. As in the general prison population, minority groups are disproportionately represented among condemned men and women although the numbers are more disparate for men. While the general population of the country is approximately 13% African American, 29% of women and 41% of men on death row are black. Among the six women executed in the modern period, four were white and two were African American.

Earlier in this chapter, we considered the data showing that women typically commit fewer violent crimes than men. When they do engage in violence, women are more likely to attack people known to them, which suggests that female violence is often placed within the context of a relationship rather than as a random event. If one reads the list of offenses for which women on death row have been convicted, there is no doubt many have done horrendous things. However, the list of offenses also shows, not surprisingly, a sizeable percentage of women condemned for murders within their own families. Some would argue that killing a relative is more horrible than killing a stranger, and therefore it deserves the harshest punishment. Yet women are much more likely than men to be on death row because of a family-related murder. For example, in California of twelve women sentenced to death as of 2001, seven (58%) had killed family members. In North Carolina, half of the women on death row had killed husbands or boyfriends. In Texas, 57% were convicted of murdering family members; in Florida, the number is two out of three. These statistics bear out the contention that, at the most extreme level of sanctions, women are punished for different offenses than men.

The differing characteristics of their crimes may help to explain why a larger percentage of women than men get off death row alive. For both sexes, only 9% of those condemned to death are actually executed. About a third of death penalty cases are either reversed or granted sentencing relief by courts. Among this group, women have been more successful than men in appealing their sentences.[64] Some scholars have argued that women are spared execution because of chivalry, a form of gender bias that favors women. According to this analysis, courts are reluctant to strap a woman to the gurney and kill her by lethal injection.[65] Other research proposes that women have been more successful in contesting death sentences because they raise their appeals more quickly. The very rarity of capital punishment for women makes each case newsworthy. Advocates are more likely to be aware of higher-profile cases, and such publicity may speed the appeal process. Elizabeth Rapaport makes a strong argument that the high reversal rate of women's death sentences is related to actual errors in the lower courts, rather than simply to extralegal factors. Trial courts sometimes fail to see that a female defendant has little history of violence prior to the current offense or that the aggravating factors are less severe than for a male counterpart. Most critically, there may be "gender patterned mitigating factors" not considered at trial, such as a history of battering or coercion by a male accomplice.[66] In other words, if a defense attorney failed to raise or explain issues such as abuse before the original sentence, that failure may be a major factor in granting relief.

The highly publicized 1998 case of Karla Fay Tucker in Texas generated a wide-ranging discussion of executive clemency, especially as it might apply to a condemned woman. Although Governor George W. Bush was inundated with requests to commute Tucker's death sentence, some of them from his supporters on the Christian right, Bush ultimately decided to let the execution proceed. In this case the arguments were not that Tucker had been denied a fair trial or that her defense had failed to raise relevant facts. Rather, the pleas to spare her life focused mostly on her prison conversion to Christianity, her work to help rehabilitate other inmates, and implicitly, on that fact that she was a woman. During the post-*Furman* period, before Tucker, only one woman had been executed. Velma Barfield had been put to death in North Carolina in 1984. Some say Governor Bush's rejection of the clemency appeals for Tucker was a victory for formal equality. Her case was treated without regard to her sex, simply as a "routine" execution.

It may be argued that after Karla Fay Tucker's execution, governors realized that they could ignore the "chivalry factor" and deny appeals for executive clemency for women without fear of political repercussion. During the 1990s, however, several governors did commute women's death sentences—not, apparently because of chivalry, but because of factors believed to mitigate the defendant's guilt. As Illinois Governor Jim Edgar stated when he spared the life of Guinivere Garcia in 1996, her crime was "not a typical murder." Garcia had shot her ex-husband in what appeared to be an example of separation assault. Likewise, Governor Richard Celeste of Ohio commuted eight death sentences just before he left office. Included in the group were four women and four men. The governor cited race, mental capacity, and questions about actual guilt as reasons for clemency. Celeste had also ordered a review of all Ohio cases where battered women had killed their abusers to determine whether the courts had properly considered the implications of abuse. Although none of them had been on death row, he ordered the release of 28 women convicted of that offense.[67]

It would be unreasonable to argue that women should be spared any appropriate punishment, even the death penalty, simply because of their sex. Such a view would clearly violate the standards of equal protection. It is not unreasonable, however, to advocate that all sanctions—including the ultimate sanction of taking a convicted person's life—should be applied in ways that take into account every relevant factor. Our research has shown that gender is such a relevant factor, and that to be fair and credible, all the elements of the criminal justice system charged with punishing crime must be gender responsive.

CHAPTER SEVEN

Regulating Reproduction

This chapter revisits several themes developed earlier—how laws affecting women have been made without women's formal participation in the process; how a society with a patriarchal legal framework defines appropriate female behavior and exerts control over women's lives, and how tensions separate the public and private spheres. It will focus particularly on the social control of reproductive matters and reexamine the issue of a woman's right to control her own body. One might ask, if a woman does not have the right to make decisions regarding her own body, who does? And more specifically, why should someone else have that right? This discussion follows from earlier examinations of issues regarding women's bodily integrity. We have argued that everyone has the right to be free from assault, that one's personal relationships do not diminish that right. Does the same principle apply in thinking about reproduction? Do women have the same absolute right to autonomy when it comes to childbearing, or does pregnancy diminish one's stature as an autonomous person?

The gender roles that prevail in any society or historical period will determine how those questions are answered. In a strongly patriarchal society with clearly defined gender expectations, the law will not recognize a woman's right to make independent reproductive decisions. Certainly under coverture there were no provisions for women to exercise such bodily integrity. Yet long after the most overt elements of coverture have been repealed, Americans continue to struggle over a woman's right to make reproductive decisions. If decisions are taken out of individual women's hands, they are likely to be delegated not to individual husbands but to the state. The notion that the state may play a role in reproductive decisions seems to contradict the idea of family privacy. Nonetheless, state involvement takes several forms in the contemporary world. The most obvious struggles have occurred over the regulation of abortion, but similar issues of control over pregnancy have arisen in conjunction with drug use and other dangerous behavior by expectant mothers.

Before examining the history of reproductive regulation in the United States, we need to be aware that this issue forces one to confront contradictions. An obvious contradiction that often arises in political discussions is how opponents of abortion who describe themselves as "pro-life" can favor other policies, such as the death penalty. Conversely, why do some abortion rights supporters ignore the claims of innocent fetuses while opposing the execution of convicted criminals? These questions force one to examine definitions of human life and the proper role of the state in its preservation.

Within the framework of this book, it would also be wise to consider in particular some contradictions related to gender. Taub and Schneider note that while the separate spheres notion was accompanied by an "ideological glorification of domestic roles," this meant two different things. On the one hand, the state refused to intervene in the private sphere even to protect women from abuse or injury. On the other hand, the glorification of domestic roles resulted in legislation denying women the right to decide whether to have children—a clear intervention in family life.[1] One might wonder why, if nature had determined that women should be mothers, it was necessary for the state to enforce that natural behavior. Carol Smart would argue that the family was (and may still be) the site of women's oppression, including male domination over female sexuality and reproduction.[2] Women cannot reach their full human potential as long as that domination persists. Catherine MacKinnon proposes that any sort of forced maternity is an example of sex inequality and subordination, and laws that contribute to this subordination are by definition violations of equal protection.[3]

We are faced with a dilemma—in previous chapters we have argued for a larger public role in domestic relations to ensure that women and children do not become victims behind a veil of family privacy. In this chapter we will ask whether a larger public role in domestic relations can be a two-edged sword if it also diminishes a woman's right to decide about her own bodily integrity. It is also important to look at race and class in considering the acceptability of reproductive regulation. For middle-class women the issue is often whether they have the free choice not to bear a child. But poor and minority women are frequently defined as selfish, immature, maladjusted, or irresponsible if they do have children.[4] We will return to the concept of subordination and how it relates to reproductive choice in our final analysis.

Historical Background

In her study of the history of birth control in the United States, Linda Gordon argues that a broad definition of motherhood is necessary to maintain a patriarchal society. Originally men set rules for maternity as a way of ensuring that property was passed along to legitimate heirs. But motherhood is more than the biology of child bearing, it also has a social meaning that involves the notion that mothers are responsible for the nurturing of children beyond the physical necessity of birth and nursing. Finally, in most societies, motherhood is invested with a moral necessity—the belief that having children is a woman's proper destiny. During the nineteenth century, Americans developed a newly idealized definition of motherhood. As the Industrial Revolution removed a great deal of productive work from the home, family roles changed. In earlier agricultural societies, families typically worked together in production—parents and children all remained close to home. With industrialization, men usually went to work outside the home in offices or factories, women remained at home where they did less "production" and more child rearing and "homemaking." These roles not only developed, they were idealized as the natural order, especially by the influential middle class. Men and women had different roles; they occupied "separate spheres." They were not just different; they were opposites. (The expression "the opposite sex" suggests this concept that men and women have qualities that are the reverse of one another.) One example of this gendered opposition is the notion that while it was natural for men to be motivated by their sex drives, the comparable instinct in women was mothering.[5] It is within this historical setting that the first real legal restrictions were placed on contraception and abortion in the United States.

Contrary to the notion that birth control and abortion were "invented" in the twentieth century, those practices are as old as human society. The real story is that they were repressed in the nineteenth century and emerged again into the open in the last half of the twentieth. Many societies have had traditions of infanticide, most often of female babies, either for religious or for economic reasons. Infanticide, however, has traditionally been condemned by Christian teaching because infants who are born not only have a soul, but, without baptism, they would be condemned to hell. But historically—until the mid-nineteenth century—abortion was perfectly legal and not a subject of religious concern, as long as it took place before "quickening." Quickening or fetal movement was believed to be the point at which human life began. Before that stage, women might use potions, instruments, or severe exercise to try to end a pregnancy. Likewise, many forms of contraception go back as far as the ancient world where condoms, withdrawal, pessaries (devices inserted into the vagina), and douching were used.[6] Frequently information about contraception and abortion was transmitted through midwives or through other informal networks of women.

Around the mid-nineteenth century, certain vocal groups, especially physicians "discovered" abortion. In the 1860s and 1870s, Americans also "discovered" that commercial infanticide or baby farming was taking place.[7] Historians disagree about the reasons for this new awareness and concern about threats to the family ideal, but several explanations seem to be relevant. Family size, especially among the middle and upper classes, was shrinking. One can see a decrease from an average of eight children per family in the late 1700s to three per family in 1900.[8] Smaller families along with some dismantling of the old laws of coverture—women's property rights, better educational opportunities, agitation for the vote—were alarming trends to some social conservatives. Changes in the ethnic and racial makeup of the county worried others, as immigrants came to the United States in record numbers and African Americans were freed from slavery.

For some or all of these reasons, three main arguments developed to justify limitations on reproductive rights. Some politicians promoted the notion of "race suicide," the idea that the "fittest" members of society were limiting their families, while the poor and minorities had lots of children. The outcome would be a country in which the old Anglo-Saxon "races" were outnumbered and outvoted by the less desirable newcomers. According to this view, women of the better classes must be stopped from controlling their fertility. A related argument held that women had become too selfish. They were out pursuing frivolous or disruptive activities—shopping or going to meetings—and refusing to take up their natural role as mothers. If women could not see where their duty lay, presumably lawmakers would show them, by removing their choices about childbearing. If those two explanations suggest rather racist and sexist reasons for banning contraception and abortion, the third reason relates to professional self-interest. In the mid-nineteenth century, the medical profession was in a state of flux. Approaches to health care ranged over the spectrum from herbal cures to macrobiotic diets to midwifery to chiropractic to "regular" medicine. The regulars—virtually all men who had attended college and earned a medical license—wanted to assert control of the practice of medicine from those they considered "quacks." Among the areas they most hoped to monopolize were obstetrics and gynecology, and this meant taking control of childbirth and related matters from midwives. As part of this struggle, doctors were among the most vocal advocates of prohibiting contraception and abortion. They reasoned that women's health demanded that they fulfill their natural role—motherhood—and that they should seek the services of professionals in the process.[9]

Reva Siegel expands on the doctors' role in banning various reproductive controls. She notes that the medical profession tried to discredit the idea of quickening as the beginning of human life in favor of the view that the progression from embryo to man (they typically used male terms) is one continuous process. From this perspective, conception is the important event, and the mother's role in childbearing is minimized to being a vessel or carrier of the fetus. It is ironic, in a way, that physicians made this argument at a time when society idealized motherhood. But by doing so, they raised their own status. It became a doctor's place to stand between a woman and the state, to determine what was best for her. In a way, Siegel sees women becoming legal wards of physicians when it came to childbirth. She also argues that this new form of control occurred just when older forms of coverture were being repealed. The power of doctors and states over women's reproductive choice became a new way to control women in the absence of formal coverture laws.[10] By the last quarter of the nineteenth century, states passed a variety of laws banning or restricting contraception and abortion. The federal government, in the form of the Comstock Laws, prohibited sending any information about birth control or abortion through the mail. Any material discussing those subjects, no matter how clinical, was classified as obscene.[11]

In contrast to these paternalistic approaches, advocates of women's rights also addressed the issue of childbearing. Most nineteenth-century feminists did not openly advocate contraception or abortion. They proposed instead "voluntary motherhood." As discussed in earlier chapters, women's rights advocates wanted to remake marriage so that women would enjoy dignity and power within the relationship. Among the strategies they supported to reform marriage were the single standard of sexual morality and what they called voluntary motherhood. Given their awareness of battering and marital rape, it is not surprising that they believed in a woman's right to refuse sex. She should have the ability to determine, without coercion, if and when to bear children. Such a notion did not sentimentalize the family, but it did undermine the patriarchal structure of traditional marriage. Abstinence as the recommended form of contraception may seem archaic to modern readers, but the feminists had a more progressive and egalitarian notion of marriage than most of their contemporaries. Their opposition to artificial contraception was consistent with their other beliefs, as they feared such devices would simply offer more opportunities for promiscuity. Without the fear of pregnancy and the expectation of "making an honest woman of her," feminists believed men would be more inclined to seduction and adultery. With or without birth control, women would be the losers as long as the double standard remained or if the male standard became the only one.

An organized challenge to the laws against contraception and abortion came in the early twentieth century. Then the opposition came not from feminists but from radicals who wanted to remake the family and the whole social structure. Margaret Sanger, whose name is most closely associated with the organized birth control movement, began her political career as a socialist. She argued that poor women needed a way to limit their family size for purely economic reasons. Sanger and her supporters also challenged the Comstock Laws on free speech grounds.

In 1938, a federal court found that the applying the obscenity laws to birth control was unconstitutional because contraception was a medical matter.[12] Therefore, First Amendment rights of speech and association were violated by prohibiting its circulation. This ruling removed the federal legal bans on birth control, although the states were still free to regulate as they saw fit. The decision made no mention of women's right to control child bearing but reflected the standard twentieth century attitude that doctors should manage access to reproductive technology. That perception remained dominant until the women's movement that began in the 1960s restored the connection between women's reproductive choices, challenges to male supremacy, and full participation in society.

Controlling the Unfit

In the early 1900s, nativism and racism entered the discussion of contraception when those who believed in "improving the race" argued in favor of reproductive control of the unfit. Chapter Five discussed the belief that promiscuity and feeblemindedness were linked. For some, sexual activity among young girls was evidence of low intelligence and depravity—traits that could supposedly be inherited—rather than a possible symptom of abuse and vulnerability. Following this line of thinking, a number of states passed eugenics laws allowing for the sterilization of the "defective." These laws provide some extreme examples of reproductive control, and, although they could be applied to either male or female subjects, the evidence is clear that they were most commonly invoked against poor women and minorities.

Perhaps the most notorious case testing these eugenics laws came from Virginia in 1927. In *Buck v. Bell*,[13] (See Appendix Ten) the Court ruled on an equal protection challenge. The superintendent of the State Colony for Epileptics and Feeble Minded ordered that Carrie Buck, an eighteen-year-old "feeble-minded white woman," be sterilized. Buck was described as the daughter of a "feeble-minded mother in the same institution" and the mother of an "illegitimate feeble-minded child." The apparent issue was whether the state's interest in preventing Carrie Buck from future reproduction overrode her personal liberty. The opinion considers several points: the operation was safe, and the institution followed its procedures for deciding to perform the surgery. More interesting are the questionable assumptions that support the decision, including the statement that "heredity plays an important part in the transmission of insanity, imbecility, etc." On that basis, the Court found that Carrie Buck was the "probable potential parent of socially inadequate offspring, likewise afflicted." This was not simply a tragedy, but a public concern, as the court believed that fertile defective persons, if discharged, "would become a menace." Society would be "swamped with incompetents." If the unfit were sterilized, they might be safely discharged. The menace Carrie Buck posed to society was her ability to have "socially inadequate offspring." The Court believed the state was justified in taking preventive measures. "It is better for all the world, if instead of waiting to execute degenerate offspring for crime, or to let them starve for their imbecility, society can prevent those who are manifestly unfit from continuing their kind....Three generations of imbeciles are enough." Finally, the Court dismissed the equal protection argument that institutionalized persons were treated differently than similarly situated feeble-minded persons on the outside. "So far as the operations enable those who otherwise must be kept confined to be returned to the world, and thus open the asylum to others, the equality aimed at will be more nearly reached." Thus one could imagine a revolving door, where those deemed unfit to reproduce were institutionalized and sterilized, then released, allowing others to come in and take their places.

Buck v. Bell shocks the contemporary conscience in its contemptuous dismissal of the humanity of those considered inferior. It also fails to recognize the gendered implications of the policy it endorses, given the belief in the link between feeblemindedness and sexual activity in girls and women. Its blindness to the particular effects on women is revealed in the sentence, "The principle that sustains compulsory vaccination is broad enough to cover cutting the Fallopian tubes."

Privacy and Reproductive Rights

Almost sixty years after *Buck v. Bell* the Supreme Court looked again at cases dealing with reproductive issues and set a course that identified choices about pregnancy in a constitutional right to privacy. The first major case in this line was *Griswold v. Connecticut*.[14] Dating from the mid-nineteenth century, Connecticut had on its books a law that banned the use of contraceptives.[15] Although the law was not enforced, Planned Parenthood raised a challenge to its constitutionality. In finding the anti-contraception measure unconstitutional, the Supreme Court articulated a right to privacy that included decisions about childbearing. The majority found that although the Bill of Rights does not specifically mention privacy, the right is implicit in the First, Fourth, Fifth, and Ninth Amendments. The First Amendment protects a right to association, which, the court held, included the marital association. The Fourth prohibits unreasonable searches, which seems to imply that there are zones of privacy, areas off limits to the state. They also found an area of privacy in the Fifth Amendment's protection against self-incrimination. Presumably, the Constitution allows some information to be kept secret. The Ninth Amendment provides that the people retain rights not given to the states, thus suggesting that there are more rights than those specifically enumerated in the Constitution. In *Griswold*, the court focused on privacy within a marital relationship. "Would we allow the police to search the sacred precincts of marital bedrooms for telltale signs of the use of contraceptives? The very idea is repulsive to the notion of privacy surrounding the marriage relationship."

Thus although the *Griswold* ruling cleared away the anachronistic law that prohibited the use of birth control, it did so by asserting that the law was wrong because it interfered with decisions that should be made by married couples and doctors. The court objected to legislation that "operates directly on an intimate relation of husband and wife and their physician's role in one aspect of that relation." Missing from *Griswold* is any notion that reproductive decisions are matters of women's rights. The court came closer to that analysis seven years later in *Eisenstadt v. Baird*.[16]

William Baird had given a lecture at Boston University at which he displayed a variety of birth control devices. At the end, he gave a package of contraceptive foam to a young woman in the audience and ran afoul of a Massachusetts law that permitted only physicians and pharmacists to distribute contraceptives and only to married persons. In *Eisenstadt*, the Court found that privacy regarding birth control matters did not rest in the relationship of husband and wife but in the individual. "If the right of privacy means anything, it is the right of the individual, married or single, to be free from unwarranted governmental intrusion into matters so fundamentally affecting a person as the decision whether to bear or beget a child." The ruling stated that by treating married and unmarried persons differently (with respect to birth control), Massachusetts violated the equal protection clause of the Fourteenth Amendment. As in *Griswold*, the court did not talk about gender as a factor in decisions about pregnancy. Rather they held that each individual, female or male, must make a decision about bearing or begetting a child. Nor, according to this decision, did marriage make a difference. A married woman had just as much right to choose contraception as did a single woman. Thus *Eisenstadt* should be seen as one of the final nails in the coffin that held the remains of coverture.

A year after *Eisenstadt*, the Court made one of its most far-reaching and controversial rulings regarding women's reproductive rights in *Roe v. Wade*, in which they found unconstitutional a Texas law that prohibited abortions except to save a mother's life.[17] The justices followed the tradition of the birth control cases by identifying the right to choose abortion with the right to privacy, not with a prohibition against sex discrimination. However in *Roe*, the ruling did not provide for an absolute right to privacy or an absolute right to choose. Instead, a woman's liberty is weighed against the state's interest in protecting the life of future citizens. The decision sets that balancing process within a trimester framework that describes the nine-month gestation period. Essentially the woman's right to choose is weighted most heavily in the earliest period. As the pregnancy progresses, the state's interest grows and her liberty decreases. During the last trimester, the state may prohibit abortions except to protect the life or health of the mother. In 1973, medical opinion held that the last trimester coincided with viability—the time when the fetus could survive on its own.

Some have suggested that the issue of abortion could better be argued on Fourteenth Amendment equal protection grounds rather than as a privacy issue. From this perspective, the denial of the right to choose could be seen as an exercise of male power over reproductive decisions. Siegel argues that if legislation contributes to maintaining a hierarchy based on gender, as restrictions on abortion do, it is a violation of equal protection. In this view, constraints on reproductive choice single out women for burdensome and invasive public regulation. Such laws injure women by "compelling" motherhood. The obligations of motherhood may then be used to justify women's subordination and exclusion from full citizenship.[18]

In any case, the immediate effect of *Roe v. Wade* was to wipe out state laws that banned abortion. The major source of debate ever since has been how much and what type of abortion regulation states may impose without depriving a woman of her constitutional right to choose.

Probably the most significant of the post-*Roe* decisions was *Planned Parenthood of Southeastern Pennsylvania v. Casey* in 1992.[19] (See Appendix Eleven). During the nineteen years since its first abortion decision, the membership of the Court had changed to include several more conservative justices. Nonetheless, in a very complicated ruling, they reaffirmed what they called the "essential holding" of *Roe*, the constitutional protection of a woman's right to terminate a pregnancy

tion of a woman's right to terminate a pregnancy before viability. At issue in this case was a Pennsylvania law regulating abortions that required a 24-hour waiting period, parental consent for minors, spousal consent for married women, and rather elaborate reporting procedures for clinics. The Court upheld all of the regulations except the spousal consent provision. The majority concluded that those restrictions did not place an "undue burden" on a pregnant woman's rights. The undue burden standard was meant to replace the trimester framework in determining how to balance the woman's liberty against the state's interest in "potential human life." Besides reaffirming *Roe* and promulgating a new test for constitutionality, Casey included several other points of interest. The opinion notes additional reasons for upholding a woman's right to privacy in reproductive matters because her "suffering is too intimate and personal for the State to insist...upon its own vision of the woman's role, however dominant that vision has been in the course of our history and our culture. The destiny of the woman must be shaped to a large extent on her own conception of her spiritual imperatives and her place in society...." In other words, the state cannot use its power to force women to follow traditional roles. This reasoning suggests that some members of the Court are aware of reproductive choice as a matter of equal protection as well as a matter of privacy.

Two other points about *Casey* merit attention. The Court found the spousal notification provision unconstitutional. They recognized the prevalence of domestic violence and other forms of coercion, "millions of women in this country who are victims of regular physical and psychological abuse at the hands of their husbands," and of marital rape, "many women who are pregnant as a result of sexual assaults by their husbands." They believed that such violence would prevent a substantial number of women from procuring an abortion "as surely as if the Commonwealth had outlawed abortion in all cases." Aside from the threat of abuse, the court found the spousal notification requirement "consonant with the common law status of married women [coverture] but repugnant to our present understanding of marriage and the rights secured by the Constitution. Women do not lose their constitutionally protected rights when they marry." They concluded that the Constitution protects everyone, regardless of sex or marital status, from "the abuse of governmental power, even where the power is employed for the supposed benefit of a member of the individual's family." This part of the decision seems clearly to establish full citizenship status for women, to separate their rights from their relationships. It offers a hopeful basis for future development.

The ruling also reaffirmed that state regulations on abortion must provide exceptions to protect a mother's life and health. Many pro-life advocates, including Justices Rehnquist, Scalia, and Thomas, argue that the health exception amounts to "abortion on demand." Their position is that doctors will support any claims a woman makes about needing an abortion for health-related reasons. This skeptical view of doctors as pawns in the hands of women seems at odds with the tradition of physicians as gatekeepers of women's reproductive rights. Also underlying their position is a notion of women and fetuses as adversaries. This not only devalues the well-being of the mother it also implies hostility and deception on the part of mothers. Similar attitudes are reflected in laws that seek to punish pregnant women for acting in ways that are believed to endanger a fetus. Some of these policies will be discussed in the next section.

One other abortion decision by the Supreme Court merits out attention, the 2000 ruling, *Stenberg v. Carhart*, in which the Court overturned a Nebraska law banning "partial birth abortions" unless necessary to preserve a mother's life.[20] The emotional term "partial birth abortion," coined by pro-life groups, is not medical language. According to doctors, its meaning is so vague the law could have prohibited a number of early-term abortion procedures. The Supreme Court, in a 5 to 4 ruling, declared the Nebraska law unconstitutional on the grounds that the regulation was written in such ambiguous language that it placed an undue burden on a woman's right to choose an abortion before fetal viability. The majority also found the law's failure to provide an exception for the health of the mother violated the principle established in *Roe* and *Casey*. Many pro-choice advocates were troubled by the attempt to criminialize a specific method of abortion. That approach could take the decision to terminate a pregnancy away from a woman and her doctor. It could turn the clock back to the pre-*Roe* days when the state legislature had veto power over procedures affecting women's health.

Criminalizing Pregnant Women

The regulation of women's reproductive rights has taken a variety of forms. Historically, laws that prohibited birth control and abortion effectively compelled women to become mothers regardless of their own wishes. Other legislation has been designed to regulate women's conduct during pregnancy, raising issues of equal protection. Does the state have a compelling interest in controlling the behavior of potential mothers? What methods of control may be acceptable? Are some women subjected to more control because their race and/or class exposes their conduct to greater scrutiny? Do we still find some of the assumptions of *Buck v. Bell*, suggesting that some women are, by definition, unfit mothers?

Policies that regulate the conduct of pregnant women and hold them legally responsible for fetal harm may assume several things. Some believe that all women are able to produce healthy offspring any time and that they should be held accountable or even punished if they do not. Others may argue that fetuses are persons with the same rights as any other person, protected by law, or at least that fetuses have rights to certain protections. In this view, certain groups of pregnant women are likely to be irresponsible. These women need a certain amount of public control over their behavior. In some cases, judges and physicians have referred to expectant mothers as "fetal environments," making their interests clearly secondary to those of the fetus.[21] A number of scholars have argued that holding a pregnant woman legally responsible for fetal harm assumes that, by choosing to carry a pregnancy to term and not to abort, she has forfeited her right to bodily integrity. If this is the case, the state can intrude into her body without her consent.[22]

During the last decade, concerns over the use of illegal drugs, especially crack and cocaine, which are believed to cause serious harm to developing fetuses, have inspired laws to hold using mothers accountable. A variety of legal actions against women who use drugs while pregnant have been instigated as fetal protection measures. Some states have instituted criminal proceedings under laws that prohibit child abuse and neglect or laws that forbid the delivery of illegal drugs to minors. Many of these cases have been thrown out because they misapply laws that were made for other purposes. An example was a 1992 Florida case, *Johnson v. State.*[23] Ms. Johnson had used cocaine over a period of three years during two pregnancies. When her second child was born, she was charged with the crime of delivering drugs to a minor based on the transmission of cocaine through the umbilical cord during the thirty to ninety seconds between the baby's delivery and the time the cord was cut. Her conviction was overturned by the Court of Appeals. They noted that the intent of the legislation was to prevent adults from providing drugs to children. Nothing in the law addressed the transmission of substances through the umbilical cord. The court also found that the policy undermined Florida's policy of "keeping families together" if it had the result of incarcerating mothers when other alternatives were available. Prosecution of mothers, the court found, was the least effective response to drug use, especially as they were likely to be sick, fragile and in need of neonatal care. It would be preferable, as the American Medical Association and the American Public Health Association advised, to make drug treatment available to at-risk pregnant women. Similar prosecutions were overturned in Michigan, Ohio, New York, and Kentucky.

Cocaine use also provoked the South Carolina program for drug testing pregnant women at issue in *Ferguson v. Charleston*, discussed in the first chapter of this book. With the background of reproductive rights issues examined in this chapter, another look at that case is in order. The Supreme Court decided the case on Fourth Amendment grounds—did the drug tests carried out at the Medical University of South Carolina (MUSC) Hospital violate the constitutional ban on unreasonable searches and seizures? The hospital turned over the test results to the local police, who then charged the women with distributing an illegal substance to a person under the age of eighteen and with child abuse. Such charges were possible because South Carolina law states that any live fetus is a "person" and enjoys legal protections. Between 1989 and 1993, thirty pregnant women were arrested under this program. As one attorney for the women described, "Our clients went to the hospital to get medical help, and instead they got jail. Rather than provide them with treatment for the disease of drug addiction, the hospital staff collaborated with the police to search pregnant women and new mothers and send them to jail, bound in chains and shackles."[24]

The Supreme Court found that the MUSC program violated the Fourth Amendment by using nonconsensual searches, without warrants or probable cause, for law enforcement purposes. The state's argument that its real purpose was to promote maternal and fetal health by getting the mothers off drugs did not persuade the Court that the searches were permissible. The decision closed down one program, but many of the assumptions that lay behind the MUSC policy are likely to persist. One issue is whether expectant mothers have fewer constitutional rights than other Americans. Although the Court upheld Fourth Amendment protections in this case, many of the laws that allow regulation of the behavior of pregnant women seem to imply that bearing a child means a woman has a lesser expectation of privacy.

The notion that somehow by becoming pregnant a woman loses or forfeits some of her constitutional protections is connected with the perception that she has become more like an incubator and less like an autonomous person. In other words, there is an equal protection issue. Her drug use is not viewed like the drug use of other adults—as behavior that harms the user—but like the act of a parent who has abused a child. At a moral level, this approach may make sense. Most people find it appalling that an expectant mother would jeopardize the well-being of her future child by using drugs (or for that matter by smoking, drinking alcohol, or skydiving). But there is a vast legal gap between irresponsible behavior and child abuse. A pregnant woman is not identical with a parent. Unlike a mother or father who can take some time off from childcare to take a nap, go jogging, or have a drink, during pregnancy a woman can never stop "parenting." Thus, as Sherry Colb argues, if the government's goal is to monitor fetal protection, it might be "viewed as unreasonably seizing the pregnant woman for the duration of her pregnancy."[25] If the Supreme Court is right and that option is unacceptable, then there must be alternatives to using child abuse laws to discourage drug use among pregnant women.

Implicit in the willingness to "seize" pregnant women who use drugs are other equal protection issues. Margo Ely notes that the public is rightly concerned with maternal substance abuse, but "women do not become subject to government surveillance simply because they become pregnant—unless they live in South Carolina, are poor and African-American, and seek prenatal care at a state hospital."[26] As the Charleston case showed, such programs are likely to be carried out in public hospitals, where the patients are predominantly poor and members of minority groups. More affluent women and those with private health insurance will enjoy better prenatal care and an expectation of confidentiality in dealing with their physicians. The plaintiffs in the case argued that because the South Carolina policy was carried out only at MUSC and because it only tested for cocaine, not for the whole range of harmful drugs, it had a disparate impact on African American women. They produced evidence that 68% of maternity patients who tested positive for any drug were African American, while 90% of those who tested positive for cocaine were African American.[27] In addition, the criteria for testing, such as little or no prenatal care, preterm labor, and birth defects, could be correlated with poverty as well as with drug use. It could be argued that such a program shows a greater willingness to compromise the rights of pregnant minority women, perhaps a sense that they were not to be trusted to be good mothers. Vivian Berger concluded that the treatment of the women in Charleston showed "a total lack of respect." Some of them were taken directly from the delivery room, still bleeding and in pain, in handcuffs and shackles. One was kept for three weeks before delivery in an unsanitary prison cell. "It's hard to believe that the authorities would behave so callously if the vast majority of affected patients were not impoverished women of color."[28] Such racial bias does not occur because individuals target other individuals based on race. No one is saying that the personnel at MUSC consciously picked black women to test and punish. Rather the racism may be found in the fabric of a system where race correlates with economic status and with the value placed on respecting one's dignity.[29]

Although the issue was not raised in the South Carolina case, some commentators have argued that prosecuting mothers and not fathers for prenatal drug use is another form of inequality. Some evidence suggests that drug-using fathers can have a damaging effect on the genetic makeup of a child. Fathers may also bear some responsibility for a mother's involvement in drugs, through abuse, coercion, or encouragement.[30]

With all its inequities, one might still maintain that the Charleston policy and others like it are necessary evils that serve the goal of protecting the unborn. But do such punitive programs even do that? As Justice Ginsberg pointed out during oral arguments, four of the women were arrested after giving birth. It was hard to see how those arrests had any impact on fetal health. The Court also found that criminal sanctions against pregnant women may well have negative effects on their health and that of the fetus, by discouraging them from seeking prenatal care for fear of arrest. Holding the mothers criminally responsible for their addictions implies that they had an alternative, that if they wished to get clean, there were effective, affordable drug treatment programs available to them. But the evidence is overwhelming that there are not sufficient treatment programs, that the good ones are oversubscribed, that many will not take pregnant women for liability reasons, that childcare is seldom available for residential programs, and that programs are often designed for a male model of behavior. Without public funds to make treatment a real option, it is hard to believe the officials who proclaim their concern for fetal health. Likewise, when babies are taken away from addicted mothers, what happens to them? In overburdened foster care systems, good homes for fragile African American and other minority children will not be easy to find.

It seems clear that punishing pregnant women does not work, either to protect their future and current children or to help them get over an addition to drugs. What such programs do is set up a conflict between the rights of individual mothers and fetuses as if they existed in isolation from the larger social problems that particularly affect the lives of poor and minority women. They also expose the limitations of the current laws regarding reproductive freedom. As Deborah Rhode notes, the Supreme Court has acknowledged that choice regarding childbearing is fundamental to women's equality. At the same time, Americans have provided few of the support structures that are necessary for women to really exercise that control. "Without funding for abortion, child care, welfare assistance, contraceptive services and medical insurance, individuals' reproductive choices will be highly constrained."[31] The choices are even more limited for the poorest women.

Some scholars see the trend toward punitive policies, rather than the types of support services Rhode describes, as a wedge to dislodge the whole structure of women's reproductive rights. If fetuses, as in South Carolina, are recognized as persons equally protected by the law from child abuse, how can they not be protected from a mother's decision to have an abortion? Wendy Chavkin, for one, sees the debate over fetal protection programs as a symbol in the larger ongoing struggle over women's roles. "The innocence ascribed to the fetus and the punitive anger expressed toward the pregnant woman considered to be its selfish adversary express metaphorically the pain and rage of those who no longer find the family to be a 'haven in a heartless world,' and who perceive the loss of the mother as central to family dissolution."[32] Her analysis allows us to place the debate over reproductive rights and the arguments about punishing pregnant women within the ongoing story of the evolution of gender and the law from the world of patriarchy and separate spheres to its modern adaptation.

This chapter began with questions about women's autonomy and reproductive rights. The idea that a woman can make decisions about pregnancy and childbearing is based on notions of personal liberty, autonomy, and privacy. Privacy has been an important concept throughout our examination of the gendered nature of law. Historically women were limited by the traditional legal interpretation, that privacy protected families—not individuals—from state intrusion. That view assumed a patriarchal family whose members had identical interests and who were represented by a male head. But stated in rulings such as *Eisenstadt* and *Roe* and implied in *Ferguson* is the concept that privacy is embodied in the individual, that each woman is autonomous. Where does this leave us? Are we then doomed to live in an adversarial world where individuals, including fetuses, struggle to assert their competing rights and interests? An alternative vision of law would balance the interests of individuals in their various roles without hierarchy or subordination but based on mutuality and connection. Elizabeth Schneider advocates a new definition of privacy that encompasses "liberty, equality, freedom of bodily integrity, automomy, and self-determination."[33] Her concept is tied to an affirmative concept of liberty which includes autonomy over one's development of intellect, interests, taste, and personality; freedom of choice in life's basic decisions, such as marriage, divorce, and contraception; and freedom from intrusion, restraint, compulsion.[34] Such a revisioned system can only be developed with full participation from women.

CHAPTER EIGHT

Concluding Thoughts

In an early part of this work, readers were introduced to the concepts of unequal enforcement and unequal protection as analytical tools for evaluating gender issues as they apply to the criminal justice system. Each chapter has provided illustrations of these themes. Victims of rape, domestic violence, stalking, and sexual harassment have often been denied the full protection of the laws. In fact, we considered that the system has only recognized the seriousness of many forms of those crimes during the latter part of the twentieth century. For centuries, the notions of separate spheres, family privacy, and assumptions about sexual access denied women the protection from violence to which they should have been entitled. The other side of the same coin is that by not prosecuting men who abused, raped, stalked, or harassed, gender was permitted to affect the enforcement of the law. By not safeguarding women and by not holding men accountable, both equal protection and equal enforcement were violated. Likewise, many women who get into trouble with the law experience both versions of inequality. The all-too-common example of the girl who escapes a violent home, then turns to prostitution and drug use, is not equally protected, nor is the law equally enforced when she and not her client or pimp is punished. Reproductive issues provided a further instance of how laws have been crafted and enforced to restrict women's choices, punishing them for bad mothering but depriving them of equal access to choices and resources. Women's active participation in the criminal justice system has also been limited by the failure to recognize their full status as citizens which includes the right to practice a profession for which one is objectively qualified. Thus up and down the criminal justice system, examples of unequal protection and unequal enforcement persist. Although evidence is strong that we have come closer to equality of protection and enforcement, stereotypes and assumptions based on a belief in masculine superiority perpetuate the gender hierarchy. If we doubt the truth of that allegation, suppose the situation were reversed. Suppose more than a quarter of men were the victims of violence at the hands of their partners, or routinely sexually harassed by their colleagues, or had their reproductive choices restricted by the state. Suppose only 14% of police officers were men or that juries had only been required to include men in the pool since 1975. Would those fantastic scenarios look like unequal protection or unequal enforcement—or both?

Deborah Rhode describes a total picture that encompasses both unequal protection and unequal enforcement. "Although subject to the law's mandates, women were, until the last quarter century, largely unacknowledged in its text, uninvited in its formulation, and uninvolved in its interpretation." Women were left out of the process of molding the law on the grounds that they were "different" from the norm, which was male. Therefore, they experienced differential treatment. Gender differences might be exaggerated, denigrated, romanticized, or deplored, but they led to inconsistent policies that might alternately be harsher or more lenient in dealing with women. Rhode notes that the "fixation on sexual difference deflected attention from the disadvantages that have followed from it."[1] The greatest disadvantage is damage to the ideal of equality.

The continuum of discrimination discussed in Chapter One gives us another tool to characterize the level of prejudice at work in the justice system. Samuel Walker and his colleagues developed the continuum that measured racial bias across a range from Pure Justice to Systematic Discrimination. How would one characterize gender bias within the system? Although there are a number of possible responses to that question, I would argue that gender discrimination falls in the range of between Institutional Discrimination and Systematic Discrimination. Granting that there have been incremental improvements in law and policy and that women's constitutional status has advanced, biases remain incorporated in American society and also in the criminal justice system that reflects its values. During the 1990s, at the behest of the National Association of Women Judges and the National Organization of Women (NOW) Legal Defense Fund, virtually every state set up a task force to investigate the "insidious effect of gender stereotyping on judicial decision making." The point was not to uncover individual incidents of bias but to evaluate whether bias "infected" the courts. Using legal and social science research and intending to reform rather than accuse, the task force studies revealed deep problems. The courts had not caught up with the nation's demographic changes, and far too many members of the legal establishment were reluctant to treat women professionally. Lawyers were likely to use "adversarial techniques based on group membership," i.e., to play upon negative stereotypes about women and members of minority groups. The American Bar Association recommended that judges subscribe to codes under which they would require attorneys "to refrain from manifesting by words or conduct, bias or prejudice based upon race, sex, religion, national origin, disability, age, sexual orientation, or socioeconomic status, against parties, witnesses, counsel, or others." By 1998, twenty-two states had adopted such codes.[2] The need to remind lawyers that manifesting prejudice is unacceptable suggests that it is being manifested frequently. The task forces were convinced that courts needed to reduce what they described as any perception of unfairness. In other words, in order for the legal system to function properly, it was necessary to build the public's confidence that the system was fair. This was a particular challenge because the law had been an instrument of discrimination and its practitioners needed to remove the "residue" of that discrimination.[3] The strong implication of the task force reports is that the state court systems still have a serious problem with gender bias—not just individual bad behavior—but a culture in which prejudice and stereotypes continue to thrive. The National Center for Women and Policing found a similar level of bias when they wrote, "hostile environments and systemic discrimination keep women from joining police agencies in more significant numbers and from being promoted up the ranks to policy-making positions."[4]

The state task forces on gender provided strong testimony to the Congressional committees that investigated the need for the Violence Against Women Act. They repeatedly made the point that state and local agencies were failing to provide adequate protection to victims of gender-motivated violence. Thirty-eight state attorneys general supported VAWA because they acknowledged that their systems were not dealing with the problem. To put it bluntly, assaults on women continue because the offenders believe the police and the courts will not take their behavior seriously, that those agencies are complicit in their sense of gender entitlement, and that they will be able to get away with it. All of this evidence strengthens the argument that gender bias remains a systematic problem within criminal justice.

You will recall that the discussion of VAWA focused on the concept that women had, under the Fourteenth Amendment, a right to bodily integrity, a right to be free from assault. Proponents of the law argued that the failure to ensure that women experienced that right—the failure to deal with violence against women—meant that women were deprived of equal protection of the laws. The reason that VAWA provided for a victim's right to sue in federal court was because, as the attorneys general agreed, the states did not provide that protection and that the problem was systemic. The civil rights remedy included in VAWA (and found unconstitutional by the Supreme Court) was a significant recognition that there is a *pattern* of gender inequality. It could be argued that as long as others exert control over women's bodies—through restrictions on reproductive choice, coerced sex, or battering—gender equality remains elusive, and the system remains biased.[5]

Those who develop feminist theory have often debated how best to address the problem of sex discrimination. Is it wiser to focus on how the law should treat men and women the same, or on how the law must respect the reality of difference? Catherine MacKinnon argues that conventional constitutional arguments about sex discrimination only reinforce the unequal status quo. As it stands, the courts permit differential treatment based on sex if it meets the test of intermediate scrutiny. If a law can be shown to have compelling justification and if the gender distinction it makes is not invidious, it will be allowed to stand. Such a standard does not rise to the level of affording women "productive lives of reasonable physical security, self-expression, individuation, minimal respect, and human dignity."[6] Rather, MacKinnon would argue that equal protection arguments permit existing gender arrangements to persist, arrangements that are based on the domination of women by men. In other words, gender differences are a sort of smoke screen that have been created to justify the subordination of women. As long as the law recognizes that those "differences" may be justified, it perpetuates the system of domination and subordination.

I would maintain that the focus on gender distinctions has had both costs and benefits for women. It depends on who is allowed to define the meaning of the differences. Too often difference is defined by looking at a male reference point, comparing women and finding them to be peculiar, deficient, or limited in some way. Historically, however, many feminists have looked at difference from a female reference point (the early policewomen were a good example) and refused to acknowledge any suggestion of inferiority. If women are deprived of their history and if feminist theory is ignored, too often women are offered only a male model of behavior. If they cannot or will not fit that model, they buy into the notion of their limitations and acquiesce in the existence of unequal treatment. This is what happened throughout our study of laws made and interpreted without women's involvement.

There is a strong case to be made for activism as a way to make the criminal justice system gender responsive and therefore closer to a model of real equal justice. There is the need for men and women who believe in the goals of feminism—the dismantling of a system based on sex discrimination—to work both for reform (changes in specific laws and practices) and transformation. The goal ought to be more than formal equality (for example, comparable drug sentences for men and women) but closer to equality of outcome that takes gender into account when determining the impact of the law.

Are such goals simply wishful thinking? One approach is to acknowledge that the greatest strides to achieving a more equal society have come when women recognized their common interests and formed organizations to pursue them. Conversely, progress always slows down when women subscribe to the model of rugged individualism. Every woman by herself cannot do much to change a structure where hierarchy and inequality have had centuries to become entrenched.

Estelle Freedman makes the case that women have exercised power in the public sphere not as individuals but as a group. She maintains that historically a major strength of feminism came from a sense of female community. Perspectives shared by women (which can include not only biological commonalities but the shared experience of exclusion or subordination) have provided a foundation for challenging the status quo. The success that Freedman describes as a phenomenon of the nineteenth and early twentieth centuries happened when women built the anti-rape and battered women's movements in the late twentieth century. As long as every woman believes her situation is exclusively her own—either her own fault or her own accomplishment—and loses a sense of sisterhood, the structures that support inequality will not be threatened. Social change only happens with organized effort that puts pressure on the legal system or the educational establishment or the media. Freedman argues that by building separate institutions such as women's clubs, colleges, settlement houses, prisons, the Women's Christian Temperance Union, the Women's Trade Union League, and the National Consumers' League, women brought their vision of justice to challenge the existing state of affairs. After 1920, when they gained the vote, many of these separate organizations were disbanded or gradually absorbed into male institutions. However, in adopting the integrationist approach, women allowed their ties with other women to fray. Without their coordinated efforts, it was easy for the legal system, as well as other institutions to neglect and devalue women's interests.[7] We observed this development in the decline of women's roles in law enforcement and corrections, in the devaluation of the importance of rape and domestic violence, in the decisions of the Supreme Court that ignored the reality of unequal protection.

A lesson from this history seems obvious. Women must maintain their own interest groups within the more gender-integrated society. Freedman's point is that separatism is compatible and even necessary for equality. It provides women with the strength and power that comes from pursuing something larger than individual goals. Rhode states that further progress toward gender equality should not focus on differences per se but on the disadvantages to women and to society that have followed from the treatment of difference.[8] It is important not to lose sight of what the earliest advocates of women's rights envisioned when they began their crusade at Seneca Falls, a dismantling of hierarchy and subordination, an end to the double standard of morality in favor of a single standard based on decency and respect. Their vision might encourage us to pursue what Martha Minow has called "the continuous work of making justice."[9]

Albert Camus wrote that "we cannot prevent a world in which children are tortured, but we can lessen the number of tortured children."[10] By acting on the need for a collective response to gender inequality, we may not prevent a world in which women suffer, but we can lessen the number of suffering women.

NOTES

Chapter One: Definitions, Examples, and Analytical Tools

1. Catherine Clinton and Michelle Gillespie, *The Devil's Lane: Sex and Race in the Early South* (New York: Oxford, 1997), xiv.
2. See Jean B. Elshtain, *Public Man, Private Woman: Women in Social and Political Thought* (Princeton, New Jersey: Princeton University, 1981).
3. Lynne Goodstein, "Women, Crime, and Criminal Justice—An Overview," in *Women, Crime, and Criminal Justice*, eds. Claire M. Renzetti and Lynne Goodstein (Los Angeles: Roxbury, 2001), 1.
4. Carol Smart, *Law, Crime, and Sexuality* (London: Sage, 1995), 2–3, 8.
5. *Ibid.*, 218–19.
6. Elizabeth Schneider, *Battered Women and Feminist Lawmaking* (New Haven: Yale, 2000), 8.
7. Karen Offen, "Feminism and Sexual Difference in Historical Perspective," in *Theoretical Perspectives on Sexual Difference*, ed. Deborah L. Rhode (New Haven: Yale, 1990) 13.
8. See Randall Kennedy, *Race, Crime, and the Law* (New York: Vintage, 1997).
9. For a useful discussion of lynching, see, for example, Edward L. Ayers, *Vengeance and Justice: Crime and Punishment in the Nineteenth Century American South* (New York: Oxford, 1984).
10. For a good synthesis of studies of race and criminal justice issues see Samuel Walker, Cassia Spohn, and Miriam DeLone, *The Color of Justice: Race, Ethnicity, and Crime in America* (Belmont, California: Wadsworth, 2000).
11. For accounts of the Till case, see Kennedy, *Race, Crime, and the Law*, 60–62; Stephen J. Whitfield, *A Death in the Delta: The Story of Emmett Till* (1988).
12. See Walker et al., *The Color of Justice*.
13. See Katherine Beckett and Theodore Sasson, *The Politics of Injustice* (Thousand Oaks, California: Pine Forge Press, 2000), 88–98.

Chapter Two: Citizenship, Constitutional Rights, and Equality: Elusive Goals

1. *Planned Parenthood of Southeastern Pennsylvania v. Casey*, 505 US 833 (1992).

2. Linda K. Kerber, *No Constitutional Right to Be Ladies: Women and the Obligations of Citizenship* (New York: Hill & Wang, 1998), xxi.
3. Jean Elshtain, *Public Man, Private Woman: Women in Social and Political Thought* (Princeton: Princeton University, 1981).
4. Mary Beth Norton, *Founding Mothers and Fathers: Gendered Power and the Framing of American Society*. New York: Knopf, 1996), 4,8–9.
5. Kerber, *No Constitutional Right*, 12.
6. Norton, *Founding Mothers*, 11. See Reva B. Siegel, "The Rule of Love: Wife Beating as Prerogative," *Yale Law* Journal 105 (June 1996), who discusses how the political vocabulary resonates with terms derived from families, such as "Founding Fathers." The term suggests both benevolence and authority in those who set up the U.S. system of government.
7. For a thorough discussion of married women's rights and obligations under coverture see Kerber, *No Constitutional Right*, Chapter 1.
8. Tapping Reeve, quoted in Kerber, 14.
9. Nadine Taub and Elizabeth M. Schneider, "Women's Subordination and the Role of Law," in *Feminist Legal Theory: Foundations*, ed. Kelly Weisburg (Philadelphia: Temple University, 1993), 13.
10. Elshtain, *Public Man*, 338.
11. Kerber, *No Constitutional Right*, 305.
12. For a good discussion of the events leading up to the Seneca Falls Convention, see Eleanor Flexner, *The Century of Struggle: The Women's Rights Movement in the United States* (Cambridge, Massachusetts: Harvard University Press, 1959).
13. Siegal, "The Rule of Love," 2130.
14. Ibid., 2181.
15. *Bradwell v. Illinois* 83 US (16 Wall.) 130 (1872).
16. *Muller v. Oregon* 208 US 412 (1908).
17. *Thompson v. Thompson* 218 US 611 (1910).
18. *Quong Wing v. Kirkendall* 223 US 59 (1912).
19. *Plessy v. Ferguson* 163 US 537 (1896).
20. *Quong Wing v. Kirkendall.*
21. *Mackenzie v. Hare* 239 US 299 (1915).
22. *Adkins v. Children's Hospital of the District of Columbia* 261 US 525 (1923).
23. *Breedlove v. Suttles* 302 US 277 (1937).
24. *Hoyt v. Florida* 368 US 57 (1961). See Kerber, No Constitutional Right for an excellent discussion of this case. We will return to this case in Chapter Three, which deals with women participating in the criminal justice system.
25. Kerber, *No Constitutional Right*, 140.
26. *Hoyt v. Florida.*
27. In this instance, the court was asking whether Florida had a rational basis for its policy of treating male and female citizens differently when it came to jury service. Was it rational to use sex as a category?

28. *Reed v. Reed* 404 US 71 (1971).
29. *Frontiero v. Richardson* 411 US 677 (1973).
30. Frontiero's case was brought under the Fifth Amendment as it challenged a policy of the federal government. The Fourteenth Amendment, which was the grounds of most sex discrimination suits, applies to actions by the states, not the federal government.
31. Congress passed the Equal Rights Amendment stating "Equality under the law shall not be denied or abridged by the United States or by any State on account of sex" in 1972. Although it appeared at first that the amendment enjoyed widespread support and would be easily ratified, opponents mounted a fierce campaign to defeat it in the states. To this day, women's full equality under the law has not been secured.
32. *Craig v. Boren* 429 US 190 (1976).
33. *Craig v. Boren* is one of the cases where the law appears to discriminate against men in favor of women. Nonetheless, it presents a question of equal protection.
34. *Taylor v. Louisiana* 419 US 522 (1975).
35. Contrary to popular opinion, the constitution does not require a jury of one's peers. Instead it requires an impartial jury, which the courts have interpreted to mean a jury taken from a pool that is representative of the community.
36. J. E. B. *v. Alabama* 92–1239 (1994).
37. When an attorney uses a peremptory strike, he or she may remove someone from the jury pool without giving a reason. The number of peremptory strikes will vary by jurisdiction.
38. *United States v. Virginia* 518 US 515 (1996).

Chapter Three: Participating in the Criminal Justice System

1. Nancy C. Jurik and Susan E. Martin, "Femininities, Masculinities, and Organizational Conflict," in *Women, Crime, and Criminal Justice*, ed. Claire M. Renzetti and Lynne Goodstein (Los Angeles: Roxbury, 2001), 266.
2. Quoted in Janis Appier, "Preventive Justice: The Campaign for Women Police," *Women and Criminal Justice* 4 no.1 (1992), 10.
3. See Sheila Rothman, *Woman's Proper Place: A History of Changing Ideals and Practices, 1870 to the Present* (New York: Basic Books, 1978).
4. Linda Kerber and Jane DeHart, eds. *Women's America: Refocusing the Past* (New York: Oxford, 1991), 239–240.
5. Appier, "Preventive Justice," 4–5.
6. Mary Hamilton, *The Policewoman: Her Service and Ideals* (New York: Frederick A. Stokes, 1924).
7. *Ibid.*, 151.
8. Appier, "Preventive Justice," 25.
9. Hamilton, *Policewoman*, 71.

10. Appier, "Preventive Justice," 11.

11. *Ibid.*, 21–22.

12. Jurik and Martin, "Femininities, Masculinities," 268.

13. Mona J. E. Danner, review of *Doing Gender, Doing Justice: Women in Law and Criminal Justice Occupations* by Susan Ehrlich Martin and Nancy C. Jurik, *Justice Quarterly* 15 no.1 (March 1998): 194–195.

14. *Dothard v. Rawlinson* 433 US 321 (1977).

15. Susan L. Miller, "Gender and Policing," in *Women, Crime, and Criminal Justice* ed. Renzetti and Goodstein, 256.

16. National Center for Women and Policing, *Equality Denied: The Status of Women in Policing* (Los Angeles: 2000), 4.

17. *Ibid.*, 4–5.

18. Bureau of Justice Statistics, *Sourcebook of Criminal Justice Statistics 1999* (Washington D.C.: 2000).

19. National Center for Women and Policing, *Equality Denied*, 2.

20. *Ibid.*

21. *Ibid.*, 5.

22. *Ibid.*

23. *Ibid.*, 5–6.

24. Susan Brownmiller, *Against Our Wills: Men, Women, and Rape* (New York: Simon and Schuster, 1975), 388.

25. United States Department of Justice, *Update of the Report of the LEAA Task Force on Women* (Washington, D.C.: 2000).

26. *Ibid.*

27. See, for example, Richard Lawrence and Sue Mahan, "Women Corrections Officers in Men's Prisons: Acceptance and Perceived Job Performance," *Women and Criminal Justice* 9 no. 3 (1988); Nancy C. Jurik, "Striking a Balance: Female Correctional Officers, Gender Role Stereotypes, and Male Prisons," *Sociological Inquiry* (1988).

28. Virginia G. Drachman, *Sisters in Law: Women Lawyers in Modern American History* (Cambridge, Massachusetts: Harvard University Press, 1998), 44–45.

29. Christina M. Rodriguez, "Clearing the Smoke-Filled Room: Women Jurors and the Disruption of an Old-Boys' Network in Nineteenth Century America," *Yale Law Journal* 108 (May, 1999), 1841.

30. Drachman, *Sisters in Law*, Chapter 6.

31. Cynthia Fuchs Epstein, *Women in Law* (Urbana, Illinois: University of Illinois, 1993), 61.

32. *Ibid.*
33. *Ibid.*, 463.
34. *Ibid.*, 382.
35. Cynthia Fuchs Epstein, "Women in the Legal Profession at the Turn of the Twenty-First Century: Assessing Glass Ceilings and Open Doors," *Kansas Law Review* 49 (May 2001).
36. Epstein, *Women in Law*, 424.
37. Joanna Grossman, "The New ABA Report on Women and Law: Why the Solutions the Report Proposes May Not Work in the Real World" (May 22, 2001) [online]: available at Findlaw.com.
38. *Ibid.*
39. Katherine T. Bartlett, *Gender and Law: Theory, Doctrine, Commentary* (Boston: Little-Brown, 1993), 627–632.
40. Epstein, "Women in the Legal Profession."
41. Karen Clanton, "Glass Ceilings and Sticky Floors: Minority Women and the Legal Profession," *Kansas Law Review* 49 (May 2001).
42. Carrie Menkel-Meadow, "Portia in a Different Voice: Speculations on a Woman's Lawyering Process," in Bartlett, *Gender and Law*, 623–626.
43. Research by Rand Jack and Dana Crowley Jack, quoted in Bartlett, *Gender and Law*, 632–633.
44. *Ibid.*, 634.
45. Epstein, "Women in the Legal Profession."
46. Susan Ehrlich Martin and Nancy Jurik, *Doing Justice, Doing Gender: Women in Law and Criminal Justice Occupations* (Thousand Oaks, California: Sage, 1996), 220.
47. Cassia Spohn, "Decision Making in Sexual Assault Cases: Do Black and Female Judges Make a Difference?" in *The Criminal Justice System and Women: Offenders, Victims, and Workers*, ed. Barbara Raffel Price and Natalie J. Sokoloff (New York: McGraw-Hill, 1995), 343–357.
48. Rodriguez, "The Smoke Filled Room," 1808.
49. Martin and Jurik, *Doing Justice*, 215.
50. Barbara Allen Babcock, "A Place on the Palladium," *University of Cincinnati Law Review* 61 (1993), 1168.
51. *Ibid.*
52. Rodriguez, "Smoke Filled Room," 1835–1835.
53. *Ibid.*, 1818; Babcock, "Place on the Palladium," 1170.

54. Quoted in Rodriguez, "Smoke Filled Room," 1824. It is a major theme in Linda Kerber, *No Constitutional Right to Be Ladies: Women and the Obligations of Citizenship* (New York: Hill & Wang, 1998) that "sparing" women their civic obligations is a component of second-class citizenship.
55. *Strauder v. West Virginia* 100 US 303 (1879).
56. *Hoyt v. Florida* 368 US 57 (1961). See previous discussion of this case in Chapter Two.
57. *Taylor v. Louisiana* 419 US 22 (1975).
58. *Batson v. Kentucky* 476 US 79 (1986), *J. E. B. v. Alabama* 96–1939 (1994).
59. *Peters v. Kiff* 407 US 493 (1972).
60. See Nancy Cott, *The Grounding of Modern Feminism* (New Haven: Yale, 1987); and Estelle Freedman, "Separation as Strategy: Female Institution Building and American Feminism, 1870–1930," in *Women and Power in American History*, vol. II, ed. Kathryn Kish Sklar and Thomas Dublin (Englewood Cliffs, New Jersey: Prentice Hall, 1991).

Chapter Four: Women and Girls as Victims

1. Martha Mahoney, "Legal Images of Battered Women: Redefining the Issue of Separation," in *Domestic Violence Law*, ed. Nancy K. D. Lemon (St. Paul, Minnesota: West, 2001), 16–18.
2. *Ibid.*
3. Elizabeth A. Stanko, *Intimate Intrusions: Women's Experience of Male Violence* (London: Routledge, 1985), 17.
4. *Ibid.*, 10–15.
5. Catherine A. MacKinnon, "Toward Feminist Jurisprudence," in *Feminist Jurisiprudence*, ed. Patricia Smith (New York: Oxford, 1993), 614–615.
6. Joanne Belknap, *The Invisible Woman: Gender, Crime, and Justice* (Belmont, California: Wadsworth, 2001), 213.
7. Stanko, *Intimate Intrusions, 166*; Susan Brownmiller, *Against Our Wills: Men, Women, and Rape* (New York: Simon and Schuster, 1975), 389.
8. Linda Gordon, *Heroes of Their Own Lives: The Politics and History of Family Violence* (New York: Viking, 1988), 27.
9. Traci C. West, *Wounds of the Spirit: Black Women, Violence, and Resistence Ethics* (New York: New York University Press, 1999), 55.
10. *Ibid.*, 5.
11. Patricia Tjaden and Nancy Thoennes, *Full Report of the Prevalence, Incidence, and Consequences of Violence Against Women* (Washington, D.C.: National Institutes of Justice, 2000).

12. Clare Dalton and Elizabeth M. Schneider, *Battered Women and the Law* (New York: Foundation Press, 2001), 943.
13. Diane Miller Somerville, "Rape, Race, and Castration in Slave Law in the Colonial and Early South," in *The Devil's Lane: Sex and Race in the Early South*, ed. Catherine Clinton and Michele Gillespie (New York: Oxford, 1997), 74–75.
14. Susan Estrich, *Real Rape* (Cambridge, Massachusetts: Harvard, 1987), 55.
15. See *Ibid.* and Brownmiller, *Against Our Wills*.
16. Brownmiller, *Against Our Wills*, 14.
17. See also Elizabeth A. Stanko, "Women, Danger, and Criminology," in *Women, Crime, and Criminal Justice* ed. Claire M. Renzetti and Lynne Goodstein (Los Angeles: Roxbury, 2001), 13–26.
18. Brownmiller, *Against Our Wills*, Chapter 3.
19. *Ibid.*, 391.
20. Estrich, *Real Rape*, 37–41.
21. Stanko, *Intimate Intrusions*, 38.
22. Estrich, *Real Rape*, 12.
23. Nicola Gavey, "I Wasn't Raped but...: Revisiting Definitional Problems in Sexual Victimization," in *New Versions of Victims: Feminists Struggle with the Concept*, ed. Sharon Lamb (New York: New York University, 1999), 68.
24. Susan Schecter, *Women and Male Violence: The Vision and Struggle of the Battered Women's Movement* (Boston: South End Press, 1982), 34–38.
25. Bonnie Fisher, Francis T. Cullen, and Michael G. Turner, *The Sexual Victimization of College Women* (Washington, D.C.: U. S. Department of Justice, 2000).
26. Stanko, *Intimate Intrusions*, 39.
27. Maria Bevacqua, *Rape on the Public Agenda: Feminism and the Politics of Sexual Assault* (Boston: Northeastern University, 2000), 119–121.
28. For a longer discussion of the terminology, see Kathleen J. Ferraro, "Woman Battering: More Than a Family Problem," in *Women, Crime, and Criminal Justice*, ed. Renzetti and Goodstein, 135–153.
29. The "rule of thumb" came to America as part of English common law. The case most often cited as an example of its application is *State v. Rhodes* 61 NC 453 (1868), in which a North Carolina court refused to intervene with a wife beater "unless in cases where permanent or malicious injury is inflicted or threatened or the condition of the party is intolerable. For however great are the evils of ill temper, quarrels, or even personal conflicts inflicting only temporary pain, they are not comparable with the evils which would result from raising the curtain, and exposing to public curiosity and criticism, the nursery and the bed chamber."
30. Gordon, *Heroes of Their Own Lives*, 4–5, 26.

31. Elizabeth Pleck, *Domestic Tyranny: The Making of Social Policy Against Family Violence from Colonial Times to the Present* (New York: Oxford, 1987), 21.
32. *Ibid.*, 52–53.
33. Myra C. Glenn, *Campaigns Against Corporal Punishment: Prisoners, Sailors, Women and Children in Antebellum America* (Albany: State University of New York Press, 1984), 64–80.
34. See Reva B. Siegel, "The Rule of Law: Wife Beating as Prerogative," *Yale Law Journal* 105 (June 1996) for an excellent discussion of the substitution of privacy for coverture.
35. Pleck, *Domestic Tyranny*, 111–119.
36. Glenn, *Campaigns Against Corporal Punishment*, 65.
37. Quoted in *Ibid.*, 69.
38. Pleck, *Domestic Tyranny*, 102–105.
39. Jerome Nadelhoft, "Wife Torture," *Journal of American Culture* 10 (Fall 1987), 39–59.
40. Gordon, *Heroes of Their Own Lives*, 7–12.
41. *Ibid.*, 56–57.
42. Schecter, *Women and Male Violence*, 21–14; Pleck, *Domestic Tyranny*, 159.
43. Schecter, *Women and Male Violence*, 57–58.
44. Elizabeth M. Schneider, *Battered Women and Feminist Lawmaking* (New Haven: Yale, 2000), 22–23.
45. Pleck, *Domestic Tyranny*, 196. Italics added.
46. Tjaden and Thoennes, *Violence Against Women Survey*.
47. See a discussion and rebuttal of this view in Schneider, *Battered Women*, 24–25.
48. See Russell P. Dobash et al., "Separate and Intersecting Realities: A Comparison of Men's and Women's Accounts of Violence Against Women," in *Battered Women and the Law*, ed. Dalton and Schneider, 126–127.
49. Angela Browne, "Reshaping the Rhetoric: The Nexus of Violence, Poverty, and Minority Status in the Lives of Women and Children in the United States," in *Domestic Violence Law*, ed. Lemon, 133–134.
50. See Ferraro, "Woman Battering."
51. Mahoney, "Legal Images of Battered Women," 27–28.
52. *Ibid.*; See also Karla Fischer, Neil Vidmar, and Rene Ellis, "The Culture of Battering and the Role of Mediation in Domestic Violence Cases," in *Battered Women and the Law*, ed. Dalton and Schneider, 57–64.
53. Victoria Nourse, "Passion's Progress: Modern Law Reform and the Provocation Defense," in *Domestic Violence Law*, ed. Lemon, 614–616.

54. Zanita E. Fenton, "Domestic Violence in Black and White: Racialized Gender Stereotypes in Gender Violence," in *Ibid.*, 149–150; Linda Ammons, "Mules, Madonnas, Babies, Bathwater, Racial Imagery and Stereotypes: The African-American Woman and the Battered Woman Syndrome," in *Ibid.*, 151–153.

55. Jenny Rivera, "Domestic Violence Against Latinas by Latino Males: An Analysis of Race, National Origin, and Gender Differences," in *Ibid.*, 155–170.

56. Beverly Horsburgh, "Lifting the Veil of Secrecy: Domestic Violence in the Jewish Community," in *Ibid.*, 179–182.

57. Judith Armotta, "Getting Beyond the Law's Complicity in Intimate Violence Against Women," in *Ibid.*, 39–40.

58. Joan Zorza, "The Criminal Law of Misdemeanor Domestic Violence 1970–1990," in *Ibid.*, 527.

59. *Ibid.*, 531–535.

60. Barbara J. Hart, "Arrest: What's the Big Deal?" in *Ibid.*, 490–492.

61. Deborah Epstein, "Redefining the State's Response to Domestic Violence: Past Victories and Future Challenges," in *Ibid.*, 28–38.

62. Donna Wills, "Domestic Violence: The Case for Aggressive Prosecution," in *Ibid.*, 579–584.

63. Amy Karon, Susan Keilitz, and Sharon Denaro, "Domestic Violence Courts: What Are They and How Should We Manage Them?" in *Ibid.*, 640–653.

64. Hart, "Arrest," 490–492.

65. Christopher D. Maxwell, Joel H. Garner, and Jeffrey A. Fagan, "The Effects of Arrest on Intimate Partner Violence: New Evidence from the Spouse Assault Replication Program," *National Institutes of Justice Research in Brief* (Washington D.C.: US Department of Justice, June 2001).

66. Hart, "Arrest," 489–490.

67. T. Marie Walls, "Civil Orders of Protection and the Victim of Abuse: Recent Changes in the Family Abuse Legislation," *In Our Vision* (Williamsburg, Virginia: Virginians Against Domestic Violence, Summer 1998).

68. Joan Zorza and Nancy K. D. Lemon, "Two Thirds of Civil Protection Orders Are Successful," in *Domestic Violence Law*, ed. Lemon, 309–312.

69. Kit Kinports and Karla Fischer, "Orders of Protection in Domestic Violence Cases: An Empirical Assessment of the Impact of Reform Statutes," in *Ibid.*, 285.

70. Merle H. Weiner, "Domestic Violence and the Per Se Standard of Outrage," in *Ibid.*, 275.

71. Schneider, *Battered Women*, 13.

72. Jorial Foltz, "Community Teams," *In Our Vision* (Williamsburg, Virginia: Virginians Against Domestic Violence, Spring 2000).

73. Janet M. Bowermaster, "Relocation Custody Disputes Involving Domestic Violence," in *Domestic Violence Law*, ed. Lemon, 378–390.

74. Demie Kurz, "Women, Welfare, and Domestic Violence," *Social Justice* 25, no.1 (1998), 105–122.

75. Mary Ann Dutton, "How Battered Women Cope," *National Institutes of Justice Journal* (April 2001): 20.

76. West, *Wounds of the Spirit*, 78–88.

77. Dorothy Q. Thomas and Michele E. Beasley, "Domestic Violence as a Human Rights Issue," in *Battered Women and the Law*, ed. Dalton and Schneider, 993–1002.

78. Marina Angel, "Criminal Law and Women: Giving the Abused Woman Who Kills a Jury of Her Peers," *American Criminal Law Review* 33 no 2 (Winter 1996): 34.

79. Rhonda Copelon, "Recognizing the Egregious in the Everyday: Domestic Violence as Torture," in *Battered Women and the Law*, ed. Dalton and Schneider, 1005.

80. Tjaden and Thoennes, *Violence Against Women Survey*.

81. *Ibid.*

82. Fisher, Cullen, and Turner, *Sexual Victimization of College Women*.

83. Dalton and Schneider, "Stalking and Domestic Violence," in *Battered Women and the Law*, 666–668.

84. *Petersen et al. v. State of* Alaska, 930 P2nd 414 (1996) quoted in *Ibid.*, 683.

85. Caroline A. Forell and Donna M. Matthews, *A Law of Her Own: The Reasonable Woman as a Measure of Man* (New York: New York University Press, 2000), 130.

86. Carol Pateman, *The Sexual Contract* (Stanford, California: Stanford University, 1988), 142.

87. Louise F. Fitzgerald et al., "Why Didn't She Just Report Him?" *Journal of Social Issues* 51 (1995), 119–121.

88. *Ibid.*

89. 42 USC Sec 2000e-2(a)(1).

90. *Meritor Savings Bank v. Vinson* 477 US 57 (1986).

91. *Harris v. Forklift Systems* 510 US 17 (1993).

92. See Debra A. DeBruin, "Identifying Sexual Harassment: The Reasonable Woman Standard," in *Violence Against Women: Philosophical Perspectives*, ed. Stanley G. French, Wanda Teays, and Laura M. Purdy (Ithaca: Cornell University Press, 1998), 107–122; Forell and Matthews, *A Law of Her Own*.

93. *Oncale v. Sundowner Offshore Services* 523 US 75 (1998).

94. *Faragher v. City of Boca Raton* 524 US 775 (1998).

95. Quoted in Catherine MacKinnon, *Sex Equality* (New York: Foundation Press, 2001), 1029.

96. Peter Aronson, "Silent Suffering Kills Sex Cases," *National Law Journal*, July 23, 2001.

97. R. Robin McDonald, "Are We Too Vulgar to Be Actionable?" *National Law Journal*, July 23, 2001.

98. Robert C. Post and Reva B. Siegel, "Equal Protection by Law and Federal Antidiscrimination Legislation After *Morrison* and *Kimel*," *Yale Law Journal* 110 (December 2000), 525.

Chapter Five: Victims and Offenders: Gender as the Link

1. Darrell Steffensmeier and Lisa Broidy, "Explaining Female Offending," in *Women, Crime, and Criminal Justice*, ed. Claire M. Renzetti and Lynne Goodstein (Los Angeles: Roxbury, 2001), 111–112.

2. *Ibid.*, and Joycelyn M. Pollock, *Criminal Women* (Cincinnati, Ohio: Anderson, 1999), 23–25.

3. Barbara Meil Hobson, *Uneasy Virtue: The Politics of Prostitution and the American Reform Tradition* (Chicago: University of Chicago Press, 1990), 187–191.

4. Pollock, *Criminal Women,* 123. See also Traci C. West, *Wounds of the Spirit: Black Women, Violence, and Resistance Ethics* (New York: New York University Press, 1999), Chapter 4.

5. See, for example, Freda Adler, *Sisters in Crime* (New York: McGraw-Hill, 1975) and Rita Simon, *The Contemporary Woman and Crime* (Washington D.C.: National Institutes of Mental Health, 1975).

6. Pollock, *Criminal Women*, 35.

7. *Ibid.*, 73.

8. *Ibid.*, 141–142.

9. Meda Chesney-Lind, *The Female Offender: Girls, Women, and Crime* (Thousand Oaks: California: Sage, 1997), 4–5.

10. *Ibid.*, 158.

11. *Ibid.*, 135.

12. Kathleen Daly, *Gender, Crime, and Punishment* (New Haven: Yale, 1994), 46–48.

13. *Ibid.*, 58–59, 83–84.

14. Pollock, *Criminal Women*, 243–244.

15. *Ibid.*, 249.

16. Frances Heidensohn, *Women and Crime* (New York: New York University, 1985), 176.
17. *Ibid.*, Chapter 9.
18. Ngaire Naffine, *Female Crime: The Construction of Women in Criminology* (Sydney: Allen & Unwin, 1987), 131.
19. See, for example, Carol Gilligan, "Getting Civilized," *Fordham Law Review* 63 (October, 1994): 17–31. Gilligan is not claiming that these categories fit ALL men or ALL women, but that gender definitions encourage a perspective.
20. See Naffine, *Female Crime*, 113.
21. Steffensmeier and Broidy, "Explaining Female Offending," 126.
22. Raymond Hernandez, "Children's Sexual Exploitation Underestimated Study Finds," *New York Times*, September 10, 2001.
23. Linda Gordon, *Heroes of Their Own Lives: The Politics and History of Family Violence* (New York: Viking, 1988), 215.
24. *Ibid.*, 220.
25. *Ibid.*
26. Chesney-Lind, *Female Offender*, 25.
27. *Ibid.*, 143.
28. Marina Angel, "Criminal Law and Women: Giving the Abused Woman Who Kills a Jury of Her Peers,"*American Criminal Law Review* 33 (Winter 1996): 229–348.
29. Elizabeth A. Stanko, *Intimate Intrusions: Women's Experience of Male Violence* (London: Routledge, 1985), 89–92.Caroline A. Forell and Donna M. Matthews, *A Law of Her Own: The Reasonable Woman as a Measure of Man* (New York: New York University Press, 2000), 171.
30. See Angel, "Criminal Law and Women."
31. Mary Ann Dutton and Catherine L. Waltz, "Domestic Violence: Understanding Why It Happens and How to Recognize It," in *Domestic Violence Law*, ed. Nancy K. D. Lemon (St. Paul, Minnesota: West, 2001), 675–682.
32. Lemon, *Domestic Violence Law*, 683.
33. Paula Finley Mangrum, "Reconceptualizing Battered Woman Syndrome Evidence: Prosecution Use of Expert Testimony on Battering," in *Domestic Violence Law* ed. Lemon, 610–612.
34. Wanda Teays, "Standards of Perfection and Battered Women's Self-Defense," in *Violence Against Women: Philosophical Perspectives*, ed. Stanley G. French, Wanda Teays, and Laura M. Purdy (Ithaca: Cornell, 1998), 75.
35. Forell and Matthews, *Law of Her Own*, 172.
36. Angel, "Criminal Law and Women," 240.
37. Pollock, *Criminal Women*, 32.

38. Hobson, *Uneasy Virtue*, 86–99.

39. Prostitution is legal in Nevada and was briefly legalized in St. Louis, Missouri, in the 1870s. These remain notable exceptions to the general policy of criminalization.

40. Hobson, *Uneasy Virtue*, 25.

41. *Ibid.*, 30–31.

42. See Barbara Berg, *The Remembered Gate: Origins of American Feminism* (New York: Oxford, 1978). Estelle Freedman, *Their Sisters' Keepers: Women's Prison Reform in America, 1830–1930* (Ann Arbor: University of Michigan Press, 1984) and Hobson, *Uneasy Virtue*.

43. Carol Pateman, *The Sexual Contract* (Stanford, California: Stanford University, 1988), 196–97.

44. .Gordon, *Heroes of Their Own Lives*, 137.

45. Hobson, *Uneasy Virtue*, Chapter 9.

46. Pateman, *Sexual Contract*, 194.

47. Clelia Smyth Anderson and Yolanda Estes, "The Myth of the Happy Hooker: Kantian Moral Reflections on a Phenomenology of Prostitution," in *Violence Against Women* ed. French, Teays, and Purdy, 153.

48. *Ibid.*, 156–157.

Chapter Six: Punishing Women: The Experience of Female Offenders

1. Statistics in this section are taken from Department of Justice, Bureau of Justice Statistics, *Women Offenders* (revised October 3, 2000) by Lawrence A. Greenfield and Tracy L. Snell, Special Report.

2. See Estelle B. Freedman, *Their Sisters' Keepers: Women's Prison Reform in America, 1830–1930* (Ann Arbor: University of Michigan, 1984); Steven R. Donziger, ed., *The Real War on Crime: The Report of the National Criminal Justice Commission* (New York: Harper, 1996).

3. Barbara Owen, "Perspectives on Women in Prison," in *Women, Crime, and Criminal Justice*, ed. Claire M. Renzetti and Lynne Goodstein (Los Angeles: Roxbury, 2001), 245.

4. Kathryn Watterson, *Women in Prison: Inside the Concrete Womb* (Boston: Northeastern, 1996), 36–38.

5. *Ibid.*

6. Cathy S. Widom and Michael G. Maxfield, "An Update on the 'Cycle of Violence'," *National Institutes of Justice Research in Brief* (Washington, D.C.: Department of Justice, February 2001).

7. "Building the Case: Why Focus on Women Offenders?"in *National Symposium on Women Offenders: Conference Proceedings, December 13–15, 1999* by the Office of Justice Programs (Washington, D.C.: Department of Justice, 2000).
8. "Women's Pathways to Criminality," in *Ibid.*
9. Lori B. Girshick, *No Safe Haven: Stories of Women in Prison* (Boston: Northeastern, 1999), 34.
10. *Ibid.*, 29–30.
11. *Ibid.*, 39–47.
12. *Ibid.*, 51.
13. U.S. Department of Justice, *Update of the Report of the LEAA Task Force on Women* (Washington, D.C.: 2000).
14. Stephanie R. Bush-Baskette, "The 'War on Drugs': A War Against Women," in *Harsh Punishment: International Experiences of Women's Imprisonment*, ed. Sandy Cook and Susanne Davies (Boston: Northeastern, 1999), 213–215.
15. *Ibid.*, 216–224.
16. Amnesty International, *"Not Part of My Sentence": Violations of the Human Rights of Women in Custody* (New York: Amnesty International USA, 1999), 29.
17. Girshick, *No Safe Haven*, 66.
18. *Ibid.*, 72.
19. "Women's Prison Reform: Past, Present, and Future," *National Symposium on Women Offenders.*
20. Freedman, *Their Sisters' Keepers*.
21. *Ibid.*, 17–19; See also Barbara Meil Hobson, *Uneasy Virtue: The Politics of Prostitution and the American Reform Tradition* (Chicago: University of Chicago, 1990) 110.
22. Freedman, *Their Sisters' Keepers*, 44–45.
23. See *Ibid.*, 105; Hobson, *Uneasy Virtue*, Chapter 5.
24. See Freedman, *Their Sisters' Keepers*, Chapter 8.
25. See, for example, Joycelyn Pollock, *Criminal Women* (Cincinnati, Ohio: Anderson, 1999), 245.
26. Amnesty International, *Not Part of My Sentence*, 35–37.
27. "Building the Case: Why Focus on Women Offenders?" *National Symposium on Women Offenders.*
28. Watterson, *Women in Prison*, 21.
29. Girshick, *No Safe Haven*, 77–78.
30. *Ibid.*, 83–86; Watterson, *Women in Prison*, 79, 99.

31. Quoted in *Ibid.*, 16.
32. Quoted in Girshick, *No Safe Haven*, 101.
33. Marcia Bunney, "One Life in Prison: Perception, Reflection, and Empowerment," in *Harsh Punishment*, ed. Cook and Davies, 16–31.
34. Elizabeth Morgan, "The Violence of Women's Imprisonment: A View from the Inside," in *Harsh Punishment*, ed. Cook and Davies, 36–37.
35. *Ibid.*, 43.
36. Barbara Owen, "Women and Imprisonment in the United States: The Gendered Consequences of the U.S. Imprisonment Binge," in *Harsh Punishment*, ed. Cook and Davies, 88.
37. Amnesty International, *Not Part of My Sentence*, 39–47.
38. *Jordan v. Gardner* 986 F2nd (9th circ, 1993) in *Ibid.*, 54.
39. Additional discussion of civil rights laws and employment in the criminal justice system is included in Chapter Three.
40. "Sexual Misconduct," *National Symposium on Women Offenders*; Amnesty International, *Not Part of My Sentence*, 57–59.
41. Girshick, *No Safe Haven*, 99.
42. Watterson, *Women in Prison*, 282.
43. See Bunney, "One Life in Prison."
44. Morgan, "The Violence of Women's Imprisonment," 41.
45. Amnesty International, *Not Part of My Sentence*, 84–89.
46. Watterson, *Women in Prison*, 253.
47. Girshick, *No Safe Haven*, 99.
48. Morgan, "The Violence of Women's Imprisonment," 39.
49. Amnesty International, *Not Part of My Sentence*, 62.
50. Ibid., 64–65.
51. Executive Summary, *National Symposium on Women Offenders*.
52. Watterson, *Women in Prison*, 211.
53. "Women in Prison: Like Mother, Like Daughter," *National Symposium on Women Offenders*.
54. Donziger, *Real War on Crime*, 152–153.
55. Girshick, *No Safe Haven*, 105–106.
56. Amnesty International, *Not Part of My Sentence*, 21.
57. *Ibid.*, 21–23.
58. "Caring for the Children," *National Symposium on Women Offenders*.

59. Watterson, *Women in Prison*, 357.
60. "Effective Interventions: Looking at Gender Responsive Programming," *National Symposium on Women Offenders*.
61. Executive Summary; "Creating Systems to Support Women's Development, *Ibid*.
62. "Getting Healthy, Staying Healthy: Physical and Mental Health/Substance Abuse," *Ibid*.
63. Statistics about women and the death penalty come from Victor Streib, *Death Penalty for Female Offenders* (February 2001) [on-line at www.law.onu.edu/faculty/streib/femdeath.htm].
64. Elizabeth Rapaport, "Staying Alive: Executive Clemency, Equal Protection, and the Politics of Gender in Women's Capital Cases," *Buffalo Criminal Law Review* 4 (2001), 967–1007.
65. For an argument that the disproportionately small number of female executions is an equal protection violation, see Andrea Shapiro, "Unequal Before the Law: Men, Women, and the Death Penalty," *American University Journal of Gender, Social Policy, and the Law* (2000), 427–470.
66. Rapaport, "Staying Alive," 981.
67. *Ibid*., 983–985.

Chapter Seven: Regulating Reproduction

1. Nadine Taub and Elizabeth M. Schneider, "Women's Subordination and the Role of Law," in *Feminist Legal Theory: Foundations*, ed. D. Kelly Weisburg (Philadelphia: Temple University, 1993), 10–11.
2. Carol Smart, *Law, Crime, and Sexuality: Essays in Feminism* (London: Sage, 1995), 134–135.
3. Catherine MacKinnon, "Toward Feminist Jurisprudence," in *Feminist Jurisprudence*, ed. Patricia Smith (New York: Oxford, 1993), 617.
4. Mary Gibson, "Contract Motherhood: Social Practice in Social Context," in *The Criminalization of a Woman's Body*, ed. Clarice Feinman (New York: Haworth, 1992), 65.
5. See Linda Gordon, *Woman's Body, Woman's Right: A Social History of Birth Control in America* (New York: Penguin, 1977), Chapter 1.
6. *Ibid*., Chapter 2.
7. Unwanted, usually illegitimate infants might be placed at a "baby farm." There they would be allowed to die "natural" deaths from neglect or starvation.
8. There are many reasons why families might decide to have fewer children. Improved health care had decreased the chance of infant mortality, so more children were likely to survive to adulthood. In industrial societies, having a smaller family made economic sense. More time was devoted to raising and educating children.

Compared to agricultural societies, children did not become productive workers until a much later, especially in middle- and upper-class families.

9. Gordon discusses the bans on abortion and contraception in *Woman's Body, Woman's Right* and in *Heroes of Their Own Lives: The Politics and History of Family Violence* (New York: Viking, 1988). See also Carol Smart, *Regulating Womanhood: Historical Essays on Marriage, Motherhood, and Sexuality* (London: Routledge, 1992), 18–19; James C. Mohr, *Abortion in America: The Origins and Evolution of National Policy, 1800–1900* (New York: Oxford, 1978).
10. Reva Siegel, "Abortion as a Sex Equality Right: Its Basis in Feminist Theory," in *Mothers in Law: Feminist Theory and the Legal Regulation of Motherhood*, ed. Martha Albertson Fineman and Isabel Karpin (New York: Columbia University, 1995), 43–72.
11. Some people may be surprised to learn that the Roman Catholic Church did not formally condemn abortion until 1869. Prior to that, it accepted the idea of quickening as did most religious and secular authorities.
12. Gordon, *Woman's Body*, 321.
13. *Buck v. Bell* 274 US 200 (1927).
14. *Griswold v. Connecticut* 381 US 479 (1965).
15. The law to ban the use of contraceptives was the brainchild of P. T. Barnum, who, after his circus career, settled into Connecticut politics.
16. *Eisenstadt v. Baird* 405 US 438 (1972).
17. *Roe v. Wade* 410 US 113 (1973).
18. Siegel, "Abortion as Sex Equality," 64–65.
19. *Planned Parenthood of Southeastern Pennsylvania v. Casey* 505 US 833 (1992).
20. *Stenberg v. Carhart* 99–830 (2000).
21. Joan C. Callahan and James W. Knight, "Prenatal Harm as Child Abuse?" in *The Criminalization of a Woman's Body*, ed. Feinman, 130–131; Gibson, "Contract Motherhood in *Ibid.*, 63; Katherine T. Bartlett, *Gender and Law: Theory, Doctrine, Commentary* (Boston: Little-Brown, 1993), 839.
22. Callahan and Knight, "Prenatal Harm," 141–142.
23. *Johnson v. State* 602 So 2nd 1288 (Fla 1992).
24. Lynn Paltrow, director of National Advocates for Pregnant Women, quoted in *On the Docket* [on-line] www.medill.nwu.edu.
25. Sherry Colb, "Drug Testing Pregnant Women Is Both Counterproductive and Unconstitutional," *Findlaw's Writ*, October 25, 2000 [on-line] Findlaw.com
26. Margo Ely, "Waging War Against Drugs—and Expectant Mothers," *Chicago Daily Law Bulletin*, October 9, 2000.
27. *Ibid.*

28. Vivian Berger, "No Way to Treat a Baby," *National Law Journal*, November 13, 2000.
29. See, for example, Dorothy E. Roberts, "Punishing Drug Addicts Who Have Babies: Women of Color, Equality, and the Right of Privacy," in *Gender and Law*, ed. Bartlett, 829–833.
30. Callahan and Knight, "Prenatal Harm," 146.
31. Deborah L. Rhode, "Definitions of Difference," in *Theoretical Perspectives on Sexual Difference*, ed. Deborah L. Rhode (New Haven: Yale, 1990), 212.
32. Wendy Chavkin, "Woman and Fetus: The Social Construction of Conflict," in *The Criminalization of a Woman's Body*, ed. Feinman, 200.
33. Elizabeth M. Schneider, "The Violence of Privacy," in *The Public Nature of Private Violence: The Discovery of Domestic Abuse*, ed. Martha Albertson Fineman and Roxanne Mykitiuk (New York: Routledge, 1994), 37.
34. *Ibid.*, 51.

Chapter Eight: Concluding Thoughts

1. Deborah L. Rhode, "Definitions of Difference," in *Theoretical Perspectives on Sexual Difference*, ed. Deborah Rhode (New Haven: Yale, 1990), 198.
2. Deborah R. Hensler and Judith Resnick, "Contested Identities: Task Forces on Gender, Race, and Ethnic Bias and the Obligation of the Legal Profession," in *Ethics in Practice: Lawyers' Roles, Responsibilities, and Regulation*, ed. Deborah Rhode (New York: Oxford, 2000), 251–152.
3. *Ibid.*, 253–255.
4. National Center for Women and Policing, *Equality Denied: The Status of Women in Policing* (Los Angeles: 2000), 4.
5. In fairness to the other side of the argument, it should be noted that five members of the Supreme Court treated violence against women not as an issue of systematic injustice but like any other crime, as the unlawful acts of individuals.
6. Catherine MacKinnon, "Legal Perspectives on Sexual Difference," in *Theoretical Perspectives on Sexual Difference*, ed. Rhode, 215.
7. Estelle Freedman, "Separation as Strategy: Female Institution Building and American Feminism, 1870–1930," in *Women and Power in American History*, vol. II, ed. Kathryn Kish Sklar and Thomas Dublin (Englewood Cliffs, New Jersey: Prentice Hall, 1991), 14–20.
8. Rhode, "Definitions of Difference," 204.
9. Martha Minow, *Making All the Difference: Inclusion, Exclusion, and American Law* (Ithaca: Cornell, 1990), 389.
10. Quoted in Jean Elshtain, *Public Man, Private Woman: Women in Social and Political Thought* (Princeton, New Jersey: Princeton University, 1981), 349.

APPENDICES

APPENDIX ONE

The Seneca Falls Declaration

On July 20, 1848, the women and men who gathered at Seneca Falls, New York, adopted a Declaration of Sentiments, modeled on the Declaration of Independence, and a series of Resolutions. An edited version follows.

We hold these truths to be self-evident: that all men and women are created equal; that they are endowed by their Creator with certain inalienable rights; that among these are life, liberty, and the pursuit of happiness; that to secure these rights governments are instituted, deriving their just powers from the consent of the governed....But when a long train of abuses and usurpations, pursuing invariably the same object evinces a design to reduce them under absolute despotism, it is their duty to throw off such government, and to provide new guards for their future security. Such has been the patient sufferance of the women under this government, and such is now the necessity which constrains them to demand the equal station to which they are entitled.

The history of mankind is a history of repeated injuries and usurpations on the part of man toward woman, having in direct object the establishment of an absolute tyranny over her. To prove this, let facts be submitted to a candid world.

He has never permitted her to exercise her inalienable right to the elective franchise.

He has compelled her to submit to laws, in the formation of which she has no voice.

He has withheld from her rights which are given to the most ignorant and degraded men—both natives and foreigners.

Having deprived her of this first right of a citizen, the elective franchise, thereby leaving her without representation in the halls of legislation, he has oppressed her on all sides.

He has made her, if married, in the eye of the law, civilly dead.

He has taken from her all right in property, even to the wages she earns.

He has made her, morally, an irresponsible being, as she can commit many crimes with impunity, provided they be done in the presence of her husband. In the covenant of marriage, she is compelled to promise obedience to her husband, he becoming to all intents and purposes, her master—the law giving him power to deprive her of her liberty, and to administer chastisement.

He has so framed the laws of divorce, as to what shall be the proper causes, and in case of separation, to whom the guardianship of the children shall be given, as to be wholly regardless of the happiness of women—the law, in all cases, going upon a false supposition of the supremacy of man, and giving all power into his hands.

After depriving her of all rights as a married women, if single, and the owner of property, he has taxed her to support a government which recognizes her only when her property can be made profitable to it.

He has monopolized nearly all the profitable employments, and from those she is permitted to follow, she receives but a scanty remuneration. He closes against her all the avenues to wealth and distinction which he considers most honorable to himself. As a teacher of theology, medicine, or law, she is not known.

He has denied her the facilities for obtaining a thorough education, all colleges being closed against her.

He allows her in Church, as well as State, but a subordinate position, claiming Apostolic authority for her exclusion from the ministry, and with some exceptions, from any public participation in the affairs of the Church.

He has created a false public sentiment by giving to the world a different code of morals for men and women, by which moral delinquencies which exclude women from society are not only tolerated, but deemed of little account in man.

He has usurped the prerogative of Jehovah himself, claiming it as his right to assign for her a sphere of action, when that belongs to her conscience and to her God.

...[I]n view of the unjust laws above mentioned, and because women do feel themselves aggrieved, oppressed, and fraudulently deprived of their most sacred rights, we insist that they have immediate admission to all the rights and privileges which belong to them as citizens of the United States.

In entering upon the great work before us, we anticipate no small amount of misconception, misrepresentation, and ridicule; but we shall use every instrumentality within our power to effect our object.

[A series of resolutions followed and concluded with the following.]

Resolved: That the speedy success of our cause depends upon the zealous and untiring efforts of both men and women, for the overthrow of the monopoly of the pulpit, and for the securing to woman an equal participation with men in the various trades, professions, and commerce.

APPENDIX TWO

Bradwell v. Illinois

83 US (16 Wall.) 130 (1872)

Although Justice Miller wrote the opinion in which the Supreme Court denied Myra Bradwell's claim that, under the Fourteenth Amendment, Illinois could not deny her a license to practice law, Justice Bradley's concurring opinion has become more famous. Bradley's concurrence offers an outstanding example of a defense of coverture and the "separate spheres" thinking that provided "reasonable" grounds for denying women access to full citizenship.

The claim...under the fourteenth amendment of the Constitution, which declares that no State shall make or enforce any law which shall abridge the privileges and immunities of citizens of the United States...assumes that it is one of the privileges and immunities of women as citizens to engage in any and every profession, occupation, or employment in civil life.

It certainly cannot be affirmed, as an historical fact, that this has ever been established as one of the fundamental privileges and immunities of the sex. On the contrary, the civil law, as well as nature herself, has always recognized a wide difference in the respective spheres and destinies of man and woman. Man is, or should be, woman's protector and defender. The natural and proper timidity and delicacy which belongs to the female sex evidently unfits it for many of the occupations of civil life. The constitution of the family organization, which is founded in the divine ordinance, as well as in the nature of things, indicates the domestic sphere as that which properly belongs to the domain and functions of womanhood. The harmony, not to say identity, of interests and views which belong, or should belong, to the family institution is repugnant to the idea of a woman adopting a distinct and independent career from that of her husband. So firmly fixed was this sentiment in the founders of the common law that it became a maxim of that system of jurisprudence that a woman had no legal existence separate from her husband, who was regarded as her head and representative in the social state; and notwithstanding some recent modifications of this civil status, many of the special rules of law flowing from and dependent upon this cardinal principle still exist in full force in most States. One of these is, that a married woman is incapable, without her husband's consent, of making contracts which shall be binding on her or him....

It is true that many women are unmarried and not affected by any of the duties, complications, and incapacities arising out of the married state, but these are exceptions to the general rule. The paramount destiny and mission of woman are to fulfill the noble and benign offices of wife and mother. This is the law of the Creator. And the rules of civil society must be adapted to the general constitution of things, and cannot be based upon exceptional cases.

APPENDIX THREE

Muller v. Oregon

208 US 412 (1908)

The Supreme Court upheld an Oregon law that established maximum hours for women working in certain industries. They paid particular attention to the arguments put before them in the "Brandeis Brief," which cited empirical data that long hours were harmful to women's health. Although the ruling benefited working women in the short run by permitting reduced hours, it does rest upon some stereotypical concepts of gender.

Justice Brewer for the Court

That woman's physical structure and the performance of maternal functions place her at a disadvantage in the struggle for subsistence is obvious. This is especially true when the burdens of motherhood are upon her. Even when they are not, by abundant testimony of the medical fraternity continuance for a long time on her feet at work, repeating this from day to day, tends to injurious effects upon the body, and as healthy mothers are essential to vigorous offspring, the physical well-being of woman becomes an object of public interest and care in order to preserve the strength and vigor of the race.

...[W]oman has always been dependent upon man...in the struggle for subsistence she is not an equal competitor with her brother.... Many words cannot make this plainer. The two sexes differ in structure of body, in the functions to be performed by each, in the influence of vigorous health upon the future well-being of the race, the self-reliance which enables one to assert full rights, and in the capacity to maintain the struggle for subsistence. This difference justifies a difference in legislation, and upholds that which is designed to compensate for some of the burdens which rest upon her.

We have not referred in this discussion to the denial of the elective franchise in the state of Oregon, for while that may disclose a lack of political equality in all things with her brother, that is not of itself decisive. The reason runs deeper, and rests in the inherent difference between the two sexes, and in the different functions in life which they perform.

APPENDIX FOUR

Thompson v. Thompson

218 US 611 (1910)

Under a District of Columbia law that provided that a married woman could sue for "trespass on her rights in property and to protect the security of her person against the wrongs and assaults of others," Jessie Thompson sought damages of $70,000 from her former husband, Charles. He had assaulted the pregnant Jessie over a period of three days. The Court determined that the law could not have meant to enact the radical policy that a woman could sue her own husband.

Justice Harlan wrote a dissent in which he maintained that the language of the law plainly permitted women to sue for wrongs and assaults, whoever perpetrated them.

Justice Day for the Court

Apart from the consideration that the perpetration of...atrocious wrongs affords adequate grounds for relief under the statutes of divorce and alimony, [Jessie Thompson's argument] would...open the doors of the courts to accusations of all sorts of one spouse against the other, and bring into public notice complaints for assault, slander, and libel, and alleged injuries to property of the one or the other, by husband against wife, or wife against husband....

Had it been the legislative purpose not only to permit the wife to bring suits free from her husband's participation and control, but to bring actions against him also for injuries to person or property as though they were strangers, thus emphasizing and publishing differences which might otherwise not be serious, it would have been easy to have expressed that intent in terms of irresistible clearness....

Nor is the wife left without remedy for such wrongs. She may resort to the criminal courts, which, it is to be presumed will inflict punishment commensurate with the offense committed. She may sue for divorce or separation and for alimony. The court, in protecting her rights and awarding relief in such cases, may consider, and so far as possible, redress her wrongs and protect her rights....

We do not believe it was the intention of Congress...to revolutionize the law governing the relation of husband and wife as between themselves.

Justice Harlan Dissented

It [the D.C. law] proceeds to authorize married women "also" to sue separately "for torts committed against them, as fully and as freely as if they were unmarried." No discrimination is made...between the persons charged with committing the tort. No exception is made in reference to the husband, if he happens to be the party charged with transgressing the rights conferred upon the wife by the statute. In other words, Congress, by these statutory provisions, destroys the unity of the marriage association as it had previously existed. It makes a radical change in the relations of man and wife as those relations were at common law....

[According to the court's interpretation of the law] Congress...is put in the anomalous position of allowing a married woman to sue her husband...for the recovery of her property, but denying her the right or privilege to sue him...for damages arising from his brutal assaults on her person. I will not assume Congress intended to bring about any such result.

APPENDIX FIVE

Adkins v. Children's Hospital of the District of Columbia

261 US 525 (1923)

The Court declared unconstitutional a law setting a minimum wage for women workers in the District of Columbia. Despite their earlier ruling in *Muller v. Oregon*, in *Adkins*, the Court found that women were no longer entitled to any special protection, that they stood on a footing that allowed them to bargain freely over wages with employers. The dissenters were skeptical that such drastic changes in women's status had occurred just because they now had the right to vote.

Justice Sutherland for the Court

But the ancient inequality of the sexes, otherwise than physical, as suggested in the Muller Case has continued "with diminishing intensity." In view of the great—not to say revolutionary—changes which have taken place since that utterance, in the contractual, political, and civil status of women, culminating in the Nineteenth Amendment, it is not unreasonable to say that these differences have now come, almost, if not quite, to the vanishing point.... [W]hile the physical differences must be recognized in appropriate cases, and legislation fixing hours or conditions of work may properly take them into account, we cannot accept the doctrine that women of mature age...require or may be subjected to restrictions upon their liberty of contract which could not lawfully be imposed in the case of men under similar circumstances. To do so would be to ignore all the implications to be drawn from the present day trend of legislation, as well as that of common thought and usage, by which woman is accorded emancipation from the old doctrine that she must be given special protection or be subjected to special restraint in her contractual or civil relationships.

[The law under consideration had provided for minimum wages adequate to provide women workers the necessary cost of living and to maintain them in good health and to protect their morals. The court found this standard too vague.]

The amount will depend upon a variety of circumstances. The individual temperment, habits of thrift, care, ability to buy necessaries intelligently, and whether the woman lives alone or with her family. To those who practice economy, a given sum will afford comfort, while to those of contrary habit the same sum will be wholly inadequate. The cooperative economies of the family group are not taken into account, though they constitute an important consideration in estimating the cost of living, for it is obvious that the individual expense will be less in the case of a member of a family than in the case of one living alone. The relation between earnings and morals is not capable of standardization. It cannot be shown that well-paid women safeguard their morals more carefully than those who are poorly paid. Morality rests upon other considerations than wages...for certainly if women require a minimum wage to preserve their morals men require it to preserve their honesty.

Justice Taft Dissented

I am not sure from a reading of the opinion whether the court thinks the authority of *Muller v. Oregon* is shaken by the adoption of the Nineteenth Amendment. The Nineteenth Amendment did not change the physical strength or limitations of women upon which [*Muller*] rests. The amendment did give women political power and makes more certain that legislative provisions for their protection will be in accord with their interests as they see them. But I do not think we are warranted in varying constitutional construction based on physical differences between men and women because of the amendment.

APPENDIX SIX

Hoyt v. Florida

368 US 57 (1961)

Gwendolyn Hoyt was convicted of killing her husband. She claimed that her due process and equal protection rights under the Fourteenth Amendment were violated by the Florida jury selection system. Under Florida law, no women could serve on a jury unless she chose to register with the circuit court. Consequently women made up only a miniscule fraction of jury pools in Florida. The Supreme Court determined that the law's differential treatment of male and female potential jurors was not unreasonable, and therefore it did not violate the Fourteenth Amendment.

Justice Harlan for the Court

We of course recognize that the Fourteenth Amendment reaches not only arbitrary class exclusions which "single out" any class of persons "for different treatment not based on some reasonable classification."...Where, as here, an exemption of a class in the community is asserted to be in substance an exclusionary device, the relevant inquiry is whether the exemption itself is based on some reasonable qualification and whether the manner in which it is exercisable rests on some rational foundation.

[They cannot conclude that Florida's statute is unreasonable.] Despite the enlightened emancipation of women from the restrictions and protections of bygone years, and their entry into many parts of community life formerly considered to be reserved to men, woman is still regarded as the center of home and family life. We cannot say that it is constitutionally impermissible for a State, acting in pursuit of the general welfare, to conclude that a woman should be relieved from the civic duty of jury service unless she herself determines that such service is consistent with her own special responsibilities.

APPENDIX SEVEN

Frontiero v. Richardson

411 US 677 (1973)

When Sharron Frontiero, an Air Force officer, applied for housing and medical benefits for her husband, she was told she must prove that he depended upon her for more than 50% of his support. The spouses of male officers, on the other hand, automatically qualified for benefits. The military assumed that husbands supported wives. Clearly the policy involved a difference in treatment based on sex. The court determined that the differential treatment of male and female service personnel amounted to unconstitutional discrimination. Ruth Bader Ginsberg, at the time a lawyer with the American Civil Liberties Union, argued for Frontiero.

The opinion in *Frontiero* is complicated because all the justices agreed that the policy was discriminatory, but they disagreed about the basis for that decision.

Justice Brennan Announced the Ruling

There can be no doubt that our Nation has had a long and unfortunate history of sex discrimination. Traditionally, such discrimination was rationalized by an attitude of "romantic paternalism" which, in practical effect, put women not on a pedestal, but in a cage.... It is true, of course, that the position of women in America has improved markedly in recent decades. Nevertheless, it can hardly be doubted that, in part because of the high visibility of the sex characteristic women still face pervasive, although at times more subtle, discrimination in our educational institutions, in the job market and perhaps most conspicuously, in the political arena.

Moreover, since sex, like race and national origin, is an immutable characteristic determined solely by the accident of birth, the imposition of special disabilities upon the members of a particular sex because of their sex would seem to violate "the basic concept of our system that legal burdens should bear some relationship to individual responsibility." And what distinguishes sex from such nonsuspect statuses as intelligence or physical disability and aligns it with the recognized suspect criteria, is that the sex characteristic frequently bears no relation to ability to perform or contribute to society. As a result, statutory distinctions between the sexes often have the effect of invidiously relegating the entire class of females to inferior legal status without regard to the actual capabilities of its individual members.

APPENDIX EIGHT

United States v. Virginia

518 US 515 (1996)

The Virginia Military Institute (VMI) a state-supported college, had admitted only male students since its founding in 1839. In 1990, a female applicant who was refused admission because of her sex challenged the all-male policy on Fourteenth Amendment equal protection grounds. After the suit, VMI created an alternative program for female students, the Virginia Women's Institute for Leadership (VWIL), at Mary Baldwin, an all-female private college. VMI argued that the VWIL program satisfied the equal protection claim.

The Supreme Court disagreed. They reiterated the ruling that any gender-based government action must meet the test of "intermediate scrutiny." There must be an exceedingly persuasive justification for treating similarly situated males and females differently. The majority of the court believed that VMI failed to provide that justification. The opinion provides a look at the history of women's exclusion from many areas of public life.

Justice Ginsberg for the Court

Through a century plus three decades of [American] history, women did not count among voters composing "We the People"; not until 1920 did women gain a constitutional right to the franchise. And for half a century thereafter, it remained the prevailing doctrine that government, both federal and state, could withhold from women opportunities accorded men as long as any "basis in reason" could be conceived for the discrimination....

[Since *Reed v. Reed*, the Court] has repeatedly recognized that neither federal nor state government acts compatibly with the equal protection principle when a law or official policy denies to women, simply because they are women, full citizenship stature—equal opportunity to aspire, achieve, participate in and contribute to society based on their individual talents and capacities.

Without equating gender classifications, for all purposes, to classification based on race or national origin, the court, in post-*Reed* decisions has carefully inspected official action that closes a door or denies opportunity to women (or to men). To summarize the court's current directions for cases of official classification based on gender: Focusing on the differential treatment or denial of opportunity for which relief is sought, the reviewing court must determine whether the proffered justification is "exceedingly persuasive." The burden of justification is demanding and rests entirely on the State. The State must show "at least that the [challenged] classification serves 'important governmental objectives and that the discriminatory means employed' are 'substantially related to the achievement of those objectives'." The justification must be genuine, not hypothesized or invented post hoc in response to litigation. And it must not rely on overbroad generalizations about the different talents, capacities, or preferences of males and females....

"Inherent differences" between men and women, we have come to appreciate, remain cause for celebration but not for denigration of the members of either sex or for artificial constraints on an individual's opportunity. Sex classifications may be used to compensate women "for particular economic disabilities they have suffered," to "promote equal employment opportunity," to advance full development of the talent and capacities of our Nation's people. But such classifications may not be used, as they once were, to create or perpetuate the legal, social, and economic inferiority of women....

State actors controlling gates to opportunity...may not exclude qualified individuals based on "fixed notions concerning the roles and abilities of males and females."...

The notion that admission of women would downgrade VMI's stature, destroy the adversative system and with it, even the school, is a judgment hardly proved, a prediction hardly different from other "self-fulfilling prophecies," once routinely used to deny rights or opportunities. When women first sought admission to the bar and access to legal education, concerns of the same order were expressed....

VMI's mission [is] to produce "citizen soldiers," individuals "imbued with love of learning, confident in the functions and attitudes of leadership, possessing a high sense of public service, advocates of the American democracy and free enterprise system, and ready...to defend their country in time of national peril."

Surely that goal is great enough to accommodate women, who today count as citizens in our American democracy equal in stature to men.

APPENDIX NINE

Dothard v. Rawlinson

433 US 321 (1977)

Dianne Rawlinson's application to become a prison counselor in Alabama was rejected because she weighed less than the 120 pounds required for the position. Rawlinson sued under Title VII of the Civil Rights Act of 1964, claiming that the law discriminated on the basis of sex. Rawlinson's position was that the height (5 feet 2 inches) and weight (120 pounds) requirements discriminated against female applicants. She also alleged that size was not a "bona fide occupational qualification." Rawlinson also challenged another provision that prohibited women from working in contact positions in maximum security male prisons. The Court overturned the height and weight requirements but permitted Alabama to maintain its ban on women in contact positions.

Justice Stewart's Opinion for the Court

The gist of the claim that the statutory height and weight requirements discriminate against women does not involve an assertion of purposeful discriminatory motive....Once it is shown that the employment standards are discriminatory in effect, the employer must meet "the burden of showing that any given requirement [has] a manifest relationship to the employment in question."

[The state argues that the height and weight requirements are job related.] These requirements, they say, have a relationship to strength, a sufficient but unspecified amount of which is essential to effective job performance as a correctional counselor....[H]owever, they produced no evidence correlating the height and weight requirements with the requisite amount of strength thought essential to good job performance. Indeed, they failed to offer evidence of any kind in specific justification of the statutory standards.

If the job-related quality that the appellants identify is bona fide, their purpose could be achieved by adopting and validating a test for applicants that measures strength directly. Such a test, fairly administered, would fully satisfy the standards of Title VII because it would be one that "measure[s] the person for the job and not the person in the abstract."

[The Court finds that sex is a bona fide occupational qualification for a contact position in the maximum security prison.] The environment in Alabama's penitentiaries is a peculiarly inhospitable one for human beings of whatever sex. Indeed, a Federal District Court has held that the conditions of confinement in the prisons of the State, characterized by "rampant violence" and a "jungle atmosphere" are constitutionally intolerable. The record in the present case shows that because of inadequate staff and facilities, no attempt is made in the four maximum security male penitentiaries to classify or segregate inmates according to their offense or level of dangerousness....

Consequently, the 20% of the male prisoners who are sex offenders are scattered throughout the penitentiaries' dormitory facilities.

The essence of a correctional counselor's job is to maintain prison security. A woman's relative ability to maintain order in a male, maximum security, unclassified penitentiary of the type Alabama now runs could be directly reduced by her womanhood. There is a basis in fact for expecting that sex offenders who have criminally assaulted women in the past would be moved to do so again if access to women were established within the prison. There would also be a real risk that other inmates, deprived of a normal heterosexual environment, would assault women guards because they were women.... The likelihood that inmates would assault a woman because she was a woman would pose a real threat not only to the victim of the assault but also to the basic control of the penitentiary and protection of its inmates and other security personnel. The employee's very womanhood would thus directly undermine her capacity to provide the security that is the essence of a correctional counselor's responsibility.

Justice Marshall Wrote a Dissent

What would otherwise be considered unlawful discrimination against women is justified by the court, however, on the basis of the "barbaric and inhumane" conditions in Alabama prisons, conditions so bad that state officials have conceded that they violate the constitution. To me this analysis sounds distressingly like saying two wrongs make a right....

The court's error in statutory construction is less objectionable, however, than the attitude it displays toward women. Though the court recognizes that possible harm to women guards is an unacceptable reason for disqualifying women, it relies instead on an equally speculative threat to prison discipline supposedly generated by the sexuality of female guards. There is simply no evidence in the record to show that women guards would create any danger to security in Alabama prisons significantly greater that that which already exists....

No prison guard relies primarily on his or her ability to ward off an inmate attack [and] to maintain order. Guards are typically unarmed and sheer numbers of inmates could overcome the normal complement. Rather, like all other law enforcement officers, prison guards must rely primarily on the moral authority of their office and the threat of future punishment for miscreants.... [C]ommon sense, fairness, and mental and emotional stability are the qualities a guard needs to cope with the dangers of the job...Well qualified and properly trained women, no less than men, have these psychological weapons at their disposal....

It appears that the real disqualifying factor in the court's view is "the employee's very womanhood."...The court refers to the large number of sex offenders in Alabama prisons, and to "the likelihood that inmates would assault a woman because she was a woman."...In short, the fundamental justification for the decision is that women as guards will generate sexual assaults. With all respect, this rationale regrettably perpetuates one of the most insidious of the old myths about women, that women, wittingly or not, are seductive sexual objects. The effect of the decision, made I am sure with the best of intentions, is to punish women because their very presence might provoke sexual assaults. It is women who are made to pay the price in lost job opportunities for the threat of depraved conduct by prison inmates. Once again "the pedestal upon which women have been placed has...upon closer inspection, been revealed as a cage." It is particularly ironic that the cage is erected here in response to feared misbehavior by imprisoned criminals.

APPENDIX TEN

Buck v. Bell

274 US 200 (1927)

The Court found that Carrie Buck's Fourteenth Amendment rights were not violated when she was surgically sterilized, against her will, while a resident at the Virginia State Colony for Epileptics and Feeble Minded.

Justice Holmes for the Court

[The law in question provides] that the health of the patient and the welfare of society may be promoted in certain cases by the sterilization of mental defectives...that the Commonwealth is supporting in various institutions many defective persons who if now discharged would become a menace but if incapable of procreating might be discharged with safety and become self-supporting with benefit to themselves and to society; and that experience has shown that heredity plays an important part in the transmission of insanity, imbecility, etc.

We have seen more than once that the public welfare may call upon the best citizens for their lives. It would be strange if it could not call upon those who already sap the strength of the State for these lesser sacrifices...in order to prevent our being swamped with incompetence. It is better for all the world if, instead of waiting to execute degenerate offspring for crime, or to let them starve for their imbecility, society can prevent those who are manifestly unfit from continuing their kind. The principle that sustains compulsory vaccination is broad enough to cover cutting the Fallopian tubes. Three generations of imbeciles are enough.

APPENDIX ELEVEN

Planned Parenthood of Southeastern Pennsylvania v. Casey

505 US 833 (1992)

In this case, the Court tried once again, as it had during the two decades since *Roe v. Wade* to define more precisely the balance between a woman's right to privacy and the state's interest in maternal and fetal health. The issues seem to come down to a consideration of what regulations a state may make a) without interfering with a woman's broad right to choose in the early stages of pregnancy; b) to protect the potential life of the fetus especially later in the pregnancy; and c) to protect the mother's health and life. Some, including Chief Justice Rehnquist and Justices Scalia and Thomas, argue that there is no constitutional right to privacy, that the attempt to balance states' interests and women's rights is futile. They would repeal *Roe* and permit each state to make whatever laws it chose regulating or even banning abortion.

In *Casey*, six members of the court declined to overturn *Roe v. Wade*. Instead, they struggled to find language and rules to provide states with clear guidelines that protected the constitutional right to reproductive choice. They upheld several of the Pennsylvania regulations: informed consent; a 24-hour waiting period; parental consent for minors seeking abortions; and stringent reporting requirements for clinics. However, they found a provision requiring spousal notification unconstitutional. On that subject, the court made a particularly strong statement denouncing the common law notion of patriarchal marriage.

Justice O'Connor, Justice Kennedy, and Justice Souter Delivered the Opinion of the Court

[The Court determined] that *Roe's* essential holding be retained and reaffirmed as to each of its three parts: (1) a recognition of a woman's right to choose to have an abortion before fetal viability and to obtain it without undue interference from the State, whose pre-viability interests are not strong enough to support an abortion prohibition or the imposition of substantial obstacles to the woman's effective right to elect the procedure; (2) a confirmation of the State's power to restrict abortions after viability, if the law contains exceptions for pregnancies endangering a woman's life or health; and (3) the principle that the State has legitimate interests from the outset of the pregnancy in protecting the health of the woman and the life of the fetus that may become a child....

Our law affords constitutional protection to personal decisions relating to marriage, procreation, contraception, family relationships, child rearing, and education. Our cases recognize the right of the individual, married or single, to be free from unwarranted government intrusion into matters so fundamentally affecting a person as the decision whether to bear or beget a child. Our precedents "have respected the private realm of family life which the state cannot enter." These matters, involving the most intimate and personal choices a person may make in a lifetime, choices central to personal dignity and autonomy, are central to the liberty protected by the Fourteenth Amendment. At the heart of liberty is the right to define one's own concept of existence, of meaning, of the universe, and of the mystery of human life. Beliefs about these matters could not define the attributes of personhood were they formed under compulsion of the State....

Though abortion is conduct, it does not follow that the State is entitled to proscribe it in all instances. That is because the liberty of the woman is at stake in a sense unique to the human condition, and so, unique to the law. The mother who carries a child to full term is subject to anxieties, to physical constraints, to pain that only she must bear. That these sacrifices have from the beginning of the human race been endured by woman with a pride that enobles her in the eyes of others and gives to the infant a bond of love cannot alone be grounds for the State to insist that she make the sacrifice. Her suffering is too intimate and personal for the State to insist, without more, upon its own vision of the woman's role, however dominant that vision has been in the course of our history and our culture. The destiny of the woman must be shaped to a large extent on her own conception of her spiritual imperatives and her place in society....

A finding of an undue burden is a shorthand for the conclusion that a state regulation has the purpose or effect of placing a substantial obstacle in the path of a woman seeking an abortion of a nonviable fetus. A statute with this purpose is invalid because the means chosen by the State to further the interest in potential life must be calculated to inform the woman's free choice, not hinder it....

The spousal notification requirement is likely to prevent a significant number of women from obtaining an abortion. It does not merely make abortions a little more difficult or expensive to obtain; for many women, it will impose a substantial obstacle. We must not blind ourselves to the fact that a significant number of women who fear for their safety and the safety of their children are likely to be deterred from procuring an abortion as surely as if the Commonwealth had outlawed abortion in all cases....

We recognize that a husband has a deep and proper concern and interest...in his wife's pregnancy and in the growth and development of the fetus she is carrying. With regard to the children he has fathered and raised, the court has recognized his "cognizable and substantial" interest in their custody. If this case concerned a State's ability to require a mother to notify the father before taking some action with respect to a living child raised by both, therefore, it would be reasonable to conclude, as a general matter, that the father's interest in the welfare of the child and the mother's interest are equal.

Before birth, however, the issue takes on a different cast. It is an inescapable biological fact that state regulation with respect to the child the woman is carrying will have a far greater impact on the mother's liberty than on the father's. The effect of state regulation on a woman's protected liberty is doubly deserving of scrutiny in such a case, as the State has touched not only upon the private sphere of the family, but upon the very bodily integrity of the pregnant woman. The court has held that when the wife and the husband disagree on this decision, the view of only one of the two marriage partners can prevail. Inasmuch as it is the woman who physically bears the child and who is the more directly and immediately affected by the pregnancy, as between the two, the balance weighs in her favor. This conclusion rests upon the basic nature of marriage and the nature of our Constitution: [T]he marital couple is not an independent entity with a mind and heart of its own, but an association of two individuals, each with a separate intellect and emotional makeup. If the right of privacy means anything, it is the right of the individual, married or single, to be free from unwarranted governmental intrusion into matters so fundamentally affecting a person as the decision whether to bear or beget a child. The Constitution protects individuals, men and women alike, from unjustified state interference, even when that interference is enacted into law for the benefit of their spouses....

For the many women who are victims of abuse inflicted by their husbands, or whose children are the victims of such abuse, a spousal notice requirement enables the husband to wield an effective veto over his wife's decision. Whether the prospect of notification itself deters such women from seeking abortions, or whether the husband through physical force or psychological pressure or economic coercion, prevents his wife from obtaining an abortion until it is too late, the notice requirement will often be tantamount to [a] veto requirement. The women most affected by this law—those who most reasonably fear the consequences of notifying their husbands that they are pregnant—are in the gravest danger....

[The spousal notification section] embodies a view of marriage consonant with the common law status of married women, but repugnant to our present understanding of marriage and of the nature of the rights secured by the Constitution. Women do not lose their Constitutionally protected liberty when they marry. The Constitution protects all individuals, male or female, married or unmarried, from the abuse of governmental power, even where that power is employed for the supposed benefit of a member of the individual's family.

Chief Justice Rehnquist, Justice Scalia, and Justice Thomas Dissented

We believe that *Roe* was wrongly decided, and that it can and should be overturned.

APPENDIX TWELVE

Film and Fiction

Students and I have often found it helpful to examine issues related to gender and justice through films and fiction. Analyzing an individual story, even if the events themselves are not "true," allows one to visualize and empathize in ways all the statistics and scholarly data may not. What follows is, admittedly, a subjective selection of novels, stories, and movies that deal with concepts considered in this book. I provide the list in the hope that others will use it and build on it as a way of engendering discussion in and out of class.

Inclusion and Equality

Susan Glaspell's short story "A Jury of Her Peers" is deservedly a popular choice for looking at how men and women can view the same situation (the home of a woman accused of killing her husband) and reach very different conclusions. I find it a good place to start a discussion that considers—among other things—why women's perspective is critical to the criminal justice system. A more extensive treatment of a legal system in which women are excluded and subordinated "for their own protection" is Margaret Atwood's antiutopian novel, *The Handmaid's Tale*. It can also stimulate discussion of reproductive choice.

Working in the System

As Paul Bergman and Michael Asimow, the authors of *Reel Justice: The Courtroom Goes to the Movies* (Kansas City: Andrews and McMeel, 1996) point out, female lawyers on film are seldom impressive. They sleep around—with clients, law professors, opposing attorneys, or their supervisors—thus reinforcing some pretty negative stereotypes about successful women. Some are just stupid in the courtroom, doing things like planting evidence. They are likely to lose all objectivity and become emotionally overwrought. It's useful to go back to a 1949 movie, *Adam's Rib*, in which Katharine Hepburn defends a woman accused of attempting to murder her cheating husband. Despite some questionable points of law, the film is ahead of its time in portraying a strong minded, competent attorney with a successful personal life.

TV shows, such as "Law and Order" and "NYPD Blue" portray some strong female police officers. Few films do as well. An exception is Sheriff Margie in *Fargo*, who is tenacious, brave, decent—and pregnant.

Victims

The film, *The Accused*, is based loosely on a gang rape that took place in New Bedford, Massachusetts in 1983. Although the movie version reaches a different legal conclusion than the actual trial, it succeeds in illustrating powerful rape myths and the degradation of the victim. The character played by Jodie Foster argues eloquently that her voice should be heard if justice is to be served. *We Were the Mulvaneys*, a novel by Joyce Carol Oates, examines a family's disintegration after the daughter is raped by an acquaintance. Margaret Atwood's short story, "Rape Fantasies," offers a very different view. A Toronto office worker, put off by her coworkers' sexual fantasies, tells some of her own. They feature scenarios in which the victim subverts the potential violence through her common sense.

"The Burning Bed," a made-for-TV movie, provides a strong vision of a victim of battering who kills her abuser. Novels by Amy Tan, such as *The Kitchen God's Wife*, offer a look at domestic violence in a cross-cultural context.

Victims/Offenders

Thelma and Louise gives the viewer a chance to consider the complex relationship between victims and offenders. Both women were victims of rape, both lost faith in the system to rectify injustice. Their final act of suicide may be interpreted either as courage or as despair.

Punishing Women

Although a student once complained to me that she was bored because the film is in black and white, *I Want to Live* makes a powerful statement about gender and punishment, specifically the death penalty. The film is drawn from the story of Barbara Graham, executed in California in 1954. Allowing for developments in criminal procedure since the mid-1950s, students can examine a host of gendered assumptions that influenced the case, whether or not Graham was guilty.

On the surface of Zora Neale Hurston's "The Conscience of the Court," it appears that the white-controlled system metes out justice to the black woman on trial. Hurston's more subtle message calls the fairness of the court into question.

Reproduction and Motherhood

Students have found it interesting to discuss Nadine Gordimer's story, "Happy Event," as it deals with the law and reproductive issues, as well as race and class. The story is set in South Africa, but raises universal questions. "Customs of the Country" by Madison Smartt Bell is set in rural Virginia. An uneducated woman, whose husband got her addicted to drugs, lost custody of her son. She gradually comes to see that the court will never give him back. In frustration, she hits the abusive husband next door over the head with a frying pan and takes off for the city.

BIBLIOGRAPHY

Adler, Freda. *Sisters in Crime*. New York: McGraw-Hill, 1975.

Alschuler, Albert W., and Deiss, Andrew G. "A Brief History of the Criminal Jury in the United States." *University of Chicago Law Review* 61 (Summer, 1994): 867–928.

Ammons, Linda. "Mules, Madonnas, Babies, Bathwater, Racial Imagery and Stereotypes: The African-American Woman and the Battered Woman Syndrome." In *Domestic Violence Law*, edited by Nancy K. D Lemon. St. Paul, Minnesota: West, 2001.

Amnesty International. "*Not Part of My Sentence*": *Violations of the Human Rights of Women in Custody*. New York: Amnesty International, USA, 1999.

Anderson, Clelia Smyth, and Estes, Yolanda. "The Myth of the Happy Hooker: Kantian Moral Reflections on a Phenomenology of Prostitution." In *Violence Against Women: Philosophical Perspectives*, edited by Stanley G. French, Wanda Teays, and Laura M. Purdy. Ithaca: Cornell University Press, 1998.

Angel, Marina. "Criminal Law and Women: Giving the Abused Woman Who Kills a Jury of Her Peers," *American Criminal Law Review* 33 (Winter 1996): 229–348.

Appier, Janis. "Preventive Justice: The Campaign for Women Police, 1910–1940," *Women and Criminal Justice* 4 (1992): 3–36.

Armatta, Judith. "Getting Beyond the Law's Complicity in Intimate Violence Against Women," In *Domestic Violence Law*, edited by Nancy K. D. Lemon. St. Paul, Minnesota: West, 2001.

Babcock, Barbara Allen. "A Place in the Palladium: Women's Rights and Jury Service," *University of Cincinnati Law Review* 61 (1993): 1139–1181.

Bart, Pauline, and Moran, Eileen Geil, eds. *Violence Against Women: The Bloody Footprints*. Newbury Park, California: Sage, 1993.

Bartlett, Katherine T., ed. *Gender and Law: Theory, Doctrine, Commentary*. Boston: Little, Brown, 1993.

Beckett, Katherine, and Sasson, Theodore. *The Politics of Injustice: Crime and Punishment in America*. Thousand Oaks, California: Pine Forge Press, 2000.

Belknap, Joanne. *The Invisible Woman: Gender, Crime, and Justice*. Belmont, California: Wadsworth, 2001.

Berg, Barbara. *The Remembered Gate: Origins of American Feminism*. New York: Oxford University Press, 1978.

Berger, Vivian. "No Way to Treat a Baby," *National Law Journal* (November 13, 2000).

Bevaqua, Maria. *Rape on the Public Agenda: Feminism and the Politics of Sexual Assault*. Boston: Northeastern University Press, 2000.

Bowermaster, Janet M. "Relocation Custody Disputes Involving Domestic Violence." In *Domestic Violence Law*, edited by Nancy K. D. Lemon. St. Paul, Minnesota: West, 2001.

Browne, Angela. "Reshaping the Rhetoric: The Nexus of Violence, Poverty, and Minority Status in the Lives of Women and Children in the United States." In *Domestic Violence Law*, edited by Nancy K. D. Lemon. St. Paul, Minnesota: West, 2001.

Brownmiller, Susan. *Against Our Wills: Men, Women and Rape*. New York: Simon and Schuster, 1975.

Bunney, Marcia. "One Life in Prison." In *Harsh Punishment: International_Experiences of Women's Imprisonment*, edited by Sandy Cook and Susanne Davies. Boston: Northeastern University Press, 1999.

Bush-Baskette, Stephanie R. "The 'War on Drugs': A War Against Women?" In *Harsh Punishment: International Experiences of Women's Imprisonment*, edited by Sandy Cook and Susanne Davies. Boston: Northeastern University Press, 1999.

Callahan, Joan C. and Knight, James W. "Prenatal Harm as Child Abuse?" In *The Criminalization of a Woman's Body*, edited by Clarice Feinman. New York: Haworth Press, 1992.

Campbell, Jacquelyn C. "Wife Battering: Cultural Contexts Versus Western Social Sciences." In *Domestic Violence Law*, edited by Nancy K. D. Lemon. St. Paul, Minnesota: West, 2001.

Caron, Susan, MacDonald, Peter, and Zeya, Suma. "Enforcing Domestic Violence Protective Orders Throughout the Country: New Frontiers of Protection for Victims of Domestic Violence." In *Domestic Violence Law*, edited by Nancy K. D. Lemon. St. Paul, Minnesota: West, 2001.

"Can the Court Recover?" *Time* (December 25, 2000).

Caputi, Jane. "The Sexual Politics of Murder." In *Violence Against Women: The Bloody Footprints*, edited by Pauline B. Bart and Eileen Geil Moran. Newbury Park, California: Sage, 1993.

Chafe, William H. *Women and Equality: Changing Patterns in American Culture*. New York: Oxford University Press, 1977.

Chavkin, Wendy. "Woman and Fetus: The Social Construction of Conflict." In *The Criminalization of a Woman's Body*, edited by Clarice Feinman. New York: Haworth Press, 1992.

Chesney-Lind, Meda. *The Female Offender: Girls, Women, and Crime*. Thousand Oaks, California: Sage, 1997.

Clanton, Karen. "Glass Ceilings and Sticky Floors: Minority Women in the Legal Profession." *Kansas Law Review* 49 (May 2001): 761–775.

Claybrook, Joan. "Women in the Marketplace." In *The Corporate Victimization of Women*, edited by Elizabeth Szockyj and James G. Fox. Boston: Northeastern University Press, 1996.

Clinton, Catherine, and Gillespie, Michele, eds. *The Devil's Lane: Sex and Race in the Early South*. New York: Oxford University Press, 1997.

Cohen, Jane Maslow. "Private Violence and Public Obligation: The Fulcrum of Reason." In *The Public Nature of Private Violence: The Discovery of Domestic Abuse*, edited by Martha Albertson Fineman and Roxanne Mykitiuk. New York: Routledge, 1994.

Colb, Sherry. "Drug Testing Pregnant Women Is Both Counterproductive and Unconstitutional," *Findlaw's Writ* (October 25, 2000).

———. "Why the Senate Should Refuse Even to Consider the Unborn Victims of Violence Act of 2001," *Findlaw's Writ* (June 2, 2001).

Cook, Sandy, and Davies, Susanne, eds. *Harsh Punishment: International Experiences of Women's Imprisonment*. Boston: Northeastern, 1999.

Copelon, Rhonda. "Recognizing the Egregious in the Everyday: Domestic Violence as Torture." In *Battered Women and the Law*, edited by Clare Dalton and Elizabeth M. Schneider. New York: Foundation Press, 2001.

Courtwright, David T. *Violent Land: Single Men and Social Disorder from the Frontier to the Inner City*. Cambridge, Massachusetts: Harvard University Press, 1996.

Cott, Nancy. *The Grounding of Modern Feminism*. New Haven: Yale University Press, 1987.

Coyle, Marcia. "Fourth Amendment Focus of Justice," *National Law Journal* (October 9, 2000).

Crowell, Nancy A., and Burgess, Ann W., eds. *Understanding Violence Against Women*. Washington, D.C.: National Academy Press, 1996.

Dalton, Clare, and Schneider, Elizabeth M., eds. *Battered Women and the Law*. New York: Foundation Press, 2001.

Daly, Kathleen. *Gender, Crime, and Punishment*. New Haven: Yale University Press, 1994.

Danner, Mona J. E. "Review of *Doing Justice, Doing Gender: Women in Law and Criminal Justice*." *Justice Quarterly* 15:1 (March 1998): 193–197.

Davies, Susanne, and Cook, Sandy. "The Sex of Crime and Punishment." In *Harsh Punishment: International Experiences of Women's Imprisonment*, edited by Sandy Cook and Susanne Davies. Boston: Northeastern University Press, 1999.

DeBruin, Dabra A. "Identifying Sexual Harassment: The Reasonable Woman Standard." In *Violence Against Women: Philosophical Perspectives*, edited by Stanley G. French, Wanda Teays, and Laura M. Purdy. Ithaca: Cornell University Press, 1998.

Dobash, Russell P.,et al. "Separate and Intersecting Realities: A Comparison of Men's and Women's Accounts of Violence Against Women." In *Battered Women and the Law*, edited by Clare Dalton and Elizabeth M. Schneider. New York: Foundation Press, 2001.

Donziger, Steven R., ed. *The Real War on Crime: The Report of the National Criminal Justice Commission*. New York: Harper, 1996.

Drachman, Virginia G. *Sisters in Law: Women Lawyers in Modern American History*. Cambridge, Massachusetts: Harvard University Press, 1998.

Dutton, Mary Ann, and Woltz, Catherine L. "Domestic Violence: Understanding Why It Happens and How to Recognize It." In *Domestic Violence Law*, edited by Nancy K. D. Lemon. St. Paul, Minnesota: West, 2001.

Dutton, Mary Ann. "How Battered Women Cope," *National Law Journal* (April 16, 2001).

Elshtain, Jean. *Public Man, Private Woman: Women in Social and Political Thought*. Princeton, New Jersey: Princeton University Press, 1981.

Ely, Margo L. "Waging War Against Drugs—and Expectant Mothers," *Chicago Daily Law Bulletin* (October 9, 2000).

Epstein, Cynthia Fuchs. *Women in Law*. Urbana, Illinois: University of Illinois Press, 1993.

———. "Women in the Legal Profession at the Turn of the Twenty-first Century: Assessing Glass Ceilings and Open Doors." *Kansas Law Review* 49 (May 2001): 733–760.

Epstein, Deborah. "Effective Intervention in Domestic Violence Cases: Rethinking the Role of Prosecutors, Judges, and the Court System." In *Domestic Violence Law*, edited by Nancy K. D. Lemon. St. Paul, Minnesota: West, 2001.

———. "Redefining the State's Response to Domestic Violence: Past Victories and Future Challenges." In *Domestic Violence Law*, edited by Nancy K. D. Lemon. St. Paul, Minnesota: West, 2001.

Eskow, Lisa R. "The Ultimate Weapon? Demythologizing Spousal Rape and Reconceptualizing Its Prosecution." In *Domestic Violence Law*, edited by Nancy K. D. Lemon. St. Paul, Minnesota: West, 2001.

Estrich, Susan. *Real Rape*. Cambridge, Massachusetts: Harvard, 1987.

Farkas, Mary Ann. "Correctional Officer Attitudes Toward Inmates in a 'Get Tough' Era." *Journal of Criminal Justice* 27:6 (1999): 495–506.

———. "Inmate Supervisory Style: Does Gender Make a Difference?" *Women and Criminal Justice*. 10:4 (1999): 25–45.

Feinman, Clarice, ed. *The Criminalization of a Woman's Body*. New York: Haworth, 1992.

Felkenes, George, and Lasley, James R. "Implications of Hiring Women Police Officers: Police Administration Concerns May Not Be Justified." *Policing and Society*. 3 (1992): 41–50.

Fenton, Zanita E. "Domestic Violence in Black and White: Racialized Gender Stereotypes in Gender Violence." In *Domestic Violence Law*, edited by Nancy K. D. Lemon. St. Paul, Minnesota: West, 2001.

Ferraro, Kathleen J. "Woman Battering: More Than a Family Problem." In *Women, Crime, and Criminal Justice: Original Feminist Readings*, edited by Claire M. Renzetti and Lynne Goodstein. Los Angeles: Roxbury, 2001.

Fineman, Martha A., and McCleskey, Martha T., eds. *Feminism, Media, and the Law*. New York: Oxford University Press, 1997.

Fineman, Martha Albertson, and Karpin, Isabel, eds. *Mothers in Law: Feminist Theory and the Legal Regulation of Motherhood*. New York: Columbia University Press, 1995.

Fineman, Martha Albertson and Mykitiuk, Roxanne, eds. *The Public Nature of Private Violence: The Discovery of Domestic Abuse*. New York: Routledge, 1994.

Finkelman, Paul. "Regulation of Race and Sex in the Colonial South." In *The Devil's Lane: Sex and Race in the Early South*, edited by Catherine Clinton and Michelle Gillespie. New York: Oxford University Press, 1997.

Finley, Lucinda M. "The Pharmaceutical Industry and Women's Health." In *The Corporate Victimization of Women*, edited by Elizabeth Szockyj and James G. Fox. Boston: Northeastern University Press, 1996.

Fischer, Karla, Vidmar, Neil, and Ellis, Rene. "The Culture of Battering and the Role of Mediation in Domestic Violence Cases." In *Battered Women and the Law*, edited by Clare Dalton and Elizabeth M. Schneider. New York: Foundation, 2001.

Fisher, Bonnie, Cullen, Francis T., and Turner, Michael G. *The Sexual Victimization of College Women*. Washington, D.C.: U.S. Department of Justice, 2000.

Fitzgerald, Louise F., et al. "Why Didn't She Just Report Him?" *Social Issues* 51 (1995): 117–151.

Flexner, Eleanor. *Century of Struggle: The Women's Rights Movement in the United States*. Cambridge, Massachusetts: Harvard University Press, 1959.

Flowers, Ronald Barri. *Women and Criminality: The Woman as Victim, Offender, and Practitioner*. New York: Greenwood, 1987.

Foltz, Joriel. "Community Teams," *In Our Vision*. Williamsburg, Virginia: Virginians Against Domestic Violence, Summer 2000.

Forell, Caroline A., and Matthews, Donna M. *A Law of Her Own: The Reasonable Woman as a Measure of Man*. New York: New York University Press, 2000.

Forman, Deborah. "What Difference Does It Make? Gender and Jury Selection." *UCLA Women's Law Journal*, 35 (1992): 35–84.

Fox, James G. "Law, Policy, and Social Change." In *The Corporate Victimization of Women*, edited by Elizabeth Szockyj and James G. Fox. Boston: Northeastern, 1996.

Fox-Genovese, Elizabeth. *Feminism Without Illusions: A Critique of Individualism*. Chapel Hill: University of North Carolina Press, 1991.

Frankel, Noralee, and Dye, Nancy S., eds. *Gender, Class, Race, and Reform in the Progressive Era*. Lexington, Kentucky: University of Kentucky Press, 1991.

Freedman, Estelle. "Separation as Strategy: Female Institution Building and American Feminism, 1870–1930." In *Women and Power in American History*, vol. II, edited by Kathryn Kish Sklar and Thomas Dublin. Englewood Cliffs, New Jersey: Prentice-Hall, 1991.

———. *Their Sisters' Keepers: Women's Prison Reform in America, 1830–1930*. Ann Arbor, Michigan: University of Michigan Press, 1984.

———. "Theoretical Perspectives on Sexual Difference: An Overview." In *Theoretical Perspectives on Sexual Difference*, edited by Deborah L. Rhode. New Haven: Yale University Press, 1990.

French, Stanley G., Teays, Wanda, and Purdy, Laura M. *Violence Against Women: Philosophical Perspectives*. Ithaca: Cornell University Press, 1998.

Gavey, Nicola. "I Wasn't Raped but . . .": Revisiting Definitional Problems in Sexual Victimization." In *New Versions of Victims: Feminists Struggle with the Concept*, edited by Sharon Lamb. New York: New York University Press, 1999.

Gibson, Mary. "Contract Motherhood: Social Practice in Social Context. " In *The Criminalization of a Woman's Body*, edited by Clarice Feinman. New York: Haworth, 1992.

Gilligan, Carol. "Getting Civilized." *Fordham Law Review* 63 (October, 1994): 17–31.

Girshick, Lori B. *No Safe Haven: Stories of Women in Prison*. Boston: Northeastern University Press, 1999.

Glenn, Myra C. *Campaigns Against Corporal Punishment: Prisoners, Sailors, Women and Children in Antebellum America*. Albany: State University of New York Press, 1984.

Goldfarb, Sally F. "Violence Against Women and the Persistence of Privacy." In *Battered Women and the Law*, edited by Clare Dalton and Elizabeth M. Schneider. New York: Foundation, 2001.

Gondolf, Edward, and Fisher, Ellen. "The Survivor Theory." In *Domestic Violence Law*, edited by Nancy K. D. Lemon. St. Paul, Minnesota: West, 2001.

Gordon, Linda. *Heroes of Their Own Lives: The Politics and History of Family Violence*. New York: Viking, 1988.

———. *Woman's Body, Woman's Right: A Social History of Birth Control in America*. New York: Penguin, 1977.

Grossman, Joanna. "The New ADA Report on Women and Law: Why the Solutions the Report Proposes May Not Work in the Real World," *Findlaw's Writ* (May 22, 2001).

———. "Pregnancy and Partnership: A Law Firm Partner's Anti-Discrimination Suit," *Findlaw's Writ* (December 19, 2000).

———. "Sexual Harassment in Law Firms: Why It Still Exists, and Why Firms Haven't Taken Steps to Prevent It and to Decrease Their Own Liability," *Findlaw's Writ* (November 10, 2000).

Hamilton, Mary E. *The Policewoman: Her Service and Ideals*. New York: Frederick A. Stokes, 1924.

Hanna, Cheryl. "The Paradox of Hope: The Crime and Punishment of Domestic Violence." In *Domestic Violence Law*, edited by Nancy K. D. Lemon. St. Paul, Minnesota: West, 2001.

Hart, Barbara J. "Arrest: What's the Big Deal?" In *Domestic Violence Law*, edited by Nancy K. D. Lemon. St. Paul, Minnesota: West, 2001.

Heidensohn, Frances. *Women and Crime*. New York: New York University Press, 1985.

Hensler, Deborah R., and Resnick, Judith. "Contested Identities: Task Forces on Gender, Race, and Ethnic Bias and the Obligation of the Legal Profession." In *Ethics in Practice: Lawyers' Roles, Responsibilities, and Regulation*, edited by Deborah L. Rhode. New York: Oxford University Press, 2000.

Hire, Garth E. "Holding Husbands and Lovers Accountable for Rape: Eliminating the Defendant Exception in Rape Shield Laws." In *Domestic Violence Law*, edited by Nancy K. D. Lemon. St. Paul, Minnesota: West, 2001.

Hobson, Barbara Meil. *Uneasy Virtue: The Politics of Prostitution and the American Reform Tradition*. Chicago: University of Chicago Press, 1990.

Holder, Kerry Anne, Nee, Claire, and Ellis Thomas. "Triple Jeopardy? Black and Asian Women Police Officers' Experiences of Discrimination." *International Journal of Police Science and Management* 3:1 (2000): 68–87.

Horsburgh, Beverly. "Lifting the Veil of Secrecy: Domestic Violence in the Jewish Community." In *Domestic Violence Law*, edited by Nancy K. D. Lemon. St. Paul, Minnesota: West, 2001.

Inciardi, James A., Lockwood, Dorothy, and Pottieger, Anne E. *Women and Crack Cocaine*. New York: Macmillan, 1993.

Jacobson, Neil S., and Gottman, John M. "Myth #2: All Batterers Are Alike." In *Battered Women and the Law*, edited by Clare Dalton and Elizabeth M. Schneider. New York: Foundation, 2001.

Jagger, Alison M. "Sexual Difference and Sexual Equality." In *Theoretical Perspectives on Sexual Difference*, edited by Deborah L. Rhode. New Haven: Yale University Press, 1990.

Janeway, Elizabeth. *Powers of the Weak*. New York: Alfred A. Knopf, 1980.

Jones, Ann. *Next Time She'll Be Dead: Battering and How to Stop It*. Boston: Beacon, 1994.

Jurik, Nancy C. "Striking a Balance: Female Correctional Officers, Gender Role Stereotypes, and Male Prisons," *Sociological Inquiry* (1998): 291–305.

Jurik, Nancy C., and Martin, Susan E. "Femininities, Masculinities and Organizational Conflict: Women in Criminal Justice Occupations." In *Women, Crime, and Criminal Justice: Original Feminist Readings*, edited by Claire M. Renzetti and Lynne Goodstein. Los Angeles: Roxbury, 2001.

Karon, Amy, Keilitz, Susan, and Denaro, Sharon. "Domestic Violence Courts: What Are They and How Should We Manage Them?" In *Domestic Violence Law*, edited by Nancy K. D. Lemon. St. Paul, Minnesota: West, 2001.

Kelly, Maria. "Domestic Violence and Guns: Seizing Weapons Before the Court Has Made a Finding of Abuse." In *Domestic Violence Law*, edited by Nancy K. D. Lemon. St. Paul, Minnesota: West, 2001.

Kennedy, Randall. *Race, Crime, and the Law*. New York: Vintage, 1997.

Kerber, Linda K. *No Constitutional Right to Be Ladies: Women and the Obligations of Citizenship*. New York: Hill and Wang, 1998.

Kerber, Linda, and DeHart, Jane, eds. *Women's America: Refocusing the Past*. New York: Oxford University Press, 1991.

Kessler-Harris, Alice. "Law and a Living: The Gendered Content of Free Labor." In *Gender, Class, Race, and Reform in the Progressive Era*, edited by Noralee Frankel and Nancy S. Dye. Lexington, Kentucky: University of Kentucky Press, 1991.

Kinports, Kit, and Fischer, Karla. "Orders of Protection in Domestic Violence Cases: An Empirical Assessment of the Impact of Reform Statutes." In *Domestic Violence Law*, edited by Nancy K. D. Lemon. St. Paul, Minnesota: West, 2001.

Kurz, Demie. "Women, Welfare, and Domestic Violence." *Social Justice* 25:1 (1998): 105–122.

Lamb, Sharon. "Constructing the Victim: Popular Images and Lasting Labels." In *New Versions of Victims: Feminists Struggle with the Concept*, edited by Sharon L. Lamb. New York: New York University Press, 1999.

———, ed. *New Versions of Victims: Feminists Struggle with the Concept*. New York: New York University Press, 1999.

Lanier, Mark M. "An Evolutionary Typology of Women Police Officers." *Women and Criminal Justice* 8:2 (1996): 35–57.

Lawrence, Richard, and Mahan, Sue. "Women Corrections Officers in Men's Prisons: Acceptance and Perceived Job Performance." *Women and Criminal Justice*, 9:3 (1988): 63–86.

Lemon, Nancy K. D., ed. *Domestic Violence Law*. St. Paul, Minnesota: West, 2001.

Levit, Nancy. *The Gender Line: Men, Women and the Law*. New York: New York University Press, 1998.

MacKinnon, Catherine A. "Feminism, Marxism, Method and the State." In *Violence Against Women: The Bloody Footprints*, edited by Pauline B. Bart and Eileen Geil Moran. Newbury Park, California: Sage, 1993.

———. "Legal Perspectives on Sexual Difference." In *Theoretical Perspectives on Sexual Difference*, edited by Deborah L. Rhode. New Haven: Yale University Press, 1990.

———. *Sex Equality*. New York: Foundation, 2001.

———."Toward Feminist Jurisprudence." In *Feminist Jurisprudence*, edited by Patricia Smith. New York: Oxford University Press, 1993.

Madriz, Esther. *Nothing Bad Happens to Good Girls: Fear of Crime in Women's Lives*. Berkeley: University of California Press, 1997.

Maher, Lisa. "Punishment and Welfare: Crack Cocaine and the Regulation of Mothering." In *The Criminalization of a Woman's Body*, edited by Clarice Feinman. New York: Haworth, 1992.

Mahoney, Martha. "Legal Images of Battered Women: Redefining the Issue of Separation." In *Domestic Violence Law*, edited by Nancy K. D. Lemon. St. Paul, Minnesota: West, 2001.

Mangum, Paula Finley. "Reconceptualizing Battered Woman Syndrome Evidence: Prosecution Use of Expert Testimony on Battering." In *Domestic Violence Law*, edited by Nancy K. D. Lemon. St. Paul, Minnesota: West, 2001.

Marcus, Isabel. "Reframing Domestic Violence: Terrorism in the Home." In *Battered Women and the Law*, edited by Clare Dalton and Elizabeth M. Schneider. New York: Foundation, 2001.

Martin, Susan Ehrlich, and Jurik, Nancy. *Doing Justice, Doing Gender: Women in Law and Criminal Justice Occupations*. Thousand Oaks, California: Sage, 1996.

Martin, Susan E. " 'Outsider Within' the Station House: The Impact of Race and Gender on Black Women Police." *Social Problems* 41:31 (August, 1994): 383–400.

Maxwell, Christopher D., Garner, Joel H., and Fazon, Jeffrey A. "The Effects of Arrest on Intimate Partner Violence: New Evidence from the Spouse Assault Replication Program." *National Institutes of Justice Research in Brief* (June 2001).

Menkel-Meadow, Carrie. "Portia in a Different Voice: Speculations on a Women's Lawyering Process." In *Gender and Law*, edited by Katherine T. Bartlett. Boston: Little-Brown, 1993.

Miller, Susan L. "Gender and Policing." In *Women, Crime, and Criminal Justice: Original Feminist Readings*, edited by Claire M. Renzetti and Lynne Goodstein. Los Angeles: Roxbury, 2001.

Minow, Martha. *Making All the Difference: Inclusion, Exclusion, and American Law*. Ithaca: Cornell University Press, 1990.

Mohr, James C. *Abortion in America: The Origins and Evolution of National Policy, 1800–1900*. New York: Oxford University Press, 1978.

Morgan, Elizabeth. "The Violence of Women's Imprisonment: A View from the Inside." In *Harsh Punishment: International Experiences of Women's Imprisonment*, edited by Sandy Cook and Susanne Davies. Boston: Northeastern University Press, 1999.

Murray, Virginia H. "A Comparative Survey of the Historic Civil, Common, and American Indian Tribal Law Responses to Domestic Violence." In *Domestic Violence Law*, edited by Nancy K. D. Lemon. St. Paul, Minnesota: West, 2001.

Nadelhoft, James. "Wife Torture." *Journal of American Culture* 10:3 (Fall, 1987): 39–59.

Naffine, Ngaire. *Female Crime: The Construction of Women in Criminology*. Sydney: Allen & Unwin, 1987.

———. *Feminism and Criminology*. Philadelphia: Temple University Press, 1996.

National Center for Women and Policing. *Equality Denied: The Status of Women in Policing*. Los Angeles: 2000.

Nourse, Victoria. "Passion's Progress: Modern Law Reform and the Provocation Defense." In *Domestic Violence Law*, edited by Nancy K. D. Lemon. St. Paul, Minnesota: West, 2001.

———. "Where Violence, Relationship, and Equality Meet: The Violence Against Women Act's Civil Rights Remedy." In *Domestic Violence Law*, edited by Nancy K. D. Lemon. St. Paul, Minnesota: West, 2001.

Norton, Mary Beth. *Founding Mothers and Fathers: Gendered Power and the Framing of American Society*. New York: Alfred A. Knopf, 1996.

Odem, Mary E. *Delinquent Daughters: Policing and Protecting Adolescent Female Sexuality in the United States, 1885–1920*. Chapel Hill: University of North Carolina Press, 1995.

Offen, Karen. "Feminism and Sexual Difference in Historical Perspective." In *Theoretical Perspectives on Sexual Difference*, edited by Deborah L. Rhode. New Haven: Yale University Press, 1990.

Office of Justice Programs. *National Symposium on Women Offenders: Conference Proceedings*. Washington, D.C.: Department of Justice, 1999.

Owen, Barbara. "Perspectives on Women in Prison." In *Women, Crime, and Criminal Justice: Original Feminist Readings*, edited by Claire M. Renzetti and Lynne Goodstein. Los Angeles: Roxbury, 2001.

———. "Women and Imprisonment in the United States: The Gendered Consequences of the US Imprisonment Binge." In *Harsh Punishment: International Experiences of Women's Imprisonment*, edited by Sandy Cook and Susanne Davies. Boston: Northeastern University Press, 1999.

Pateman, Carol. *The Sexual Contract*. Stanford, California: Stanford University Press, 1988.

Pleck, Elizabeth. *Domestic Tyranny: The Making of Social Policy Against Family Violence from Colonial Times to the Present*. New York: Oxford University Press, 1987.

———. "Feminist Responses to 'Crimes Against Women,' 1868–1896." *Signs* 8:3 (1983): 451–470.

Pollock, Joycelyn M. *Criminal Women*. Cincinnati, Ohio: Anderson, 1999.

Post, Robert C., and Siegel, Reva B. "Equal Protection by Law: Federal Antidiscrimination Legislation After *Morrison* and *Kimel*." *Yale Law Journal* 110 (December, 2000): 441–525.

Price, Barbara Raffel, and Sokoloff, Natalie J., eds. *The Criminal Justice System and Women: Offenders, Victims, and Workers*. New York: McGraw-Hill, 1995.

Rapaport, Elizabeth. "Staying Alive: Executive Clemency, Equal Protection, and the Politics of Gender in Women's Capital Cases." *Buffalo Criminal Law Review* 4, (2001): 967–1007.

Renzetti, Claire. "The Challenge to Feminism Posed by Women's Use of Violence in Intimate Relationships." In *New Versions of Victims: Feminists Struggle with the Concept*, edited by Sharon Lamb. New York: New York University Press, 1999.

Renzetti, Claire M., and Goodstein, Lynne, eds. *Women, Crime, and Criminal Justice: Original Feminist Readings*. Los Angeles: Roxbury, 2001.

Rhode, Deborah L. "Definitions of Difference." In *Theoretical Perspectives on Sexual Difference*, edited by Deborah L. Rhode. New Haven: Yale University Press, 1990.

——— ed. *Ethics in Practice: Lawyers' Roles, Responsibilities, and Regulation*. New York: Oxford University Press, 2000.

———, ed. *Theoretical Perspectives on Sexual Difference*. New Haven: Yale University Press, 1990.

Rivera, Jenny. "Domestic Violence Against Latinas by Latino Males: An Analysis of Race, National Origin, and Gender Difference." In *Domestic Violence Law*, edited by Nancy K. D. Lemon. St. Paul, Minnesota: West, 2001.

——— "The Violence Against Women Act and the Construction of Multiple Consciousness in the Civil Rights and Feminist Movements." In *Domestic Violence Law*, edited by Nancy K. D. Lemon. St. Paul, Minnesota: West, 2001.

Roach Anlece, Sharon L. "Women in Law: Theory, Research, and Practice." In *The Criminal Justice System and Women: Offenders, Victims, and Workers*, edited by Barbara Raffel Price and Natalie J. Sokoloff. New York: Mc-Graw-Hill, 1995.

Roberts, Dorothy E. "Punishing Drug Addicts Who Have Babies: Women of Color, Equality, and the Right of Privacy." In *Gender and Law: Theory, Doctrine, Commentary*, edited by Katherine T. Bartlett. Boston: Little, Brown, 1993.

Rodriguez, Christina M. "Clearing the Smoke-Filled Room: Women Jurors and the Disruption of an Old-Boys' Network in Nineteenth Century America." *Yale Law Journal* 108 (May, 1999): 1805–1845.

Rothman, Sheila. *Woman's Proper Place: A History of Changing Ideals and Practices 1870 to the Present*. New York: Basic Books, 1978.

Schecter, Susan. *Women and Male Violence: The Vision and Struggle of the Battered Women's Movement*. Boston: South End Press, 1982.

Schneider, Elizabeth M. *Battered Women and Feminist Lawmaking*. New Haven: Yale, 2000.

———. "The Violence of Privacy." In *The Public Nature of Private Violence: The Discovery of Domestic Abuse*, edited by Martha Albertson Fineman and Roxanne Mykitiuk. New York: Routledge, 1994.

Scully, Diana, and Marolla, Joseph. " 'Riding the Bull at Gilley's': Convicted Rapists Describe the Rewards of Rape." In *Violence Against Women: The Bloody Footprints*, edited by Pauline B. Bart and Eileen Geil Moran. Newbury Park, California: Sage, 1993.

Shapiro, Andrea. "Unequal Before the Law: Men, Women, and the Death Penalty." *American University Journal of Gender, Social Policy, and the Law* 8 (2000): 427–470.

Shiels, Marnie. "Spousal Rape Laws: Twenty Years Later." In *Domestic Violence Law*, edited by Nancy K. D. Lemon. St. Paul, Minnesota: West, 2001.

Siegel, Reva B. "Abortion as a Sex Equality Right: Its Basis in Feminist Theory." In *Mothers in Law: Feminist Theory and the Legal Regulation of Motherhood*, edited by Martha Albertson Fineman and Isabel Karpin. New York: Columbia University Press, 1995.

———. "The Rule of Love: Wife Beating as Prerogative." *Yale Law Journal* 105 (June, 1996), 2117–2207.

Simon, Rita. *The Contemporary Woman and Crime*. Washington, D.C.: National Institutes of Mental Health, 1975.

Slavin, Sarah. "Unwanted Pregnancy, Due Process of Law and Justice White." In *The Criminalization of a Woman's Body*, edited by Clarice Feinman. New York: Haworth, 1992.

Smart, Carol. *Regulating Womanhood: Historical Essays on Marriage, Motherhood, and Sexuality*. London: Routledge, 1992.

———. *Law, Crime, and Sexuality: Essays in Feminism*. London: Sage, 1995.

Smith, Patricia, ed., *Feminist Jurisprudence*. New York: Oxford University Press, 1993.

Smith-Rosenburg, Carroll. *Disorderly Conduct: Visions of Gender in Victorian America*. New York: Oxford University Press, 1985.

Somerville, Diane Miller. "Rape, Race, and Castration in Slave Law in the Colonial and Early South." In *The Devil's Lane: Sex and Race in the Early South*, edited by Catherine Clinton and Michele Gillespie. New York: Oxford University Press, 1997.

Spohn, Cassia. "Decision Making in Sexual Assault Cases: Do Black and Female Judges Make a Difference?" In *The Criminal Justice System and Women: Offenders, Victims, and Workers*, edited by Barbara Raffel Price and Natalie J. Sokoloff. New York: McGraw-Hill, 1995.

St. John, Jacqueline. "Sex, Sense, and Sensibility: Trespassing into the Culture of Domestic Violence." In *Domestic Violence Law*, edited by Nancy K. D. Lemon. St. Paul, Minnesota: West, 2001.

Stanko, Elizabeth A. *Intimate Intrusions: Women's Experience of Male Violence*. London: Routledge, 1985.

———. "Women, Danger, and Criminology." In *Women, Crime, and Criminal Justice: Original Feminist Readings*, edited by Claire M. Renzetti and Lynne Goodstein. Los Angeles: Roxbury, 2001.

Steffensmeier, Darrell, and Broidy, Lisa. "Explaining Female Offending." In *Women, Crime, and Criminal Justice: Original Feminist Readings*, edited by Claire M. Renzetti and Lynne Goodstein. Los Angeles: Roxbury, 2001.

Stevenson, George B. "Federal Antiviolence and Abuse Legislation: Toward Elimination of Disparate Justice for Women and Children." In *Domestic Violence Law*, edited by Nancy K. D. Lemon. St. Paul, Minnesota: West, 2001.

Streib, Victor L. *Death Penalty for Female Offenders* (February, 2001). [Online] Available: www.law.onu.edu/faculty/streib/femdeath.htm.

Szockyj, Elizabeth, and Fox, James G., eds. *The Corporate Victimization of Women*. Boston: Northeastern University Press, 1996.

Taub, Nadine, and Schneider, Elizabeth M. "Women's Subordination and the Role of Law." In *Feminist Legal Theory: Foundations*, edited by D. Kelly Weisberg. Philadelphia: Temple University Press, 1993.

Teays, Wanda. "Standards of Perfection and Battered Women's Self-Defense." In *Violence Against Women: Philosophical Perspectives*, edited by Stanley G. French, Wanda Teays, and Laura M. Purdy. Ithaca: Cornell University Press, 1998.

Thomas, Dorothy, and Beasley, Michele E. "Domestic Violence as a Human Rights Issue." In *Battered Women and the Law*, edited by Clare Dalton and Elizabeth M. Schneider. New York: Foundation, 2001.

Tjaden, Patricia, and Thoennes, Nancy. *Full Report of the Prevalence, Incidence, and Consequences of Violence Against Women*. Washington, D.C.: National Institutes of Justice, 2000.

U.S. Department of Justice. *Update of The Report of the LEAA Task Force on Women*. Washington, D.C.: 2000.

———. *Women Offenders* (Revised October 3, 2000) by Lawrence A. Greenfeld and Tracy L. Snell. Special Report.

Volpe, Leti. "(Mis)identifying Culture: Asian Women and the Cultural Defense." In *Domestic Violence Law*, edited by Nancy K. D. Lemon. St. Paul, Minnesota: West, 2001.

Walker, Samuel, Spohn, Cassia, and DeLone, Miriam. *The Color of Justice: Race, Ethnicity, and Crime in America*. Belmont, California: Wadsworth, 2000.

Walls, T. Marie. "Civil Orders of Protection and the Victim of Abuse: Recent Changes in the Family Abuse Legislation." *In Our Vision*. Williamsburg, Virginia: Virginians Against Domestic Violence, Summer 1998.

Wang, Karen. "Battered Asian-American Women: Community Responses from the Battered Women's Movement and the Asian-American Community." In *Domestic Violence Law*, edited by Nancy K. D. Lemon. St. Paul, Minnesota: West, 2001.

Watterson, Kathryn. *Women in Prison: Inside the Concrete Womb*. Boston: Northeastern University Press, 1996.

Weiner, Merle H. "Domestic Violence and the Per Se Standard of Outrage." In *Domestic Violence Law*, edited by Nancy K. D. Lemon. St. Paul, Minnesota: West, 2001.

Weisburg, D. Kelly, ed. *Feminist Legal Theory: Foundations*. Philadelphia: Temple University Press, 1993.

West, Robin. *Progressive Constitutionalism: Reconstructing the Fourteenth Amendment*. Durham, North Carolina: Duke University Press, 1994.

West, Traci C. *Wounds of the Spirit: Black Women, Violence, and Resistance Ethics*. New York: New York University Press, 1999.

Whitfield, Stephen. *A Death in the Delta: The Story of Emmett Till*. New York: Free Press, 1988.

Widom, Cathy S., and Maxfield, Michael G. "An Update on the 'Cycle of Violence'." *National Institutes of Justice Research in Brief*. Washington, D.C.: Department of Justice, 2001.

Wills, Donna. "Domestic Violence: The Case for Aggressive Prosecution." In *Domestic Violence Law*, edited by Nancy K. D. Lemon. St. Paul, Minnesota: West, 2001.

Zorza, Joan. "The Criminal Law of Misdemeanor Domestic Violence, 1970–1990." In *Domestic Violence Law*, edited by Nancy K. D. Lemon. St. Paul, Minnesota: West, 2001.